Chants of *The Roman Missal*

Study Edition

International Commission on English in the Liturgy

LITURGICAL PRESS
Collegeville, Minnesota

www.litpress.org

Cover design by Ann Blattner. Cover art by Martin Erspamer, OSB, a monk of Saint Meinrad Archabbey.

1 2 3 4 5 6 7 8

Library of Congress Cataloging-in-Publication Data

Catholic Church.
[Missal. English. Selections]
Chants of the Roman missal / International Commission on English in the Liturgy. — Study ed.
p. cm.
ISBN 978-0-8146-3381-6
1. Gregorian chants—Instruction and study. I. International Committee on English in the Liturgy. II. Title.

MT860.C42 2011
782.32'3—dc23 2011035343

CONTENTS

MUSIC FOR THE ENGLISH LANGUAGE ROMAN MISSAL: AN INTRODUCTION

CHANTS OF *THE ROMAN MISSAL, THIRD EDITION*

MUSIC FOR THE ENGLISH LANGUAGE ROMAN MISSAL: AN INTRODUCTION

I. SUNG VERNACULAR LITURGY IN THE LITURGICAL REFORM

For the new English language Roman Missal, the International Commission on English in the Liturgy has offered to the Conferences of Bishops of the English-speaking world chants for everything that is set to music in the *Missale Romanum, editio typica tertia* (third typical edition, 2002, 2008). The English chants provided in the Roman Missal make it possible to sing the liturgy. Sung liturgy—with sung dialogues between celebrant, deacon, or cantor and people—is an ideal of the liturgical reforms issuing from the Second Vatican Council. As no. 113 of the Constitution on the Sacred Liturgy, *Sacrosanctum Concilium*, of the Second Vatican Council states, "Liturgical worship is given a more noble form when . . . celebrated solemnly in song."[1] No. 113 of *Sacrosanctum Concilium* gives preference to uniting the ritual texts of the liturgy with music when it emphasizes that "sacred music is to be considered the more holy, the more closely connected it is with the liturgical action, whether it adds delight to prayer, fosters unity of minds, or confers greater solemnity upon the sacred rites."

The documents of liturgical reform consistently advocate sung liturgy. In doing so, the documents are calling us back to the common liturgical practice of East and West in the first millennium. It remains the practice in the Christian East to this day.

The first Roman document after the Second Vatican Council to deal comprehensively with the role of music in the reformed liturgy, the Holy See's Instruction on Music in the Liturgy, *Musicam sacram* (1967), says at no. 7:

> The amount of singing determines the gradations between the most solemn form of liturgical celebrations, in which all the parts calling for singing are sung, and the most simple form, in which nothing is sung. For the choice of parts to be sung, those should be first that of their nature are more important and particularly those sung by the priest or other ministers and answered by the congregation or sung by the priest and congregation together.[2]

There are two noteworthy principles at work in this quotation. First, there are priorities among the sung elements of the liturgy, and the highest priority is given to dialogues "sung by the priest or other ministers and answered by the congregation" and to acclamations "sung by the priest and congregation together." This means that the liturgical chants in the Missal take priority over the other musical elements of the liturgy, as important as they are, such as the antiphons, hymns or songs that are sung at the entrance, offertory, and communion, or instrumental music that enhances the liturgy at various points. Furthermore, no. 40 of the *General Instruction of the Roman Missal* offers some guidance on the extent to which these musical elements are to be used in celebrations of varying levels of solemnity when it states:

> Although it is not always necessary (e.g., in weekday Masses) to sing all the texts that are in principle meant to be sung, every care should be taken that singing by the ministers and the people not be absent in celebrations that occur on Sundays and on Holydays of Obligation.

---

1. Vatican II, *Sacrosanctum Concilium* (Dogmatic Constitution on the Sacred Liturgy), 4 December 1963, in *Vatican II: The Conciliar and Post Conciliar Documents*, ed. Austin Flannery, vol. 1., new rev. ed. (Northport, NY: Costello, 1998).

2. Sacred Congregation of Rites, *Musicam Sacram* (Instruction on Music in the Liturgy), 5 March 1967, in International Commission on English in the Liturgy, *Documents on the Liturgy, 1963–1979: Conciliar, Papal, and Curial Texts* (Collegeville, MN: Liturgical Press, 1982), 4128. See also Congregation for Divine Worship and the Discipline of the Sacraments, *General Instruction of the Roman Missal* (2002), 40.

Second, there is a pastoral thrust to the liturgical reform, as seen in the various degrees possible in the extent of singing. A fully sung liturgy is a praiseworthy ideal, but its implementation calls for prudence and pastoral sensitivity. The chants of the liturgy are sung when it is possible in a given pastoral situation, when the participants are blessed with the resources to do so well, and when it is judged that this will truly glorify God and sanctify the worshipers.

The decision to chant more or less of the liturgy should be made with several concerns in mind. Uppermost is the "full and active participation by all the people," which is "the aim to be considered before all else" according to *Sacrosanctum Concilium,* no. 14. In light of the great importance given by the Church to the singing in the celebration of the Mass, no. 40 of the *General Instruction of the Roman Missal* urges that in choosing various elements to be sung "the culture of peoples and abilities of each liturgical assembly" should be given "due consideration." Thus the sensitivities of the worshipers and the history of liturgical practice in a given place, which may make people more or less prepared for sung liturgy, should always be kept in mind.

The musical abilities of those who are to sing the ministerial chants must also be taken into account. *Musicam Sacram* addresses the importance of musical ability in no. 8 when it counsels:

> Whenever a choice of people for a sung liturgical celebration is possible, those with musical talent should obviously be preferred. . . . When no such choice is possible and the priest or minister does not have the voice to sing properly, he may recite, audibly and clearly, one or other of the more difficult parts belonging to him.

As much as the Church upholds sung liturgy, a recited proclamation is probably preferable to a poorly done sung rendition. This is not a loophole exempting ministers from striving for the ideal. Article 8 continues, "This [i.e., reciting], however, is not to be done merely to suit the personal preference of the priest or minister." In striving for the ideal of sung liturgy, a pastoral decision should be made to determine the extent to which this ideal is appropriate in a given situation and how gradually it is to be introduced with care where it is not yet the common practice.

The Church's esteem for sung liturgy is seen in the directives concerning the proclamation of the readings in the *Introduction to the Lectionary for Mass*:

> Even if the Gospel itself is not sung, it is appropriate for the greeting *'The Lord be with you,'* and *'A reading from the holy Gospel according to . . . ,'* and at the end *'The Gospel of the Lord'* to be sung, in order that the congregation may also sing its acclamations. This is a way both of bringing out the importance of the Gospel reading and of stirring up the faith of those who hear it.
>
> At the conclusion of the other readings, *'The word of the Lord'* may be sung, even by someone other than the reader; all respond with the acclamation. In this way the assembled congregation pays reverence to the word of God it has listened to in faith and gratitude.[3]

Regarding the Eucharistic Prayer, the *General Instruction of the Roman Missal* says at no. 147: "It is most appropriate that the Priest sing those parts of the Eucharistic Prayer for which musical notation is provided." Both the Latin and English editions of the Missal provide complete musical settings of Eucharistic Prayers I–IV.

To clear up any possible misunderstanding regarding the wording of the norms within the *General Instruction* or the rubrics that precede the liturgical texts in the Order of Mass and elsewhere in the Missal, no. 38 of the *General Instruction* states: "in the rubrics and in the norms that follow, words such as 'say' or 'proclaim' are to be understood either of singing or of reciting." Thus terms like "say," "acclaim" or "proclaim" in the norms and the rubrics are not intended to give preference to reciting.

3. Sacred Congregation for the Sacraments and Divine Worship, *General Introduction* to the *Lectionary for Mass* (1981), 17–18.

The English chants of the Roman Missal are intended to help the Christian people offer worthy worship as they join their voices in praise of God with the Church on earth and in heaven, for as *Sacrosanctum Concilium*, no. 8, reminds us: "In the earthly liturgy we take part in a foretaste of that heavenly liturgy which is celebrated in the Holy City of Jerusalem toward which we journey as pilgrims."

II. SINGING WELL

It is important that the singing minister render the chants as well as possible. This chapter gives practical and musical advice to help the singer.

A. Preparation of the Minister

With the proper training, preparation, practice, advice, and mutual encouragement, liturgical ministers—celebrants, deacons, cantors, and lectors—can learn to sing the chants with poised self-confidence as they work collaboratively with the ministers in their own parishes and with their diocesan office of worship. Making use of this book and the many other resources available to them (see VI. Resources, p. 61), liturgical ministers will gradually come to trust in their own abilities to introduce and sing the chants, and to rely with confidence on the congregation's generous acceptance of their efforts. The goal of careful preparation and of singing the Missal chants with confidence and with reasonable competence, of course, is to engage worshipers more fully in the sung prayer of the liturgy and to lead them more deeply into the paschal mystery made present in the eucharistic sacrifice.

B. The Meaning of the Text

Most of the chants provided in the Missal (the formulas or tones for the Prefaces, Eucharistic Prayers, and Collects), are formulaic in character, thus preserving the primacy of the texts. The liturgical text itself—its rhythm, its syntax, its structure and its semantic elements—has informed and shaped the way the chants have been applied to it. The nature of these chants calls for a style of singing that, like the chants themselves, is at the service of the text in all its aspects—rhythm, syntax, and, above all, meaning. The focus of the singer, therefore, is the sacred text, especially its meaning. Preparation for singing these chants, moreover, will involve a careful study of the text, so that when sung in a style of cantillation (a form of sung recitation or heightened speech) the meaning of each word and phrase is clearly communicated and heard in its proper context. Careful review of the text and sufficient practice of the particular chant beforehand by the celebrant will lead to a confident, natural rendition of the setting that can effectively involve the hearers in the prayer of the liturgy.

C. Pitch

Pitch is *relative* in the notation of the English Missal, not *absolute*. A standard G clef (without key signature) is used, but there is no obligation to sing at the pitch level given, and one is always free to sing at a higher or lower pitch. Some singers may wish to adjust the pitch to suit their natural vocal range or so that the chant matches the tonality or modality of a congregational piece that precedes or follows.

The following two examples—taken from the Prayer of the Faithful and the Litany of Saints of the Easter Vigil, respectively—illustrate how the notation of the Missal is not to be taken absolutely:

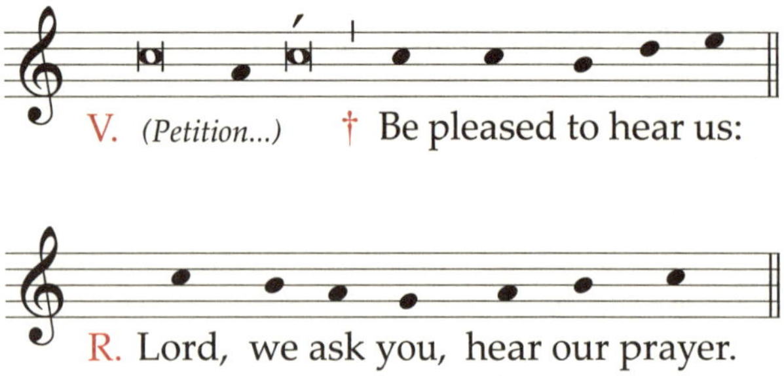

Most congregations will wish to sing this chant much lower. In congregational worship aids one is free to print chants at any pitch level.

Here are some examples of how the Preface Dialogue and Preface might be pitched so as to match the modality or tonality of the congregational *Sanctus*. The first column gives the pitches that begin the Preface Dialogue. Then the second and third columns illustrate the transition from the end of the Preface to the beginning of the *Sanctus*.

It is a good practice to imagine the pitch(es) before starting to sing. For example, the celebrant would prepare himself to sing the opening Sign of the Cross with its whole step by imagining the two pitches that begin the chant or perhaps by imagining the important higher pitch first, and then the lower and higher pitches in order:

Care must be taken so that the modality or tonality of the preceding musical piece does not put the singer in mind of the wrong modality. For the Sign of the Cross, for example, let us suppose that the opening antiphon or hymn is in the key of A major, ending on the pitches G# and A. To sing the first ministerial chant, the celebrant would have to make sure he has a G *natural* in mind, either by hearing the whole step on his own or by hearing the pitches played for him.

Pitches should be given just loud enough for the singer to hear, but not so loud as to be obtrusive.

D. Breathing

Humans breathe naturally and without thinking about it, whether awake or asleep. But to sing well, one must be intentional about inhaling deeply. The lower abdominals ought to be engaged in order to breathe deeply and support the voice. After inhaling, the singer should not try to hold air in, but to let it flow naturally and efficiently. The singer should use the breath fully for a well-supported sound, without wasting breath through an airy sound that does not fully engage the vocal mechanism.

E. Length of Phrases

The singer should feel free to adjust the phrase length and frequency of breathing, since these depend upon the singer's sense of the text and the tempo appropriate to the acoustics of the space. There are four types of bar lines in the chant of the English Missal, indicating successively larger breaks in the syntax of the text. These are the quarter bar, the half bar, the full bar, and the double bar:

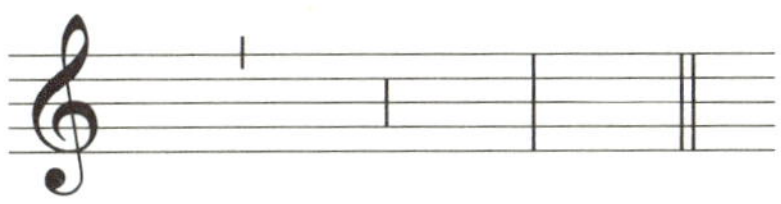

The quarter bar (above, leftmost) is a small vertical line placed on the top line of the staff. The frequency of placement of the quarter bar in the Missal chants is, for the most part, an editorial decision. The tendency is to insert more rather than fewer quarter bars to provide helpful indications to the singer who needs to breathe often. The singer must not feel absolutely bound to the bar lines as given in the Missal. The singer who is able to sing a larger portion of text without a breath should feel free to ignore any quarter bar—depending of course on the text and its syntax. Conversely, the singer who is more comfortable with shorter phrases and more frequent breathing should not hesitate to pencil in additional quarter bars or some other marking in places where the text most naturally allows for it.

It is bound to happen at times that the singer runs out of breath before reaching the phrase end or syntactical break. This need not be a problem and the singer should not worry when it happens. It is quite possible to take a very quick "catch breath" and complete the phrase without communicating an undue break in the line.

F. The Values of English Syllables

In liturgical chant, the text is rendered most effectively when the syllables receive the same nuanced rhythmic values as they would in natural speech. The cardinal rule is: sing as you speak.

The English language, even more so than Latin, has a considerable range between longer and shorter syllables.

Syllables longer by nature: **world, thanks**

Syllables shorter by nature: **to, the**

Some syllables are emphasized because of their importance for the meaning—e.g., "up" in the sentence:

We lift them **up** to the Lord.

Weaker or less important words before a stressed word or syllable tend to accelerate toward the stress, for example "to the" leading toward "Lord":

We lift them up **to the** Lord.

(acceleration)

This nuance happens naturally in good spoken proclamation of an English text (and generally without the speaker's explicit awareness). When a text is sung, the rhythmic nuance should be preserved. Each note or note group should receive the rhythmic value of its syllable, with a nuanced variety between longer and shorter syllables.

Sometimes when moving from spoken to sung rendition there is a tendency to lose the natural rhythm of the language, to even out the length of the syllables, and to decrease the tempo. The singer should resist this tendency.

Let us take this celebrant's text as an example:

Let us give thanks **to the** Lord our God.

(acceleration)

The singer should speak the text first, noting the natural acceleration of the short syllables "to the" leading to the stressed word "Lord." Then the singer should sing the same text, taking care that the syllables "to the" do not become unnaturally lengthened so that they are equal in length to "thanks" and "Lord." The natural acceleration should be preserved:

The notation of the Missal exclusively employs black note heads without stems. This notation is intended to help the singer attend to the natural rhythm of the text. There are no stems or white notes to indicate quarter note/crotchet, eighth note/quaver, half note/minim, or whole note/semibreve, since the singer is not limited to any of these rhythmic proportions.

Finally, we treat an advanced vocal technique for the more proficient singer. It concerns the rhythmic values in note groups. A note group is anything more than one note over a syllable. Here are several examples of note groups, all taken from the *Exsultet* (Easter Proclamation), above the syllables "Sound," "King's," and "tri–" :

The technique for note groups is derived from the interpretation of Latin chant as taught throughout Europe since the 1950s, especially at the Pontifical Institute of Sacred Music in Rome. Note groups are sung with movement toward the final note of the group—the second note in the case of a two-note group, the third note in the case of a three-note group, and so forth. This final note is perhaps a bit louder than the preceding note(s) in the note group, but above all it is rhythmically longer than the preceding note(s). In effect, this means that the final note of the note group is rendered with careful attention given to it before moving forward to the next syllable. The final note is the primary carrier of the syllable.

There is a practical reason for this interpretative technique, especially in larger spaces with a more reverberant acoustic. The listener perceives the first note of the group more strongly than the others because it is the first to be perceived. There is a danger that the final note of the group may be overshadowed, especially if the first note is a bit louder. Emphasizing the last note of the group by making it longer (and perhaps just a bit louder) serves to compensate for this acoustical effect and allows a balanced aesthetic perception of all the notes in the group.

In the case of longer note groups, the singer might think of the last note as the only note carrying the syllable, and the preceding notes almost as light grace notes. For example, here is a five-note group over "this," from the *Exsultet:*

The singer would first imagine the phrase as if the first word, "This," had only one pitch, the last of the group. For rehearsal purposes, it would be so sung:

Then, when the structurally important final note of the group is impressed upon the singer's consciousness, the singer would sing it somewhat like this, with quicker preceding notes:

This means, of course, that the notes within a longer group are sung more quickly than other notes such as two-note groups or individual notes over a syllable.

An important caution is necessary before the more proficient singer employs this technique. The goal must be a natural rendering of the text. Everything must flow naturally, without affectation or artificiality. It is a matter of subtle rhythmic variance, nothing more. Rhythmic variety in the sung proclamation of the text should not call attention to itself or interrupt the natural flow of the text. In rehearsal the singer might exaggerate the rhythmic differences at first, so that they are clearly in the singer's consciousness. But in the final performance, the emphases are quite slight—hardly enough to slow down the rendition. Giving attention to the final note of a note group should not obscure the text, but make it clearer and more expressive.

G. Pronunciation and Diction

To communicate the text well, the singer should pronounce the words clearly. Final consonants should be clearly enunciated, but without being overly exaggerated to cause an explosive popping sound in the microphone.

From the *Exsultet*:

Sometimes without realizing it, the singer in effect sings "nigh" and "dĕ" rather than "night" and "death." Often, when the consonant is not heard at endings of words, it is because the singer has interrupted the airflow before having reached the very end of the phrase or sentence or word. This makes the consonant disappear. The singer is reminded to include the consonant in the singing of the word, rather than switching to speech for it.

Consonants before vowels should be short and give way to the vowels. The cardinal rule is: sing on the vowel. Liquid consonants before vowels, such as M, N, L, or the characteristically American R, should be brief. In the example above, the "wh" of "when" and the "Chr" of "Christ" should be brief so as to reach the following vowels as quickly as possible.

H. Tempo

In general, chant should move along at a good pace. A fairly rapid tempo should come about naturally as the singer attends above all to the text. The singer should resist the tendency, deeply ingrained in some cases, to sing a text markedly slower than reciting it. A phrase such as the following should not take very much longer to sing than to recite:

In dialogues with a congregational response, it is best for the leader not to hold the last note very long. The last note is extended a bit, but only a bit, to round off the phrase gracefully. Holding it too long tends to put the brakes on the forward movement and hinder the timely response of the congregation. In the example above, the two notes on "hearts" would not be sung unduly slowly, nor would the last note be held out. By making the final note rather short (and concluding "hearts" with a sung "ts") and by breathing in after the final note, the celebrant cues the congregation's inhalation and timely response.

I. Special Notation: the Quilisma

One striking feature new to the revised Preface tone is the quilisma (See also section IV. Layout and Notation, p. 35). There is a quilisma in most Prefaces of the Missal. It is not difficult to sing, however. Here is an example of a quilisma on "glory," from the end of Preface II for the Sundays of Ordinary Time:

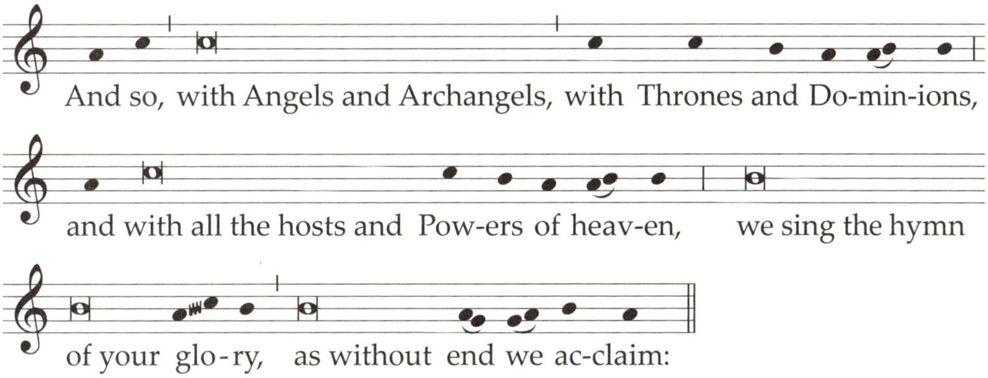

It is customary to lengthen the note before the quilisma (this is always notated as an A in the prefaces) and to sing the quilisma note (always a B) lightly, with forward movement toward the final and most important note (always a C). Here is a loose approximation of how it is sung:

For the celebrant who wishes to sing the Preface but is not yet prepared to sing the quilisma, a respectable transitional solution would be simply to sing a C instead of the three given notes:

However, by listening to recorded examples of Prefaces (see section VI. Resources), the celebrant will readily learn how to sing this feature of the Preface.

J. Accompanying Chant?

As a general rule, the celebrant's chants in the Missal are to be sung without accompaniment (cf. *Musicam Sacram*, no. 64: "Instruments are to be silent during any part sung by the priest or ministers by reason of their function"). Accompaniment may be used to support the congregation. In published accompaniment books it is standard practice to provide accompaniment for the congregational portions.

The accompanist's goal is to support the congregation and help it stay together. The accompanist must have a good sense of the rhythm and flow of the chant. The accompanist should take care that the playing of the accompaniment is not overly obtrusive or slow.

It helps the congregation to stay together if the accompaniment changes chords on accented syllables. If the acoustic is too reverberant or the congregation seems not to be staying together, the accompanist may play less legato while changing chords, inserting clear breaks before each chord to emphasize the accents. As the congregation becomes more confident, the accompaniment appropriately becomes more legato.

K. Amplification and Acoustics

Ideally, unaccompanied chant in the liturgy would be sung without any amplification, as was the case throughout most of the history of the liturgy. The human voice sounds best when it is not changed or distorted through amplification. It is more authentic when sound is heard by the listener from its true source rather than a speaker. True reverberation from a natural sound source is much to be preferred to artificial reverberation added by an amplification system, or the lack of natural reverberation in amplified sound. Unamplified singing allows communication to be more immediate and sincere. It encourages the singer to project the voice well rather than depending on artificial amplification to convey the sound.

Because of the size and acoustical properties of many churches, some amplification is necessary in many or most situations. It becomes a matter of using amplification well so as to preserve as much natural sound as possible and to minimize the distortions of amplification. The volume level should, therefore, not be set too high. In general, the amplification level should be set as low as possible, with the sound still being readily audible. Singers should be as far from the microphone as possible while still ensuring adequate amplification. Models and practices from the secular entertainment world are not always helpful, and should be resisted with intention and firm resolve.

In building or renovating worship spaces, it is essential to have acoustical considerations in mind from the outset. There should be enough hard surfaces to allow sound to travel well. The acoustics should be resonant enough so that there is no need for excessive amplification. Excessive use of sound-absorbing building materials should be avoided.

It is especially important that the chanting and singing of the congregation not be hindered by sound-absorbing materials. In order to foster their active participation in song, the members of the worshiping assembly should hear their voices joined to the resonant and full sound of the entire community. In a space where the sound of human voices is stifled and absorbed, where everything must be amplified to be heard, the Church's ideal of sung liturgy is difficult, if not impossible, to realize. But in a space with good acoustics, the singing of congregation and ministers will ring forth as they join in song "with the Angels and all the Saints."

L. Receiving Encouragement and Advice

The singing minister will benefit from the encouragement and advice of perceptive listeners. It is important that feedback be positive and not discouraging.

For the purpose of practicing the chants, it will be helpful for ministers to record their singing of the chants. By listening to the recording ministers will be given a more accurate sense of how well they are learning the chants and a greater awareness of possibilities for improvement.

M. Vocal Instruction

In order to learn the basics of good vocal technique and to develop self-confidence in singing, priests, deacons, and cantors will benefit from receiving group or individual voice lessons from professional voice teachers at colleges, universities, or high schools, and from attending workshops on singing the ministerial chants of the Mass offered by church music organizations. Singing in a church choir or community chorus is another possible way of developing good vocal technique.

III. THE GENRES OF CHANT IN THE ENGLISH MISSAL

A. Dialogues of the Order of Mass: Solemn Tone and Simple Tone

In the Order of Mass, there are two settings for the dialogues between priest and people in the English Missal: the Solemn Tone, which appears within the Order of Mass, and the Simple Tone, which appears in Appendix I: Various Chants for the Order of Mass. The Solemn Tone is more ancient, dating perhaps to the formative centuries of the liturgy in the early medieval era. The Simple Tone is more recent.

This is the Greeting in the Solemn Tone:

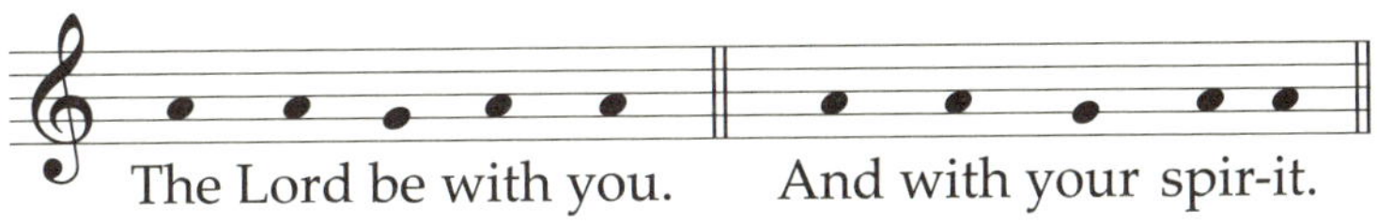

For some people today, the ancient modality of the Solemn Tone can seem foreign. Some celebrants find the Simple Tone easier to sing, precisely because of its more recent modality. The Solemn Tone, nevertheless, is the primary tone of the English Missal. Its modality is more compatible with congregational chants of the Missal, such as the third form of the Penitential Act with invocations, the *Gloria*, the Preface Dialogue and *Sanctus*, and the Doxology and Amen concluding the Eucharistic Prayer.

When the Preface Dialogue is sung, the celebrant should use the Solemn Tone if he sings the Prayer over the Offerings so as to match the modality of the Preface Dialogue.

The celebrant will sing the Order of Mass more confidently in either tone once he becomes familiar with each tone's characteristic modality. This familiarity can be acquired by listening to recordings of the chants and by practicing singing them. Over time, the tones will become second nature through frequent use in the liturgy.

Analytical knowledge of the tone's primary melodic elements and intervals is also helpful. The diagram below shows the primary melodic elements of each tone. To facilitate comparison, the Simple Tone is transposed down here so that it is centered on A, as is the Solemn Tone in its original key.

Primary melodic elements:

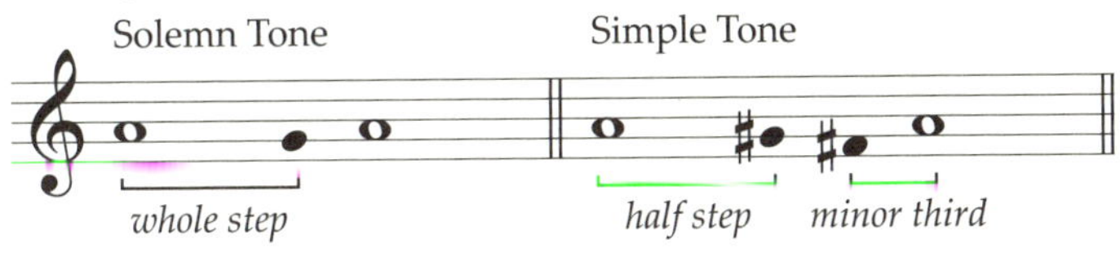

In the original key, as notated in the appendix of the Missal, the Simple Tone is centered on C:

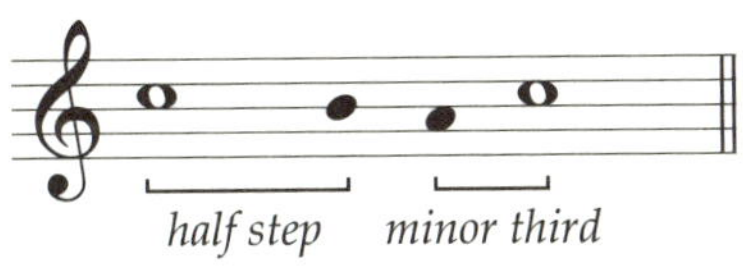

It is the whole step that gives the Solemn Tone its unique character and that can be a challenge for some singers. The singer must have this whole step firmly in mind in order to sing the Order of Mass confidently. By contrast, the Simple Tone employs a half step, which is often easier to sing. The other interval of the Simple Tone, the minor third, is also one that comes naturally to most singers.

Many Solemn Tone chants in the Order of Mass consist of nothing but the primary melodic elements A and G. Examples of this in the Introductory Rites are the third form of the Greeting,

the invitation to the Penitential Act,

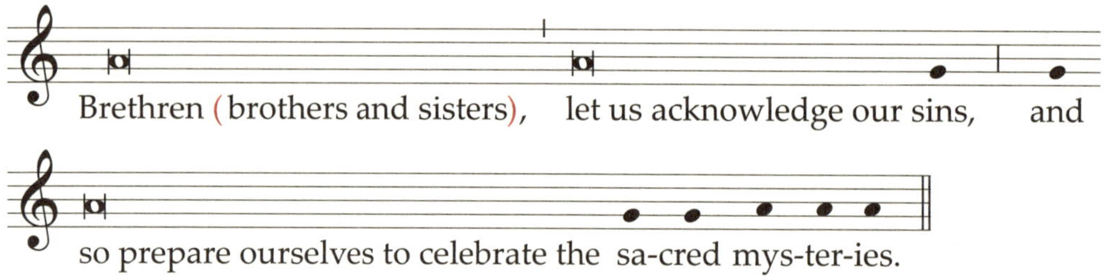

and the absolution of the Penitential Act.

The same is true of the Orations (Collect, Prayer over the Offerings, Prayer after Communion) and the Eucharistic Prayers, which will be discussed below.

Sometimes the Solemn Tone chants of the Order of Mass have an added upper note B in addition to the primary melodic elements A and G. Examples of this in the Introductory Rites are the Sign of the Cross,

and the first two forms of the Greeting.

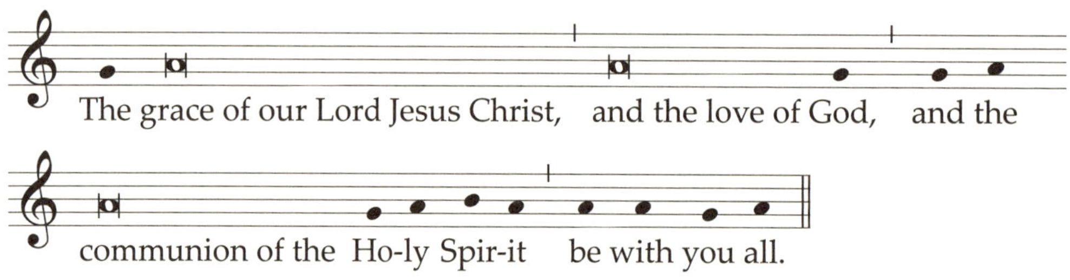

Sometimes the Solemn Tone is enhanced by an added lower note E. An example of this is the third form of the Penitential Act with invocations.

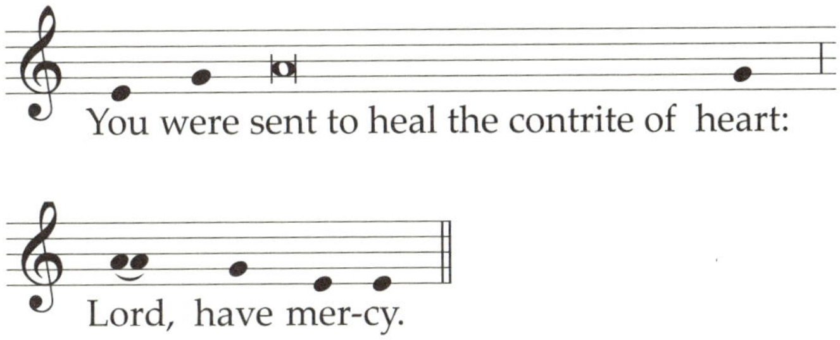

Sometimes the Solemn Tone is enhanced by the addition of both the upper note B and the lower note E—for example, in the *Gloria*.

Singers will find it easier to sing the Order of Mass in the Solemn Tone if they first get their bearings by being clear about the primary melodic elements and the added notes.

The dialogues of the Order of Mass in the Simple Tone consist of only the primary melodic elements of the tone, given above, without added notes.

B. Congregational Acclamations of the Order of Mass

The Second Vatican Council expressed the wish that the faithful "be able to say or sing together in Latin those parts of the Ordinary of the Mass which pertain to them" (*Sacrosanctum Concilium*, no. 54). The third edition of the Latin Missal (2002, 2008) provides a set of simple Latin Mass acclamations, intending that these should be learned by Catholic congregations throughout the world. The English Missal supports the intent of the Latin Missal by providing the Latin setting of acclamations such as the *Kyrie* (which comes from Greek), *Sanctus*, *Agnus Dei*, and *Pater noster*. The vernacular musical settings of these acclamations in the English Missal follow their Latin models closely to help communities sing these chants in both Latin and English. While the longer congregational chants such as the *Gloria* and Profession of Faith (*Credo*) are not included in the Latin Missal, vernacular chant settings for the English Missal were prepared based upon original Latin settings of these chants.

1) The *Kyrie*

The *Kyrie* of Mass XVI is among the easiest in the *Graduale Romanum*, and it has long been sung by congregations. In the English Missal it is closely modeled on the original melody, both in the original language and in the English adaptation (see p. 123 for the full *Kyrie* in Greek and English). This setting of the *Kyrie* is for use when the *Kyrie* is sung as a free-standing acclamation after the first two forms of the Penitential Act.

Or:

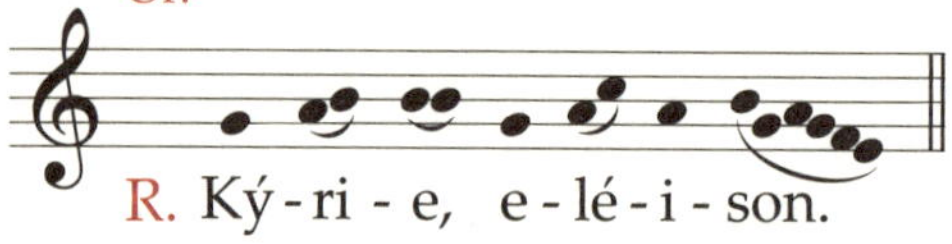

Scholars believe that the variant ending for the people's final "*Kyrie, eleison*," now optional, was originally used to provide a transition to the beginning of the sung *Gloria* that followed. Either option is always permissible. However, for days on which the *Gloria* is used, if it is not sung to a Mode IV melody beginning on E, there is no specific reason to use the variant ending. Many congregations might find it easier to repeat the cantor's melody exactly.

2) The *Kyrie* with Invocations

For the third form of the Penitential Act, there are invocations to which the congregation responds "*Kyrie, eleison*" or "Lord, have mercy."

The people reply:

Or:

This English chant is not based on the chant of the Latin Missal. It is adapted from the setting composed for the 1973 *Sacramentary* (The Roman Missal, Second Edition). This setting is well-known to most English-speaking Catholics. The melody for the invocations now has two intonation notes, E and G, to make it compatible not only with the English response ("Lord, have mercy") but also with the Greek response ("*Kyrie, eleison*").

3) The *Gloria*

The *Gloria* of Mass XV is the basis for the vernacular setting (see pp. 124–25) in the English Missal. This setting was chosen because it is one of the easiest Latin *Gloria* chants in the *Graduale Romanum*, because it is formulaic and thus easily adapted to the English language, and because its modality matches the dialogues of the Order of Mass in the Solemn Tone (see III.A above).

4) The Profession of Faith (*Credo*)

Two settings of the *Credo* from the *Graduale Romanum* have been selected as the basis for vernacular settings in the English Missal: Credo I and Credo III (see pp. 127–28, 310–11).

Credo I:

Credo III:

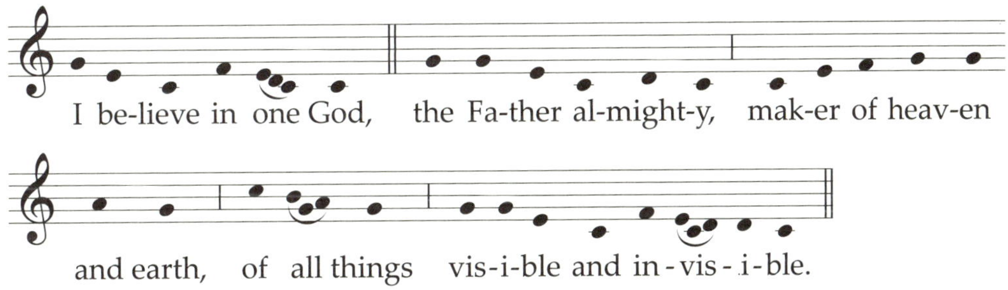

Credo I, first seen in liturgical manuscripts from the eleventh century, is quite beautiful in its ancient modality. Credo III is more recent. It is a seventeenth-century adaptation of the melodies of Mass VIII, the well-known "*Missa de Angelis*." Credo III is probably the Latin setting that has been sung the most by congregations throughout the twentieth century. This is probably because its modern modality makes it accessible to congregations. The English settings of the Creed follow the Latin melody closely in each case.

5) The *Sanctus*

The *Sanctus* chant in the Latin Missal is the setting most commonly found in congregational worship aids. The vernacular setting of the Sanctus in the English Missal follows the Latin melody closely (see p. 130).

It is important that the natural accentuation of the text be preserved in the singing of this chant ("*Sánctus*"/"Hóly"). One practical way to preserve the natural accentuation of the first word is to sing the first three notes rather like quarter notes/crotchets:

Ideally, if the celebrant chants the Preface, the congregation would begin the *Sanctus* all together from the outset, picking up the opening pitch from the conclusion of the Preface. But for practical reasons, the cantor usually intones the first word and the congregation then joins in. If the cantor sings the first word with the proper accentuation, the congregation, by imitating the cantor, may follow the natural accentuation without difficulty.

6) Memorial Acclamation

In the English Missal, the settings of the acclamation that follows the Institution Narrative of the Eucharistic Prayer make use of the basic modal/melodic elements of the Latin acclamation *Mortem tuam* (*Graduale Romanum*, no. 810, *Graduale Simplex*, no. 10; see p. 131). In the Latin Missal only *Mortem tuam* is set to music. The other two acclamations are also provided with music in the English Missal, however.

7) The Lord's Prayer (*Pater noster*)

The "Our Father" presented an interesting pastoral conundrum. In the United States, an English setting had already been widely used since the early 1970s. Similarly, Australia had its own widely used setting based on the Latin *Pater noster*. Other countries had their own settings as well. Because the translation of this prayer has not changed in the new English Missal, many would regret tampering with an element of the reformed liturgy that the people sing so well.

ICEL considered several possible solutions to this conundrum. One solution would have been to select one of the many settings currently in use. ICEL could also have refrained from proposing a revised setting, suggesting that each country retain what is presently in use. It was finally decided to offer to all the Conferences of Bishops a new setting based on the Latin *Pater noster* chant (see pp. 224–26). Each Conference of Bishops that is part of ICEL has decided which version(s) of the "Our Father" to include in their English Missal. In the United States, for example, the already-known setting has been printed in place in the Order of Mass, and the new ICEL setting is placed in Appendix I along with the other alternative settings of this chant.

8) The *Agnus Dei*

The English setting of the Lamb of God is readily suggested by the familiar Latin melody:

Some settings previously in use adapt the Latin a bit differently, but this setting places the stress correctly on "mercy" rather than "have."

9) The Prayer of the Faithful (Universal Prayer)

The English Missal provides several chant models to which the Prayer of the Faithful can be sung. The Latin models have been simplified slightly to facilitate the chanting of the English text (see p. 312).

A

B

C

D

If the Prayer of the Faithful is sung, it is especially important that the text be clearly proclaimed so it can be understood by the congregation. It is also possible to recite the petitions but sing the response.

C. The Preface Tone, Preface Dialogue, and Doxology to the Eucharistic Prayer

Not all the Prefaces are set to music in the Latin Missal, but musical settings of all of them are available in the publication *Ordo Missæ in Cantu.*[4] All the Prefaces are set to music in the English Missal.

4. *Ordo Missæ in Cantu: Iuxta Editionem Typicam Alteram Missalis Romani* (Solemnes: Abbaye Saint-Pierre, 1995).

Latin Solemn Preface Tone:

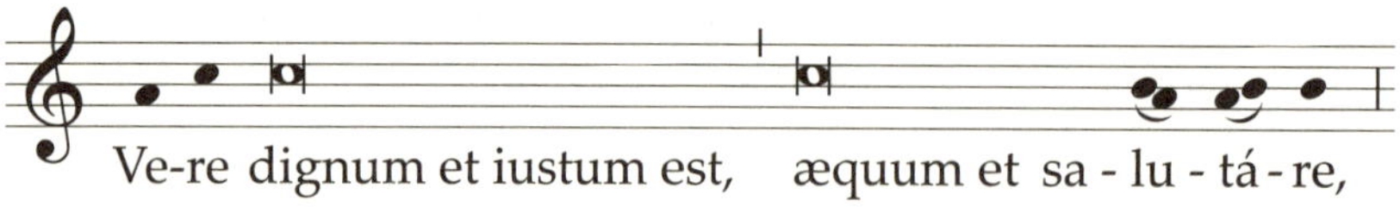

Latin simple Preface tone:

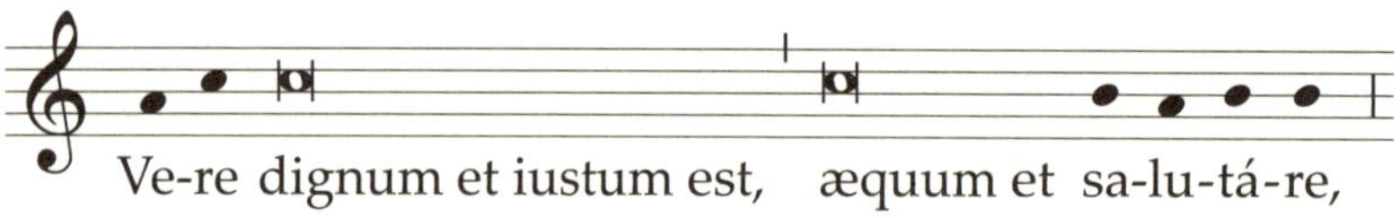

The Latin Solemn Preface Tone is more ancient, and it was the only tone in use for centuries, dating back to the formative era of the liturgy. The Simple Tone was derived from it in the eleventh and twelfth centuries.

While the Preface Tone in the previous English *Sacramentary* was based on the Latin simple Preface tone, the Preface Tone in the new English Missal is based on the Latin solemn Preface Tone. Of course, the Solemn Tone is adapted, when necessary, to fit the English text. This new, more ornate Preface Tone is similar to the well-known tone of the Easter Proclamation (*Exsultet*). Some singers report that the slightly more ornate setting is easier to sing due to its memorable melodic elements.

The new Preface Tone is illustrated here by the beginning of the Preface of Eucharistic Prayer IV:

The Simple Preface Tone appears in the English Missal only three times (see III, p. 26, below).

1) The New Preface Tone

For the celebrant singing the Preface, there are six important things to consider:

a. Each section within the Preface always begins with one note A before moving to the first reciting tone C. The celebrant should take care to respect the accentuation of the English text and proclaim it correctly. The first syllable of the reciting tone should not be accented unless it is an accented syllable. Note the variety of possibilities, all taken from Preface II for Sundays in Ordinary Time:

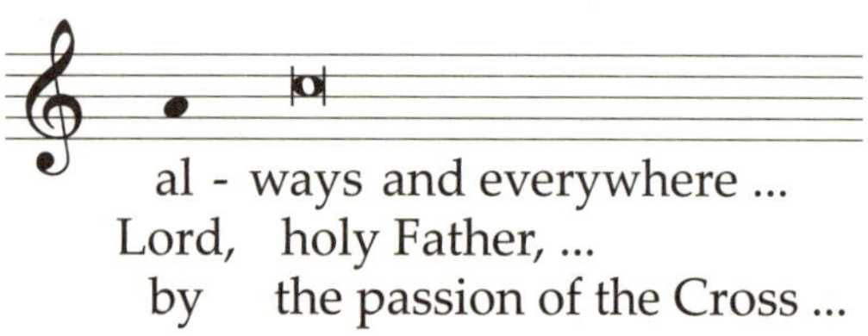

b. For the most part, the Preface departs from the reciting tone C on an accented syllable. The first note after the reciting tone is a black note C. The celebrant should watch for the first black note after the reciting tone and prepare to move to the accented syllable. Note these typical examples from the same Preface:

The nature of the English text means that sometimes the accent falls too far back for the usual text underlay. In these rare cases, the celebrant will move from the reciting tone on an unaccented syllable on the first black note B:

c. In a few cases, the second reciting tone B moves up to a single note C:

(from the Preface of the Most Holy Eucharist)

But most of the time the new Preface Tone has a more ornate run up at this point:

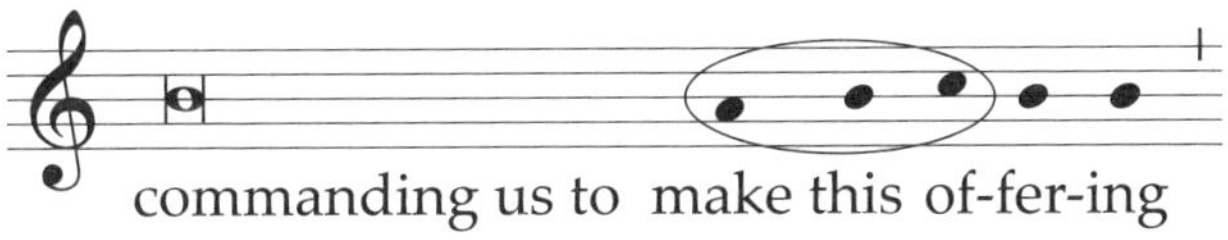

(from the Preface of the Most Holy Eucharist)

d. A fuller ornament appears in many of the Prefaces. This is a three-note figure with a "quilisma" as the second note:

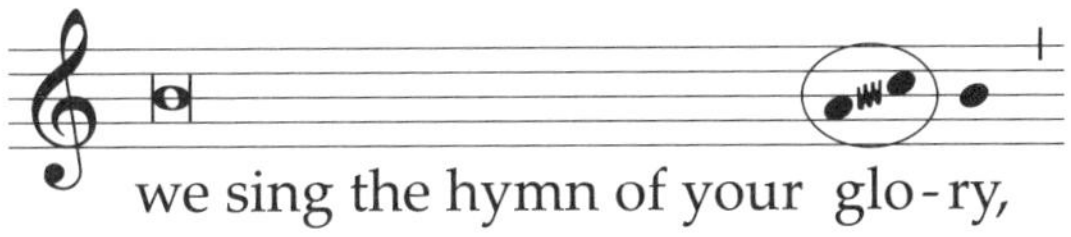

It is customary to sing these three notes by lengthening the first note, and then singing the second note lightly and quickly so as to move to the important third note (see II, pp. 14–15).

e. Here is the full melodic formula for the closing cadence in new Preface Tone:

Depending on the text, this formula is applied to the syllables in various ways, and sometimes its ending is abbreviated. Here are some examples:

(from Preface III of Easter)

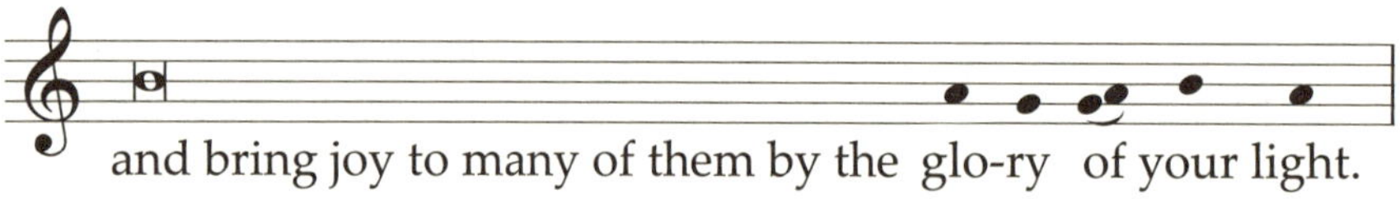

(all from Eucharistic Prayer IV)

f. In some Prefaces, there is a special melodic figure on "therefore" before the closing section of the Preface, which is similar to the Latin melodic figure employed for the words "*et ideo*" in the solemn Preface tone (see, for example, the Prefaces for Eucharistic Prayer II for Reconciliation and for June 29, Saints Peter and Paul, Apostles):

For more on the new Preface Tone, see V, pp. 46–51.

2) The Simple Preface Tone

The Latin Missal and *Ordo Missæ in Cantu* give Prefaces in both the Solemn and Simple Tones. The English Missal uses only one tone for all the Prefaces, and it is more like the Latin Solemn Tone than the Simple Tone. Only in three cases does the English Missal employ the Simple Preface Tone: the Solemn Intercessions on Good Friday, the introductory words of the baptismal liturgy at the Easter Vigil, and the Blessing of the Water at the Easter Vigil (see pp. 80–88, 102, 104–6). The Simple Tone befits the character of Good Friday, and at the Easter Vigil it serves to distinguish the baptismal liturgy from the Easter Proclamation (*Exsultet*) and the Preface of the Eucharistic Prayer. For further explanation of the Simple Preface Tone, see V, pp. 51–52.

3) Preface Dialogue and Doxology of the Eucharistic Prayer

The melodic formulas of these chants are retained from the previous *Sacramentary*, and will already be familiar to most English-speaking Catholics. They were retained not only for pastoral reasons, but also because they fit well with both the new Preface Tone and the natural accentuation of the English text.

The Preface Dialogue at the beginning of the Eucharistic Prayer is adjusted slightly, however, for the new translation:

Similarly, the Doxology of the Eucharistic Prayer uses the same melodic formulas as the previous *Sacramentary*, but adapts them to the new translation:

The Doxology is very similar to the new Preface Tone. The single note A moving to the reciting tone C on "Through" and "O" is identical to the beginning of all the Prefaces. The internal cadences on "with him, and in him" and "Holy Spirit" are treated exactly as in all the Prefaces as well. The series of pitches leading up to C "-ry and hon-" is found in nearly every Preface. Finally, the melody of the last phrase "for ever and ever" is identical to the concluding cadence formula of the new Preface Tone. By singing the new Doxology, the celebrant will become familiar with the building blocks of the new Preface tone and will find that over time singing the Preface itself will become second nature.

D. Tones for the Presidential Prayers

For the celebrant who is able to do so, it is appropriate to chant the three presidential prayers of the Mass: the Collect, the Prayer over the Offerings, and the Prayer after Communion. These texts are not marked up for singing (or "pointed") in the English Missal, but the celebrant can easily mark the texts ahead of time according to the instructions provided in Appendix I of the Missal (pp. 296–300).

The tones for the presidential prayers, in either their Solemn or Simple Tone, are musically very simple, with only a few pitches. The basic elements of the Solemn and Simple Tones here are exactly the same as in the Order of Mass (see III, pp. 17–19). When sung, these prayers consist of little more than one pitch for most of the prayer and simple melodic inflection for the musical punctuation of the text. While the explanation of how to do so in the Missal is quite detailed, it is not really that difficult to point or sing the presidential prayers.

In East and West alike, priests chanted presidential prayers for many centuries before the development of musical notation. Early liturgical books did not contain directions on how to point and sing prayers. How, then, was a priest able to chant the liturgical texts? His resources were the liturgical text, his voice, and his inherited musical tradition. He had probably heard the prayers sung since childhood.

Today, then, a priest has all of these things to draw upon, along with musical notation and a clearly explained system for pointing prayer texts. To be sure, the desire to proclaim the text expressively is more important than exacting fidelity to the rules of pointing. But the rules are there for a reason, and the priest should follow them as the norm. The rules were developed because they allow the pitches of the tone to convey the rhythm and meaning of the text. In following the rules, however, the priest should not forget that his ultimate goal is to proclaim the prayer reverently, expressing the joy in his heart, for the spiritual edification of the other worshipers.

1) The Solemn Tone for the Presidential Prayers

Let us recall the primary melodic elements of the Solemn Prayer Tone:

Primary melodic elements:

Solemn Tone

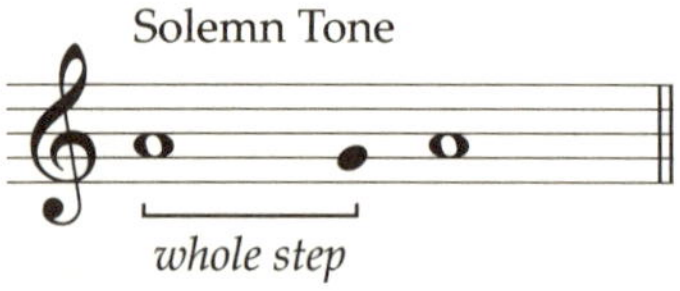

The priest who chants the prayers regularly to the Solemn Tone would ideally commit to memory the Solemn Tone invitation:

and the Solemn Tone ending:

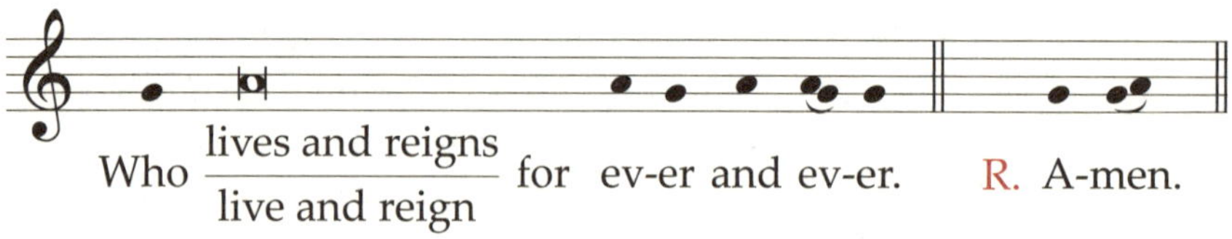

(Other possible settings of the ending, depending on the text, are given in Appendix I of the Missal.)

Then the body of the prayer is pointed as follows. This is not difficult.

a. The midway point of the prayer is decided upon (the place of the flex). Here, a judgment must be made according to the syntax of the prayer text as a whole.

b. The grave sign is placed on the syllable where the pitch descends for the flex. As described in Appendix I, this will be either the last syllable if it is accented or the syllable after the last accent. Here are several examples from Collects of the Sundays of Advent:

c. The syllable that bears the very last accent of the body of the prayer, but before the conclusion, is located. An acute accent is placed on this syllable.

d. A grave sign is placed two syllables before the last accented syllable, no matter where this happens to fall. Here are several examples from Advent Collects for placement of the grave at the end of the body of the prayer, with the acute on the final accent:

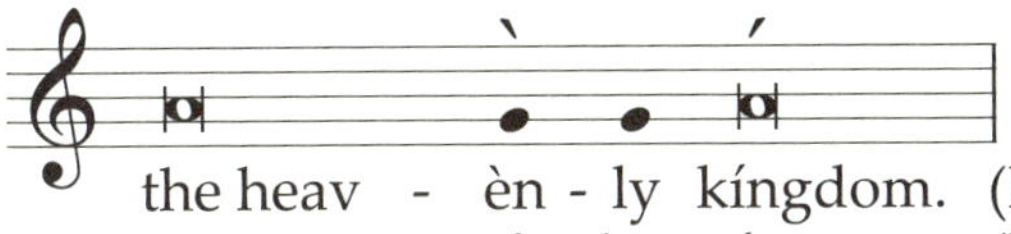

the heav - èn - ly kíngdom. (I Advent)
admittance tò his cómpany. (II Advent)
and glàd re - jóicing. (III Advent)
of his Rès - ur - réction. (IV Advent)

With this, the prayer is pointed for singing. The priest should remember that every new phrase in the solemn tone of the presidential prayers, both the opening phrase and the phrase after the flex, begins with one G before the text moves to the reciting tone on A. There is just one G, regardless of where the accents fall in the initial words of the phrase.

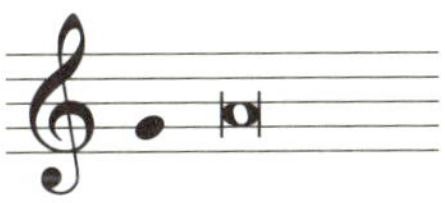

This Solemn Prayer Tone is very basic, consisting of nothing but alternation between the two pitches A and G. The priest who has this elementary tone in his ear and has spotted the midway point of the prayer will probably be able to sing the tone correctly even from a text that has not been pointed. Still, it is best always to point the prayer text ahead of time and to practice it.

There are fully notated examples of correctly pointed presidential prayers in Appendix I of the Missal. In practice, the celebrant would chant these prayers without notation from a pointed text. Here is how the text of the Collect for the First Sunday of Advent would appear when pointed for the solemn tone:

Grant your faithful, we pray, almighty God,
the resolve to run forth to meet your Christ
with righteous deeds at his comìng,
so that, gathered at his right hand,
they may be worthy to possess the heavènly Kíngdom.

There are only two graves and one acute in the entire body of the prayer when pointed for the Solemn Prayer Tone.

2) The Solemn Intercessions of Good Friday, the Blessing of the Water at the Easter Vigil, and the Eucharistic Prayers

We treat these chants at this point because these texts are all set to a tone in the Missal that is basically the same as the Solemn Presidential Prayer Tone with its pitches A and G.

For the Solemn Intercessions of Good Friday, a deacon or lay minister first sings the invitation, which expresses the intention. The simple Preface Tone is used for this invitation. Then the celebrant chants the prayer, which employs the Solemn Presidential Prayer Tone (see pp. 296–97). The Blessing of Water and the first four Eucharistic Prayers are also set to chant in the Solemn Prayer Tone.

Unlike the three presidential prayers of the Mass—the Collect, Prayer over the Offerings, and Prayer after Communion—these texts are all fully notated in the Missal. Because the pointing of these texts follows exactly the rules for the presidential prayer tones, singing these prayers with their notation will help the celebrant develop an intuitive sense for the Solemn Prayer Tone and will give him the confidence to chant the presidential prayers at Sunday Mass.

3) Solemn Anaphora Tone for Eucharistic Prayer I (Roman Canon)

The Appendix to the Order of Mass provides a "Solemn Anaphora Tone" for only one of the Eucharistic Prayers, the Roman Canon. The singer should not be confused by the terminology. The standard tone for the Eucharistic Prayers is identical to the Solemn Presidential Prayer Tone, but as indicated above, this solemn prayer tone is quite simple, consisting of nothing but the pitches A and G.

The Solemn Anaphora Tone for Eucharistic Prayer I is somewhat more ornate than the standard Eucharistic Prayer tone:

After the Preface, Eucharistic Prayer I continues at first in the standard tone. Then it transitions to the Solemn Anaphora Tone for several sections including the Institution Narrative. It then returns to the standard tone for the concluding sections up until the Doxology.

The ornate melody for the inner section of Eucharistic Prayer I in the Solemn Anaphora Tone is identical to the third setting of the Lord's Prayer in Appendix I, Tone C (see pp. 313–14). It is for this reason that Tone C of the Lord's Prayer is subtitled "Solemn Anaphora Tone."

4) The Simple Tone for Presidential Prayers

The procedure for chanting presidential prayers to the Simple Tone is quite similar to that for the Solemn Tone. As a reminder, here are the primary melodic elements of the Simple Prayer Tone, here at the pitch level used in the Missal:

Primary melodic elements:

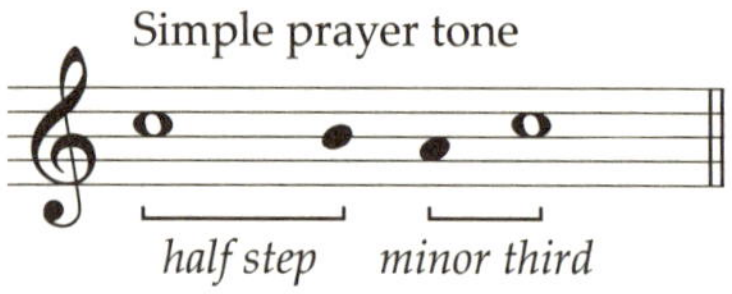

The priest who chants the prayers regularly to the Simple Tone would ideally commit to memory the simple tone invitation:

and the simple tone ending:

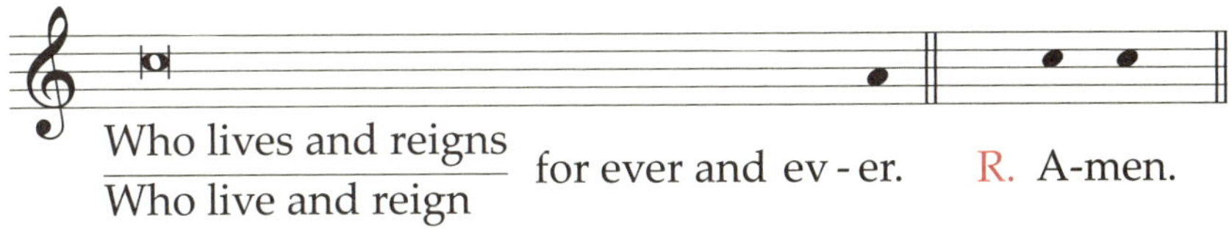

Other possible settings of the ending, depending on the text, are given in Appendix I of the Missal.

It is important to note that the Simple Tone ending always descends a minor third before the "Amen." The priest should note the difference between this and the larger descent of a perfect fifth at the end of the body of the prayer.

The body of the prayer is pointed as follows. The important thing to remember is that the Simple Tone has *three* parts for the body of the prayer, unlike the *two* parts of the Solemn Tone.

a. The midway point of the prayer is decided upon (where the *mediant* will be marked). Here, a judgment must be made according to the user's best sense of the overall syntax of the prayer text. In some cases, the midway point will be placed further back for the Simple Tone in order to provide a place prior to it for the flex (see "c." below).

b. A grave sign is placed two syllables before the last accented syllable at the mediant. Here are several examples from the Advent Collects for placement of the grave at the mediant:

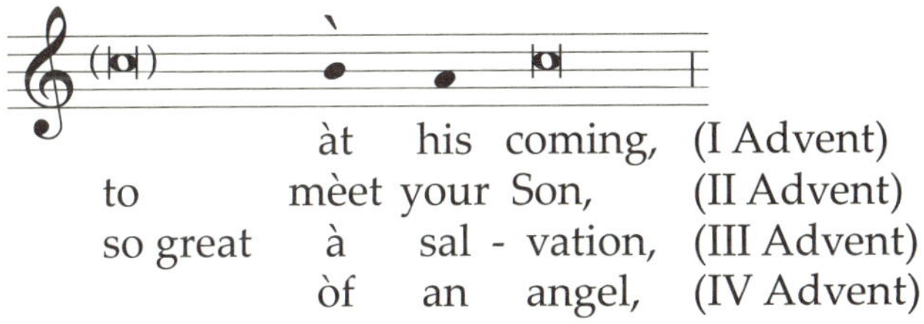

c. One selects the best place for the *flex* in the first part of the prayer, at some point before the mediant. The simple tone flex sign (+) is placed on the last syllable if it is accented, or the syllable after the last accent in other cases. Here are several examples from the Advent Collects for placement of the flex sign:

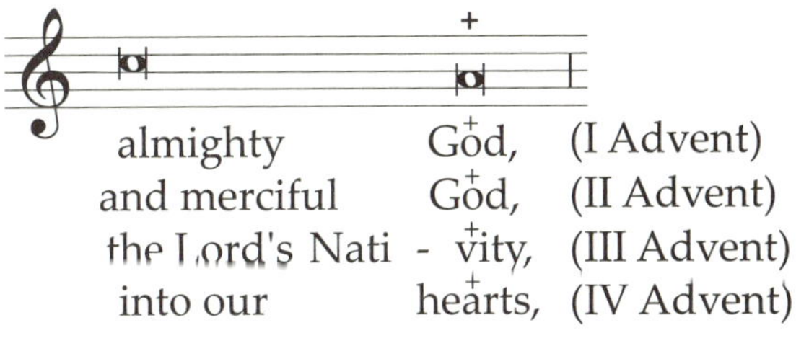

d. At the end of the body of the prayer, the double grave sign is placed on the syllable where the pitch descends. As described in Appendix I, this will be either the last syllable if it is accented, or the syllable after the last accent in other cases. Here are several examples from the Advent Collects for placement of the double grave at the end of the body of the prayer:

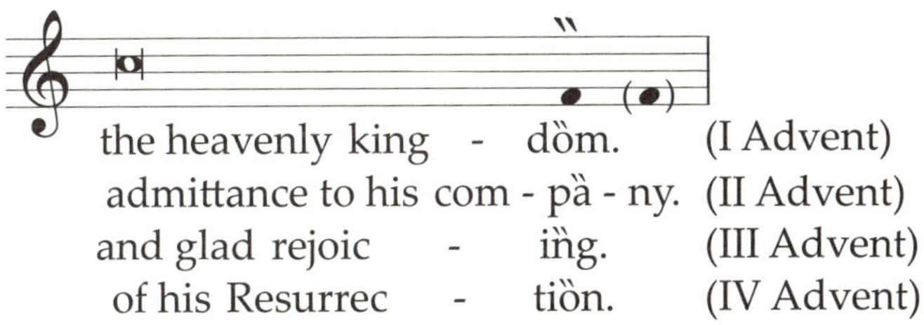

For the priest, the double grave is a reminder to descend a large interval, the perfect fifth from C to F. This is the only place in the Simple Prayer Tone where the descent is this wide, and the priest should note the difference between this and the smaller drop of a minor third, from C to A, at end of the conclusion to the prayer.

With this, the prayer is pointed for singing. The Simple Prayer Tone is somewhat easier to sing than the Solemn Prayer Tone in that every phrase begins with a C as the reciting tone, with no preceding note:

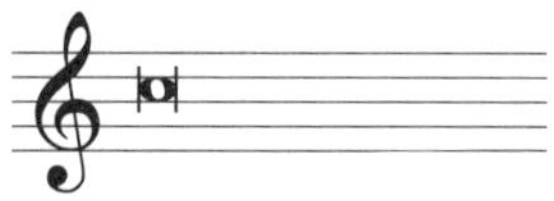

These are the steps for pointing a prayer text for the simple tone. There are fully notated examples of correctly pointed presidential prayers in Appendix I of the Missal. In practice, the celebrant would chant these prayers without notation from a pointed text. Here is how the text of the Collect for the First Sunday of Advent would appear when pointed for the simple tone:

+
Grant your faithful, we pray, almighty God,
the resolve to run forth to meet your Christ
with righteous deeds àt his coming,
so that, gathered at his right hand,
they may be worthy to possess the heavenly Kingdȍm.

There is one flex, one mediant, and one double grave in the entire body of the prayer when pointed for the Simple Prayer Tone.

Because this Simple Prayer Tone is rather easy, the priest who has the Simple Tone in his ear might find it easier simply to mark the end of the line at the three points in the body of the prayer where the text moves from the reciting note, without indicating the exact syllable. His instincts will then enable him to chant the prayer correctly as long as he has the three musical formulas in mind in the correct order:

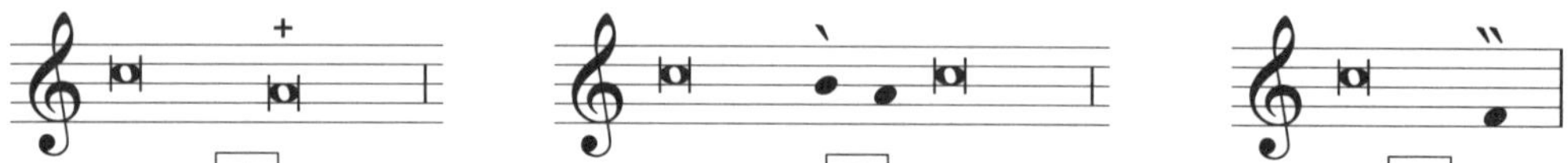

A B C

It is, of course, always best to practice the prayer ahead of time.

Here is an example of how the text of this Collect might appear for the priest who is very confident of the three formulas A, B, and C and only needs the line ends marked without exact pointing:

Grant your faithful, we pray, almighty God, |
the resolve to run forth to meet your Christ
with righteous deeds at his coming, |
so that, gathered at his right hand,
they may be worthy to possess the heavenly kingdom. ||

E. Antiphons and Versicles

In a few cases, the Latin Missal provides proper antiphons or a versicle to be sung on particular days of the year. The following chants appear in the English Missal in both Latin and English versions:

Palm Sunday:
Hosanna filio David / Hosanna to the Son of David (p. 73)

Good Friday:
Ecce lignum / Behold the wood (pp. 88–89)

Easter Vigil:
Vidi aquam / I saw water (pp. 108–9)

Presentation of the Lord:
Ecce Dominus noster / Behold, our Lord will come (p. 242)
Lumen ad revelationem / A light for revelation (p. 243)

The following chant appears in the English Missal only in English:

Easter Vigil:
Springs of water (*Benedicite fontes*) (p. 107)

Most of these antiphons would be led by the choir or a cantor. "*Ecce lignum*/ Behold, the wood," however, is a versicle, the first part of which is sung by the celebrant, deacon, or choir. The English Missal provides a vernacular setting that is melodically rich, even if it is a simplification of the Latin chant *Ecce lignum*:

Because of the importance of this chant for the Liturgy of the Lord's Passion on Good Friday, a simpler setting is also provided, in case the first setting is too difficult for some ministers. The simpler setting is designed to be used with the same response as the first setting.

F. Hymns

A hymn text is said to be "metrical" when it has a standard meter for each of its stanzas—for example, four lines of twelve syllables each, or four lines of eight syllables each. Another term for stanza is "strophe." A hymn is said to be "strophic" when its successive strophes of text can be sung to the same recurring melody, which must have the same meter as the text.

There are only three strophic metrical hymn texts in the Latin Missal:

Palm Sunday:
Gloria, laus et honor / Hymn to Christ the King: Glory and honor and praise (p. 74)

Holy Thursday Evening Mass of the Lord's Supper:
Ubi Caritas / Where true charity is dwelling (p. 78)

Good Friday:
Crux fidelis / Faithful Cross (pp. 89–91)

These hymns do not appear with music in the Latin Missal, so the English Missal similarly provides just the texts in vernacular translation. Even though they do not appear in the English Missal with music, musical settings of the English translations were prepared for this Study Edition. Since the same melody is used for each strophe of the Latin metrical text, there was no difficulty putting the metrical English hymn texts under the chant hymn melodies, which are taken from the *Graduale Romanum*.

In all three instances, the Missal indicates that these "or other suitable chants" may be sung. Other translations of these hymns are found in a variety of congregational worship aids, often with well-known hymn tunes from recent centuries. It is not intended that the new translations necessarily supplant versions already in use. But those who wish to sing the traditional Latin melodies with the English hymn texts can use the chants in this Study Edition.

G. Reading Tones

The English Missal provides tones for chanting each of the three readings of the Mass. They are all based on the Latin models, with necessary adjustments for the nature of the English language.

The reading tone for the First Reading (Old Testament, or Acts of the Apostles during the Easter Season) is similar to the Simple Presidential Prayer Tone with the characteristic drop of a perfect fifth from C to F (see III, pp. 30–32).

The reading tone for the Second Reading (or First Reading when the Mass has only one reading before the Gospel) is called the Epistle Tone. It is used for the Epistles and the Book of Revelation. It is the most ornate of the reading tones.

The reading tone for the Gospel is similar to but not quite as ornate as the Epistle Tone. The English Missal provides two tones for the Gospel, which correspond to tones B and C of the three Gospel tones provided in the Latin Missal. In the English Missal, these are called the Gospel Tone and the Solemn Gospel Tone, respectively.

A detailed explanation of how to sing the readings according to these tones is found in Appendix I of the English Missal (pp. 300–309). This explanation was necessary because English has a number of accent patterns not found in Latin. Given the relative complexity of the reading tones, it will be necessary for a reader to notate the readings entirely and to practice ahead of time. Only those who regularly chant the readings will become familiar enough with the tones to be able to sing them without notation. Appendix I also provides sample musical settings of the Old Testament Reading and Acts of the Apostles, Epistle and Book of Revelation, and Gospel as models of how to notate and chant the texts of the readings.

IV. LAYOUT AND NOTATION OF ENGLISH CHANT

The five-line notation of the English Missal is designed to help ministers sing well the chants of the Missal. It is helpful for the singer to understand the nature and particularities of this notation.

In developing the five-line notation of the Missal, attention was given to every detail. A variety of settings for the thickness of staff lines, the size of the note heads, the thickness and placement of the quarter bar, and the distance between the staff and the text were laid out for comparison. As can be seen below, all these aspects play a role in the clarity and attractiveness of the notation:

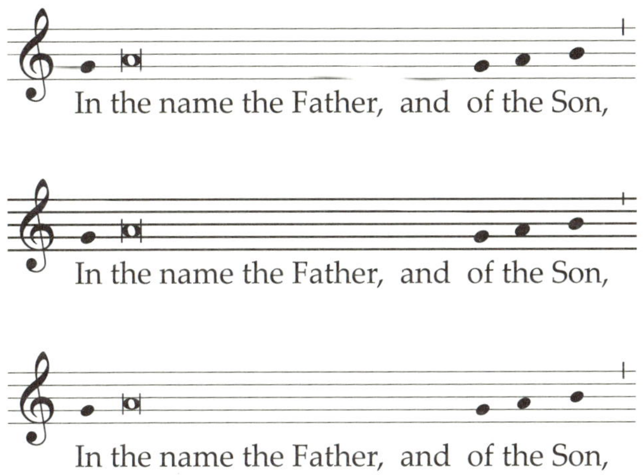

For longer chants such as the Preface, the staves of the Missal are right-hand justified, and the words are placed with standardized (normal) length between them. The line break falls wherever the text reaches the end of the line. A layout in sense lines, either with blank staff hanging over at the end of each line or with staves of varying lengths, was tried and rejected. Right-hand justification of the text, with the resulting varieties of spacing between words, was also rejected. Unlike four-line notation, the final line of a chant ends where the text and melody end, with no extra staff lines extending to the right hand margin.

Modern five-line notation is used in the English Missal because this notation is likely to be more familiar to the vast majority of liturgical ministers. It is true that the venerable four-line square-note notation of the Latin chant books is in some ways easier to read, once the singer becomes familiar with it, and it is not difficult to learn this notation. Serious consideration was given to employing four-line notation for the English chants of the Missal. But it was determined that this notation would pose a practical hindrance and psychological barrier for many singers, especially at first. It was thought more practical to avoid these dangers for the official English liturgical books. However, nothing prevents individual publishers from providing the chants in four-line square-note notation in congregational worship aids.

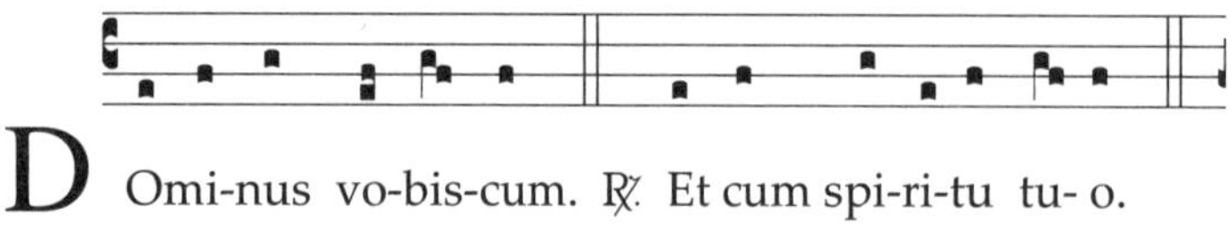

The official Latin liturgical books, both those before and after the liturgical reforms of the Second Vatican Council, use four-line square-note notation. Square-note notation has certain advantages with respect to text, and every effort has been made to bring these advantages into the five-line notation of the English Missal. In the four-line notation (see above), all note heads are black. The notes over a syllable are grouped closely together, making it clear to which syllable they belong (e.g., the two notes over each of the first two syllables of "*vobíscum*" above). This grouping of notes over a syllable suggests the primacy of the text and its syllables, whereas melodic notes spaced evenly from each other could imply melodic notes of equal rhythmic length. The individual square note, or the first note of a note group, is centered exactly over the vowel of the Latin syllable. Hyphens are placed between syllables only if this is required by the overall spacing of the text and its melody.

Some adaptation to the conventions of five-line notation are necessary, and other adaptations have been made for the sake of greater clarity. Note heads are centered over the entire English syllable, not the vowel. This follows standard five-line conventions, which accounts for English syllables that may have more than one vowel. To make the text underlay clearer, the syllables are hyphenated wherever there is a change of pitch.

In the notation of the English Missal, black notes without stems are used so as not to imply any particular rhythmic values. The rhythm is determined by the singer's sense of the text to be proclaimed (see section II, pp. 12–13). White notes are used only for reciting tones, similar to the reciting note of psalm tones. A reciting note is not used for a text less than two syllables. Here is an excerpt from the Preface to Eucharistic Prayer IV showing an intonation note (A), a reciting note (C), and black notes and note groups at the cadence.

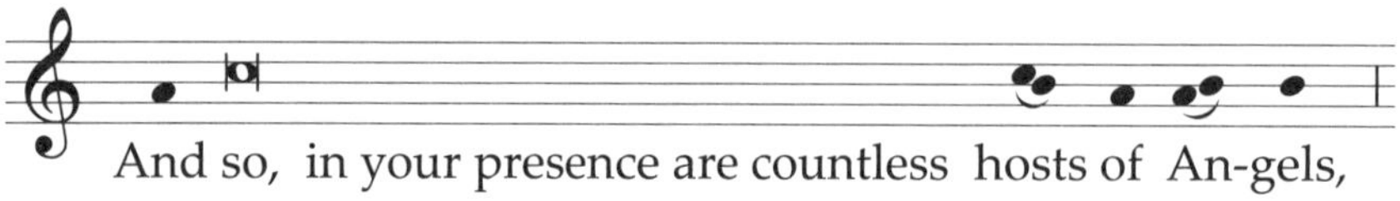

As can be seen in this example, notes in note groups (e.g. above "hosts," "An-") are spaced close together. As in the four-line notation, this clarifies the syllables to which the note groups are subordinate. Slurs marking note groups are placed under the notes so as to be closer to the text and clearer to the singer. The text is placed quite close to the staff.

Four-line square-note note notation in the Latin Missal has two particularities that required a decision in the move to five-line notation. The *liquescent* indicates a brief, light note. It is a smaller note head used at the end of a syllable. The *quilisma* is a wavy figure that is the second note of a note group.

The liquescent and the quilisma are seen in four-line notation above on the left. On the right one sees how these forms can be approximated in five-line notation. As will be seen, the liquescent appears in the English Missal only when the chant is in Latin, and the quilisma appears only in chants for the celebrant, for the most part only in the Preface.

Because the liquescent and quilisma involve subtleties of performance practice appropriate to a soloist or a trained small group, they do not appear in English congregational chants in the Missal. In Latin chant books, in fact, liquescents do appear even in simpler chants such as the *Sanctus* of Mass XVIII. This probably reflects the fact that, increasingly throughout the Middle Ages, Gregorian chant Mass Ordinaries were sung only by monastic or other choirs and no longer by the congregation. Whatever the reason, the liquescents in Latin chant are found in the five-line notation of the Missal only when it is a matter of reproducing them from the Latin four-line notation. This explains the notational difference between the Latin and English versions of the *Sanctus* in the Missal:

Latin *Sanctus*:

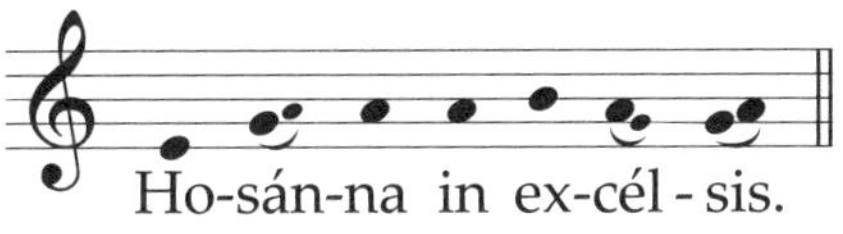

English *Sanctus*:

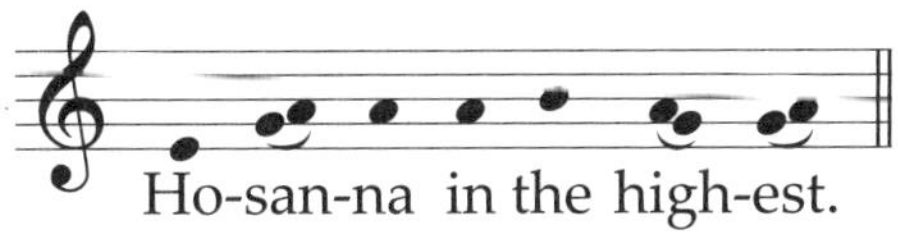

Most of the quilismas appear in the Preface, most often at its end:

The only other place the quilisma appears in the Missal is in the chant of the celebrant (or deacon or choir) at the first part of the Showing of the Holy Cross, "Behold the wood" (see II, pp. 14–15, and III, p. 33).

The aesthetics of notational layout implicitly say something about the Church's relationship to her own liturgical tradition, as well as the Church's understanding of the pastoral needs of worshiping communities. The notation of the English Missal aims to be neither iconoclastic nor archaic, neither reductively functionalist nor fussy. The user will judge whether the notation achieves that "noble simplicity" commended by the Second Vatican Council (cf. *Sacrosanctum Concilium*, no. 34).

V. DEVELOPING ENGLISH CHANT FROM LATIN MODELS

Throughout history, there have been many approaches to the adaptation of Latin chant to the English language, and there continues to be a variety of viewpoints on the topic today. To be sure, on many of the intricacies of such adaptation, there is not a general consensus. Furthermore, there are many schools of thought on how to sing chant in Latin or English—for example, on whether or not to sing accented syllables more loudly or with rhythmic lengthening. Such differences of interpretation have influenced views about how to adapt chant from Latin to English.

This chapter describes how the English chants of the Roman Missal were developed from Latin models. It is intended for the reader who wishes to understand the rationale for the decisions made, and it will help the singer to appreciate and understand the Missal chants more deeply.

A. The Process for Developing English Chant

In recent centuries, much of the adaptation of Latin chant into English has been carried out in the Anglican Communion, beginning with the Reformation in the sixteenth century, and increasing especially in the nineteenth century with "high church" movements of liturgical renewal. English chant based on Latin models has also been developed and used by other English-speaking Christians, especially those with liturgical forms of worship (e.g., Lutherans).

Interest in English chant among Roman Catholics heightened in the 1950s in anticipation of the possible future use of the vernacular in the liturgy. With the decision of the Second Vatican Council (1962–65) to admit vernacular into Roman Catholic worship, it became necessary to provide English chants for the various editions of the *Missale Romanum* (Roman Missal) and for the other ritual books.

The third edition of the *Missale Romanum* of 2002, slightly emended in 2008, has been translated into English and approved for liturgical use by Conferences of Bishops and by the Holy See. As a rule, English chants are provided for everything that is set to music in the Latin *Missale Romanum*. In many cases, following the example of the *Missale Romanum*, both simple and solemn settings are provided.

The work of preparing chant settings of the English translation was guided by several principles:

- To preserve and recover the tradition of unaccompanied singing in the Roman Rite, since the liturgy "is given a more noble form when . . . celebrated solemnly in song" (*Sacrosanctum Concilium* 113);[5]
- To facilitate "full and active participation by all the people," which is "the aim to be considered before all else" (*SC* 14);
- To take full account of the accentuation of the English language, since translators and composers "are to respect the idiom and grammar of the vernacular" in the adaptation of traditional melodies (*Musicam Sacram* 54);
- To retain vernacular chants now in use where possible, since "there must be no innovations unless the good of the Church genuinely and certainly requires them" (*SC* 23).

ICEL's music committee, comprised of renowned experts in the field of liturgical chant, undertook a detailed analysis of the Latin chants of the Missal, creating tables of accent patterns and musical formulas.

5. See also chapter 1 of this commentary, "Sung Vernacular Liturgy in the Liturgical Reform."

Likewise for the new English translation, tables of accent patterns were created, in order to arrive at the best solution where the English text has accent patterns not found in Latin (see, for example, the table of English accent patterns for the Preface, below at V.C.2).

The committee found it helpful to look at the work of other vernacular chant adaptations such as Spanish, French, and German. German-language scholarship has proven helpful, both because German-speaking scholars began investigating vernacular chant adaptation as early as the 1920s and because the German language has some similarities to English (for example, in the accent often falling on the final syllable of a phrase). The committee examined the English language chant of other Christian traditions, as well as the previous work of English chant adaptation in the Roman Catholic liturgical books of 1966, 1970, 1971, and 1973.

B. Relationship of the 2010 English Chants to the Latin Missal

The foundation for the chant in the English Missal is the chant of the Latin *Missale Romanum*. But the English chant settings of the previous 1973 *Sacramentary* were also consulted. For the most part, those texts set to chant in the Latin Missal are also set to chant in the English Missal. There are, however, a few exceptions.

The Greek Kyrie in the third form of the Penitential Act is not set to chant in the Latin *Missale Romanum*. To provide for singing this third form (in Greek and in English), a chant setting from the *Graduale Simplex* has been included (see D 1. below, p. 46). Only the incipits (first line) from the full settings of the Gloria in the *Graduale Romanum* are notated in the *Missale Romanum*. These incipits reflect the practice of the Priest intoning the Gloria. It was thought advisable to include one full setting of the English Gloria within the Order of Mass. It is based on Gloria XV. Similarly, only the incipits from the full settings of the Profession of Faith (Credo) in the *Graduale Romanum* are notated in the *Missale Romanum*, but it was thought advisable to provide English settings based on Credo I (in place in the Order of Mass) and Credo III (in Appendix I). Only the first *Mysterium fidei* acclamation is set to music in the *Missale Romanum*, but it was thought appropriate to provide chant settings for all three acclamations in English.

There are three tones for chanting the Gospel in the *Missale Romanum*, the first two being quite similar. In the English Missal only two tones are presented: a simple tone based on the second tone in the *Missale Romanum*, and a solemn tone based on the third tone in the *Missale Romanum*.

Three chants in the English Missal are newly composed or based only loosely on Latin models. First, "Behold the cross" (*Ecce lignum*) on Good Friday is based loosely on its ornate Latin model, but simplified in order to encourage the singing of this important chant. This simplified setting is still rather elaborate, so an even simpler setting based on the simple Mode VI Psalm tone is also provided. Second, "I saw water" (*Vidi aquam*) at the Easter Vigil is entirely newly composed, based on typical Mode VIII modality. It was necessary to compose a new setting because this chant is intended to be sung by the entire congregation, but the Latin chant is clearly intended for a trained schola. Third, the three *Mysterium fidei* acclamations are newly composed, based on modal structural elements of the Latin model (the chant setting of *Mortem tuam* in place in the Latin Missal).

C. Some Challenging Issues

Many practical and theoretical issues arise in the work of developing English chant from Latin models.

1) The Nature of the Accent in Latin and English

While there is fairly widespread agreement on the variety of ways the accented syllable is treated by the Gregorian composers, there is less agreement on the nature of the English accent and, consequently, the extent to which the treatment of Latin syllables can be applied to the treatment of English syllables. To explore this issue, it is necessary first to examine in some detail the compositional techniques found in Latin chant. Two issues are to be examined in the treatment of Latin accents: first, the use of note groups; second, the use of structurally important melodic pitches.

a. The Use of Note Groups with Respect to the Latin Accent

The first issue is whether or not note groups are placed consistently on accented syllables in Latin chant. In fact, they are not. Placing note groups on unaccented syllables, with a single pitch on the accented syllable, occurs often in the proper chants of the *Graduale Romanum*. It also occurs in the simpler ministerial chants of the *Missale Romanum*.

Some ministerial chants place the note group on an accent:

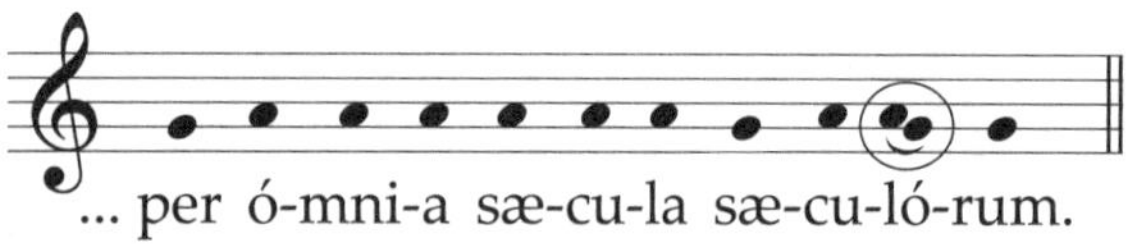

But in other cases, the note group is placed on an unaccented syllable before the accented syllable (as in the solemn tone of the Roman Canon in the first example) or after the accented syllable (as in the two examples from the Preface Dialogue and the opening phrase of the Sanctus). Note that the accented syllable (underlined in the examples below) receives a single pitch in each of these examples.

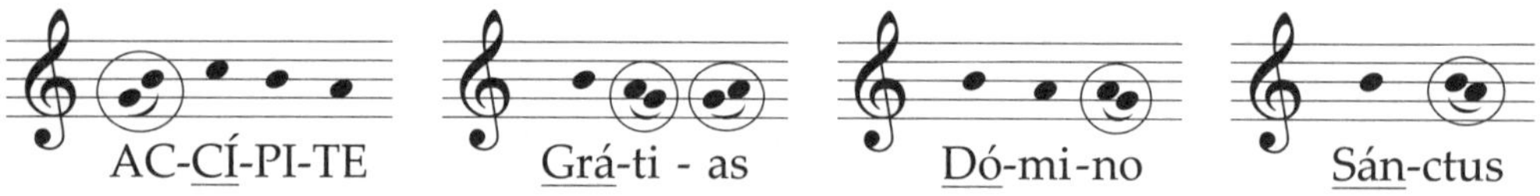

The variety of treatments, with note groups sometimes on accented syllables, sometimes not, is seen in this full line from the Preface Dialogue:

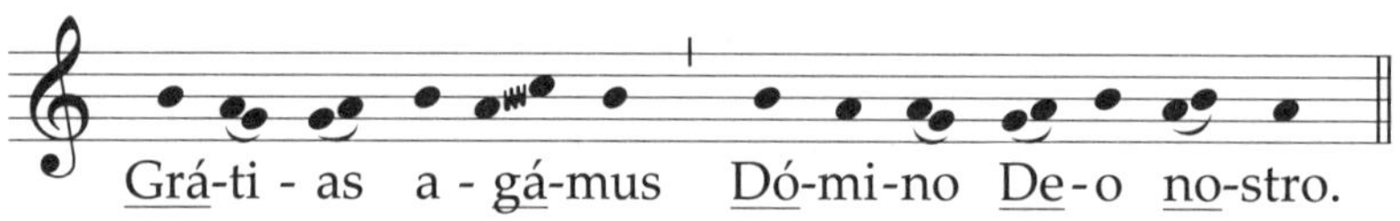

We can surmise that such varied treatment of note groups in Latin chant developed over the course of time because of the interest and vitality it lends to chant. It would be rather tiresome and sing-songy if the note groups fell on the accented syllables uniformly, as in this hypothetical example:

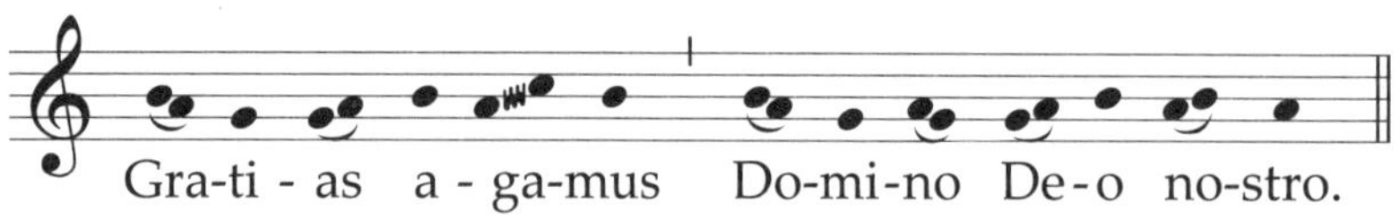

b. Structurally Important Melodic Pitches with Respect to the Latin Accent

The second issue in the treatment of the accent in Latin chant is the placement of significant melodic notes on accented syllables. This note might be significant because it is of a higher pitch, or because it is a modally important structural pitch. Oftentimes the accented syllable is treated this way in cases where the accented syllable is set to only one note.

Here is an example of a higher pitch on an accented syllable:

The Preface Dialogue, cited above, places a higher pitch on the accented syllable in both cases where this syllable is set to only one note:

In the beginning of the Gloria from Mass XV, which is the basis for the English chant Gloria in the English Missal, the pitch on the accented first syllable is low, but it is E, which is a structurally important pitch in Mode IV:

We see, then, that Latin chant often compensates for the "misplaced" note groups on unaccented syllables by placing a pitch on the accented syllable that is high or melodically important. This serves to compensate for the fact that the accented syllable does not have a note group.

In a few rare cases, it seems that the accented syllable receives no attention from the composer, neither with a note group, nor with a structurally important pitch. This appears to be the case with the very first syllable of each of the following examples—although perhaps the initial lowest pitch gives stress simply because it is in contrast melodically to what follows.

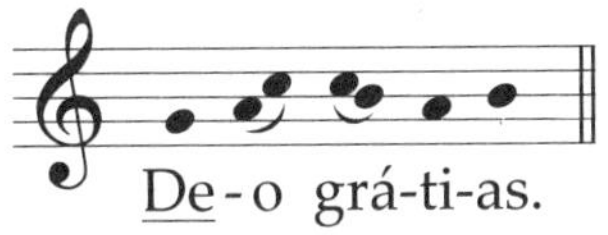

c. The Nature of the English Accent

Before discussing whether it is possible to treat the English text in the ways the Latin text is treated, it is necessary to note the principal differences between the two languages and the distinguishing characteristics of accents in English.

Latin accents tend to fall with regularity on every second or third syllable. The exceptions to this are infrequent. English accents fall much less regularly. There are two accents in a row more frequently than in Latin—for example, "in your ówn ímage." In English there are also more cases of several unaccented syllables in row—for example, "foundátion of the apóstles."

While there are differences between longer and shorter syllables in Latin, they fall within a smaller range than in English. Consider the wide range between long one-syllable English words such as "world" and "thanks" and short one-syllable words such as "to" and "the." Some English syllables are so short that it is difficult to judge how many syllables a word has for purposes of setting it to chant. For example, when set to music, should there be three syllables or two in "baptism," "family," "catholic," and "mutual"?

It is rare for the last syllable of a phrase or sentence in Latin to be accented, but this happens quite frequently in English. This difference has significant implications for the adaptation of Latin musical formulas to cadences with English text.

Finally, there is one issue about which scholars hold differing views. It concerns the weightiness of English accents in comparison to Latin accents. Following the opinion of German-speaking scholars (e.g., Thrasybulos Georgiades), some hold that English accents are heavier and carry more expressive value than Latin accents. According to this viewpoint, English accents, more than Latin accents, attract note groups to themselves. This viewpoint holds that unaccented syllables in English are not as capable of carrying note groups as are unaccented Latin syllables.

Some scholars do not acknowledge this difference between Latin and English accents and believe that one can set English chant with single pitches on accented syllables and note groups on unaccented syllables, just as in Latin chant.

Consider the opening phrase of the Preface in Latin, with its two-note group on the unaccented syllable "lu" and a single pitch on preceding syllable "sa," which is more accented.

According to the second viewpoint, which does not acknowledge the difference between Latin and English accents, it is unproblematic to transfer the musical formula to the English text at the cadence. It is considered acceptable that "our" has a single pitch, but the lighter following syllable "sal" has a two-note group:

In contrast, the approach in the English Missal is to split the two-note group so that it does not fall on an unaccented syllable, leaving a two-note group only on the accented syllable:

The issue of the nature of the English accent is an extremely important one, for it is confronted in nearly every phrase to be adapted from Latin to English. For the most part, the ICEL music committee has set the Missal chants with attention to the weight of English syllables. That is to say, English texts are not simply made to fit Latin melodies. Instead, adaptations are made to the Latin melodies and melodic formulas so that note groups generally fall on accented syllables rather than unaccented syllables.

This is not universally the case, however. As important as the weight of the English accent is in adapting Latin chant, it is not the only issue. There are other issues to consider, to which we now turn.

2) Modal Stability

There is a logic to how Gregorian melodies move forward from one structurally important modal pitch to another. Stepwise movement, or movement by small intervals such as thirds or fourths, predominates. Angular passages with large melodic jumps in various directions in rapid succession are not found in Latin chant. Large jumps, which are infrequent, are typically followed by balancing movement in the opposite direction, usually with smaller intervals. Melodic passages tend not to move exclusively in one direction without alighting upon one pitch along the way for modal stability. Or, more typically, there is movement along the way in the opposite direction, which forestalls reaching a far-off pitch too rapidly.

And yet, even as all these restraints govern how the Gregorian melody moves forward, the result is not monotonous or tiresome. The Gregorian composers knew how to move forward from one melodic pole to another with both restraint and interest. While there is restraint in melodic contour, forward movement and interest is provided by careful use of stable and unstable modal pitches in proper proportion.

Note how this phrase near the beginning of Gloria XVI, which is little more than a simple psalm tone, moves off the stable "reciting note" A to the higher, modally interesting pitch B on an accented syllable:

Ideally, this higher movement to B would be retained in the English adaptation if possible. But the corresponding English text, "and on earth peace to people of good will," does not allow for this without disturbing the modal stability. The following hypothetical setting is unsatisfactory because the melody moves too quickly in one direction from E up to B without resting on A along the way:

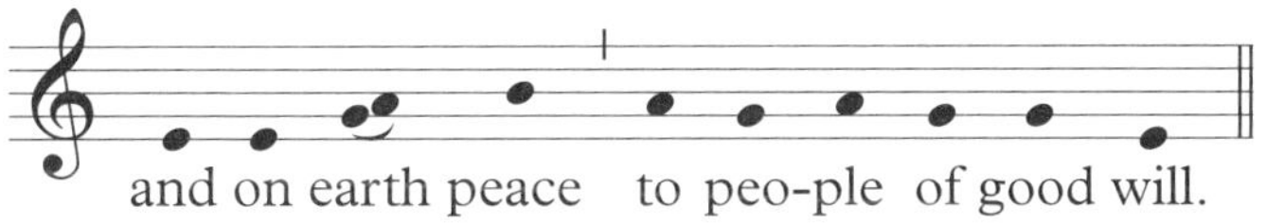

The solution in this case was to forego the higher pitch and remain on A:

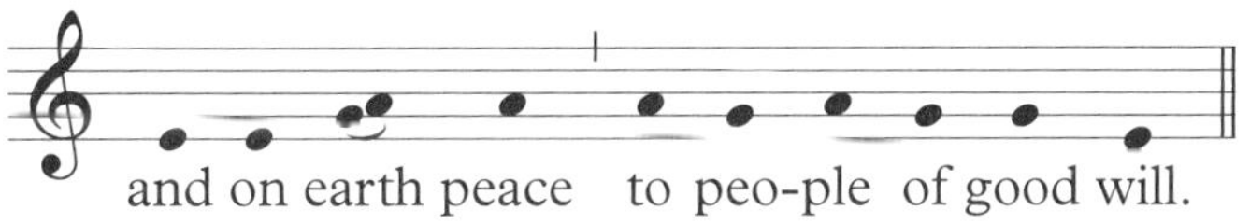

Such modal considerations played a role in the setting of the Greeting of the Introductory Rites. The setting in the previous Sacramentary/Missal could have been retained, adjusted to the revised text as follows:

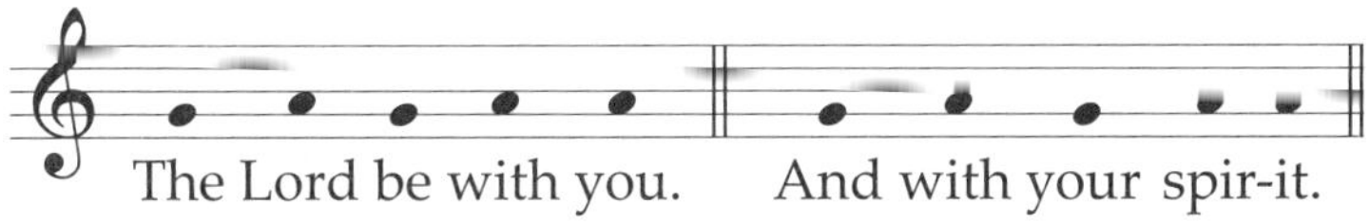

For the English Missal this solution is unsatisfactory from the standpoint of modal stability, however. The two syllables on "also" in the previous translation enabled the modal center of A to be established. But with the new text, the adaptation leads to unstable rapid alternation between G and A. For this reason, the setting in the Missal is as follows:

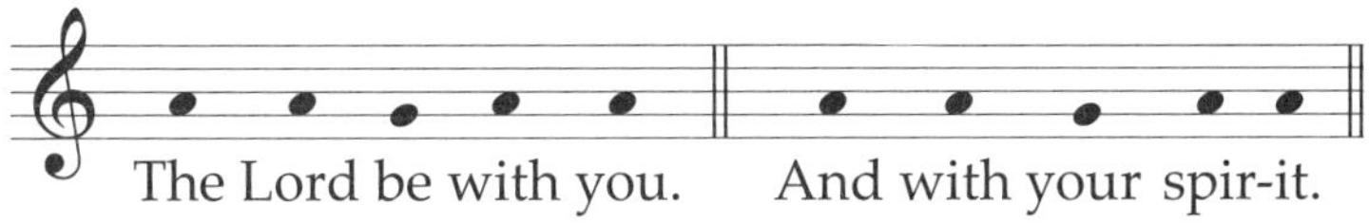

Purely from the standpoint of textual treatment, and disregarding modal or melodic implications, the setting of "to the Son of David" in the opening of this chant for Passion (Palm) Sunday might be better as follows, because it avoids the emphasis on "to" and shifts the emphasis to "Son":

But this solution was rejected because of the modal implications. Undue repetition of D detracts from the modal interest of the phrase. For this reason, the following setting, which is also more redolent of the Latin original, was selected:

An interesting challenge is posed by the common Latin formula which drops a minor third on the final unaccented syllable, as seen below in the dialogues of Passion (Palm) Sunday and the Easter Vigil:

The difficulty is that the English text, unlike the Latin, ends on an accented syllable in both cases: "Let us go forth in *peace*" and "The Light of *Christ*." Some have held, for good reason, that this final one-syllable accented word better receives its proper stress if the formula returns to the reciting note C:

Others have held, also for good reason, that there is less modal interest to the formula when it begins and ends on the same pitch (C), because the only contrasting pitch (A) is less prominent when it is not the final pitch. The alternate solution, then, is:

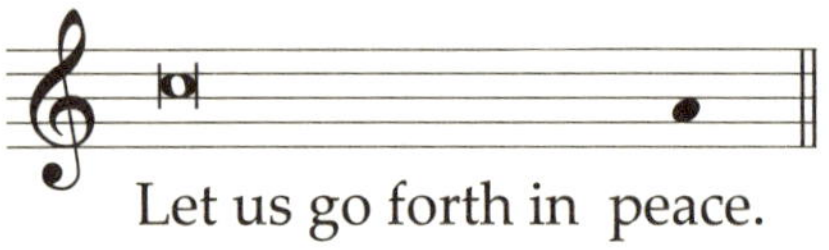

There are good reasons for either approach, and neither is clearly superior to the other. The English Missal favors the modal interest of ending on A in several cases—the invitation to process on Passion (Palm) Sunday, the Simple Tone throughout the Order of Mass, and "Let us pray" in the Simple Prayer Tone. But in other cases the English setting returns to C: "The Light of Christ," the dialogue before the Gospel in the Simple Tone, and the invitation to process on the Presentation of the Lord, though it is the same text as on Passion (Palm) Sunday. These chants can probably be sung equally well with either approach.

3) Avoidance of Distracting Melodic Motifs

It sometimes happens that the placement of note groups on accented syllables, which ordinarily serves the English text well, sets up a melodic motif that, by being striking, distracts from the text. Consider the following hypothetical settings from the Solemn Tone of the Roman Canon:

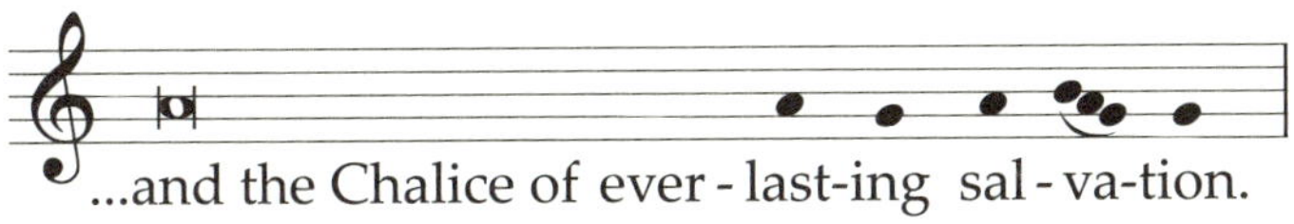

In each case, even with the most careful text-based rendition, the setting conjures the swing of a waltz on "given / up for" and "lasting sal- / va-." The setting in the Missal avoids this problem by putting note groups on unaccented syllables after the manner of Latin chant:

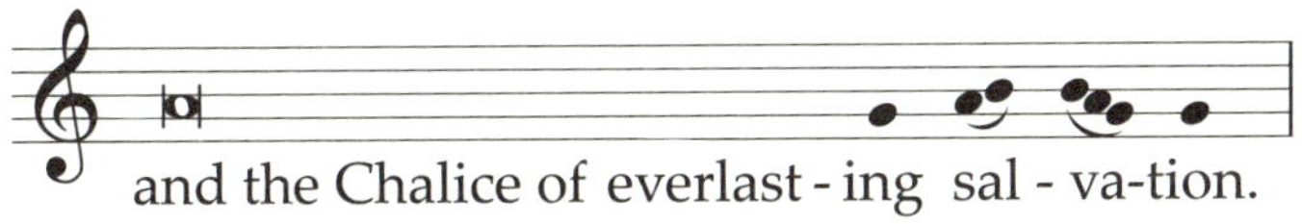

To be sure, there is a risk in this approach, and the English chant can sound affected or artificial when sung. But when a priest sings the chant carefully, noting the accentuation of the English text, it can sound natural, even if ornate. In this case, the risk was taken not only to avoid the problems of the hypothetical settings above, but also because of the nature of this particular chant. It was thought desirable that this more solemn setting be redolent of the Latin tone and the Latin manner of text underlay.

4) Usability of the Missal Chants in Practice

Sometimes one or the other above considerations (the nature of the accent in English, modal stability, and avoiding distracting melodic motifs) had to be balanced against the practical concern that the chant be usable in actual pastoral circumstances.

For example, it might seem unusual that the second Dismissal formula in the Missal has a note group on "of":

If this formula is taken in isolation, it might seem preferable to set it like this:

(the same is true of the third dismissal formula, "Go in peace, glorifying the Lord by your life").

But as much as this solution better treats the English text "Gospel of the Lord" ("by your life" in the third dismissal formula), it is less practical because it does not cue the assembly's response as well. For this reason, the cadence melody of the second and third Dismissal formulas is intentionally the same as that of the first, with the note group C-B:

The decision to place note groups mostly on accented syllables is based primarily on the nature of the English language. But it is also based on practical concerns. This manner of adaptation helps ensure that the typical priest, and not only the exceptionally talented priest, will be able to sing the Missal chants well.

D. The Setting of Some Particular English Chants

1) The *Kyrie* in the Third Form of the Penitential Act

The melody for the Greek Kyrie response is taken from the *Graduale Simplex* (452: Setting G) (see p. 123). It was selected because its modality matches the English invocation and response, which allows the same setting of the English invocations to be sung with the response in either language. It might be noted that the Gregorian setting is in mode IV* of the revised modes in the new *Antiphonale Monasticum*. In this mode, the main pitches, G and E, are a minor third from each other, and G is the reciting tone (see also III, pp. 19–20).

2) The Preface

As noted at III (p. 24) above, the revised Preface Tone in the English Missal is based upon the Latin Solemn Preface Tone, but slightly simplified as required by the English text. This new Preface Tone is used for every Preface in the Missal. Only in three cases (see III, p. 26) does the English Missal employ a simple Preface Tone. The adaptation of this Simple Tone from the Latin model is discussed below at V, pp. 51–52.

a. The New Preface Tone

This chart shows the elements of the new Preface Tone in the English Missal:

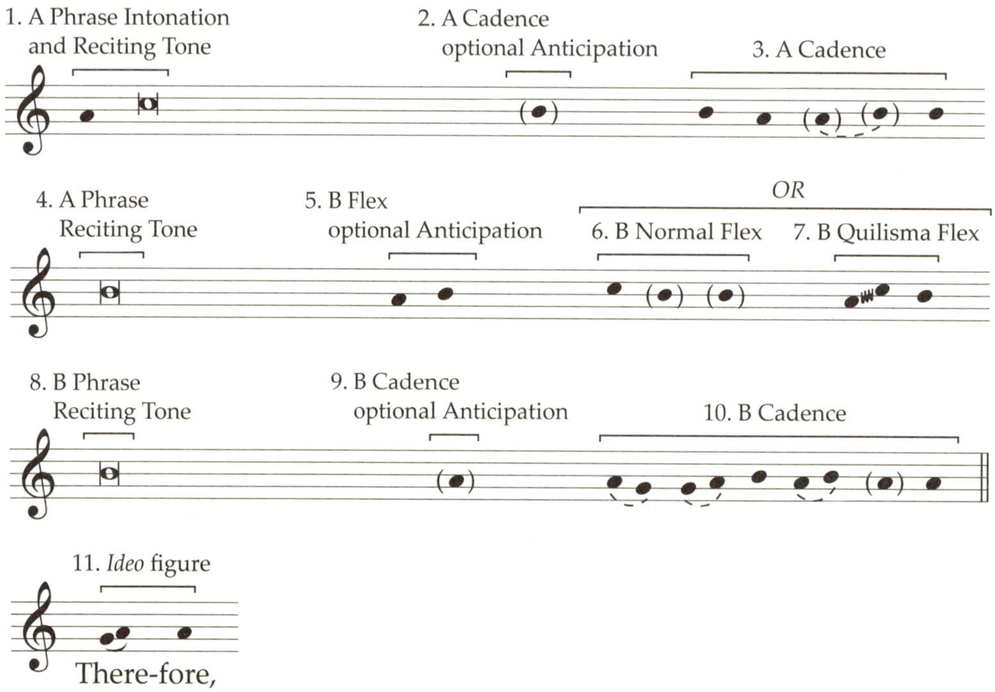

Note that the first line of music above is the "A phrase" ending with the A cadence, which can be repeated many times. The second and third lines of music above are the "B phrase." The B phrase in most cases has a flex, either a normal flex up to C, or a quilisma flex. After returning to its reciting note (third line of music above), the B phrase ends with the B cadence.

1. The intonation pitch A and the reciting pitch C

In the new Preface Tone, following the Latin Solemn Preface Tone, there is always only one A pitch before the reciting note C. This means that the singer always moves to the reciting note on the second syllable of text, whether or not this second syllable is accented.

The English Preface Tone in the previous Sacramentary/Missal sometimes had more than one anticipatory A, and other times it began directly on C. This was determined by the accents of the text. The text of the 2010 English Missal does not favor this solution, for in some cases there would need to be three or more anticipatory As, and in some cases this would result in only one or two syllables left for the reciting note C. Once the singer becomes familiar with this standard formula, it should not be difficult to render the new setting convincingly and with proper English accentuation. The singer will need to take care not to place stress on this second syllable with higher pitch in cases where it is an unaccented syllable. In singing the beginning of the Preface it is important to remember that moving from one note to another does not imply accentuation.

2. Optional pitch (B) before the A cadence

Following the Latin model, this optional pitch is inserted only when there is a three-syllable word with an accent on the first syllable (which is on C). Thus, the weak inner syllable of the three-syllable word and the final syllable each take the pitch B. This occurs infrequently, for example, on "constantly" in the Preface for the Second Sunday of Lent:

3. The A cadence

The pitches of this cadence formula can be distributed in several ways over the syllables of the text, as the chart below explains. The A phrase with its A cadence can be repeated several times before the Preface moves to the B phrase.

The first A cadence in every Preface is the following:

This setting accounts for two final accents (on "give" and "thanks"), unlike the Latin Solemn Preface Tone formula which only contains one final accent. A more "Latinate" one-accent cadence would have been:

For the A cadence in the new Preface Tone, a two-accent formula (for the final accent and penultimate accents) has been devised for the sake of the English language. Although such a two-accent formula never occurs in the Latin Prefaces, it does in the Latin *Exsultet* on *"beáta nóx"*:

This *"beata nox"* is an exception in the Latin Missal, since the Latin language rarely has an accent on the final syllable of the cadence. But English does quite often. This two-accent formula treats the various English accent patterns as follows:

Penultimate Accent — *Final Accent* **or** *Final Accent*

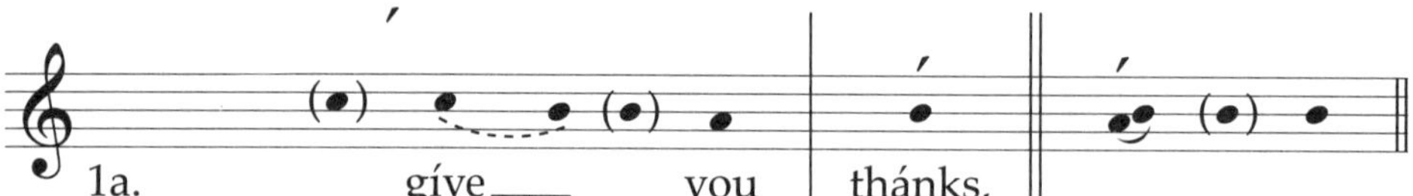

	Penultimate Accent				Final Accent	Final Accent
1a.		gíve___		you	thánks,	
1b.		sígns___		and		wón - ders,
1c.		Gód___		made		ví - si - ble.
2a.		práise	you	O	Lórd,	
2b.		wálk -	ing	in		dárk - ness.
2c.		Gód	and	hu -	- - -	- má - ni - ty.
3a.		gló -	ri - fy	your	náme,	
3b.	sér - vice	of		your		má - jes - ty,
3c.	foundátion	of	the	a -	- - -	- pós - tles,

The A cadence is notated in the English Missal so as to assist the singer in making the transition correctly from the last syllable (on the reciting pitch C) to the following syllable (on the pitch B). The following excerpt from the Preface of the Fifth Sunday of Lent shows how this transition is made clear by the placement of the first black note after the reciting tone:

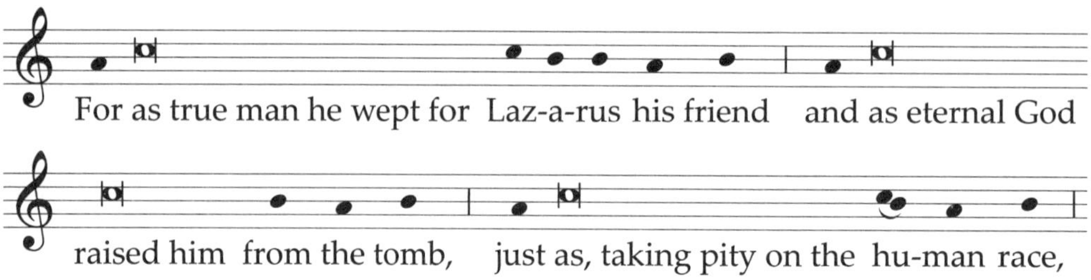

Comparison of "wept for Lazarus" and "raised him from" shows that the first black note is not always a B placed on the first syllable that changes pitch. Rather, a black note C is employed whenever the cadence begins with an accented syllable, as does "Lázarus" above. The first black note is a B only when it falls on an unaccented syllable, as seen in "from" above. In fact, since the new English Preface Tone employs a two-accent cadence formula for this part of the Preface, in most cases the first black note will be a C falling on an accent. This is seen above both in "Lazarus" and in the two-note CB on "hu–" of "human." The celebrant will become accustomed to seeing the first black note after the reciting tone and then beginning the cadential formula on an accented syllable at that point.

This explanation might make the matter seem more complicated than it is. Many singers will probably find that the Preface notation is clear and helpful without necessarily realizing why this is so.

Note that "Lazarus" is set to C B B, all notated, while the similarly accented "raised him from" is in effect set to C C B, with only the third and final syllable having a note (B) over it. This is because "Lazarus" is a three-syllable word with the accent on the first syllable, fulfilling the conditions for the optional anticipation note (no. 2).

In the rare case where there are two accents in a row at the A cadence, the new Preface tone accounts for this by placing a two-note group BA on the second to last accent, as in this example from Preface V for Sundays in Ordinary Time:

4. The reciting pitch B of the B phrase

The Latin model occasionally has an intonation pitch A before the reciting note B when the second syllable (on which the reciting tone begins) is accented. Since this occurs so infrequently in the English Prefaces, it was decided to omit it.

5. Optional anticipation

The optional anticipation is used only before the normal flex, never before the quilisma flex (which already has the pitches A and B before the high note C). This "run-up" is used whenever the combination of the accented syllable (on high C) and the preceding two syllables seem to suggest it, which is most of the time.

6. The normal flex

The high note C always falls on an accented syllable. If one or two unaccented syllables follow, they fall on the optional Bs. Quite often in English, unlike in Latin, the final syllable is accented, so that the English formula must allow for an "abrupt flex" which ends on the note C.

7. The quilisma flex

Several Prefaces have one or even two cases where the normal flex is replaced by the more ornamental quilisma flex. The three pitches of the quilisma flex (A-B-C) always fall on an accent. In fact, it is the third pitch, the high C, which is carrying this accented syllable. (For performance of the quilisma flex, see II, pp. 14–15)

8. The reciting pitch B of the B phrase

Especially when the text is rather short, it is possible that there is no flex in the B cadence. This means that the second line of music in the chart is not employed, and the setting passes from no. 3, A cadence, directly to no. 8, B phrase reciting note. When there is a flex (either no. 6 or no. 7), the B phrase returns to its reciting pitch at no. 8.

9. The optional pitch (A) before the B cadence

This is analogous to no. 2. It is used under the same conditions for a three-syllable word, but in this case taking the pitches B and A for the first two syllables, and then the note group A-G on the third syllable.

10. The B cadence

As in the A cadence, these pitches can be distributed in several ways over the cadence syllables. In its full form, the melody is:

Sometimes this full cadential formula can be used with the English text, but in other cases it must be simplified or adjusted. The treatment of the concluding cadence formula is well illustrated by examining the two excerpts below, both from the Preface of Eucharistic Prayer IV. When the English text ends on an accented syllable such as "sing" at the cadence, the melodic formula is abbreviated to a single final A. But when the English text ends with a word such as "ceasing," a fuller melodic form of the cadence is possible.

Cadence with final-syllable accent:

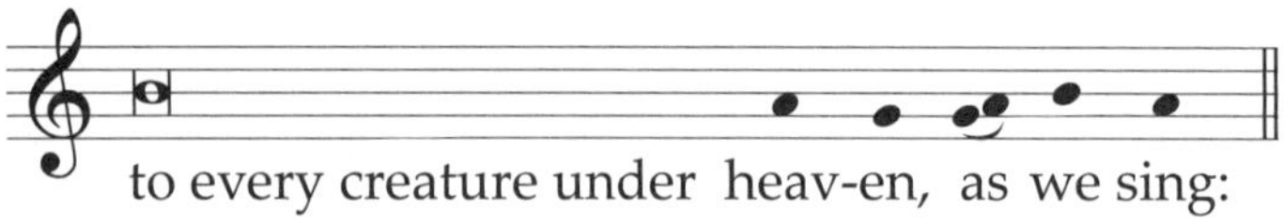

Cadence without final-syllable accent:

In this concluding cadence formula, textual considerations determine when to move from the reciting note B in order to begin the cadence formula, and whether or not to split any of the two-note groups such as AG or GA.

Compare the following examples, again from the Preface of Eucharistic Prayer IV. The first example below is the fullest cadence formula, closest to the Latin solemn tone; the others are slight modifications of it as called for by the accentuation of the English text.

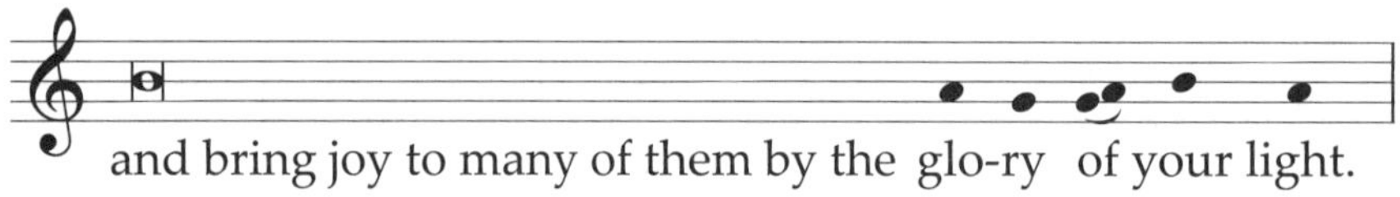

It is not easy to decide when the note group A-G of the B cadence should be split into two separate pitches. For the most part it is split in cases where the A of the split group falls on an accent, as in "glory" in the second example above. The alternative would be to retain the note group of the Latin formula, as follows:

The problem with this alternative is that the note group falls on the unaccented syllable of "glory," which poses challenges for the singer. While this hypothetical setting sets up more forward momentum and moves with greater decisiveness toward the final accent, it was finally decided that splitting the note in such cases would be easier to sing and thus preferable for priests, even though putting single pitches on each syllable of "glory" slightly stresses the unaccented syllable "of."

11. The "*ideo* figure"

This figure is so named because it appears in Latin prefaces for the text "*Et ideo.*" As in Latin Prefaces, it is used only at the beginning of the final section of the Preface before the A phrase intonation and reciting note (no. 1). It is used in the English Prefaces only for the text "therefore," whether this is a translation of "*ideo*" or another Latin word meaning "therefore." The "*ideo* figure" occurs only in a few Prefaces.

b. The Simple Preface Tone

The English Missal uses only one tone for all the Prefaces, and it is more like the Latin Solemn Tone than the Simple Tone. Only in three cases does the English Missal employ the Simple Preface Tone: the Solemn Intercessions of Good Friday, the introductory words of the baptismal liturgy at the Easter Vigil, and the Blessing of Water at the Easter Vigil.

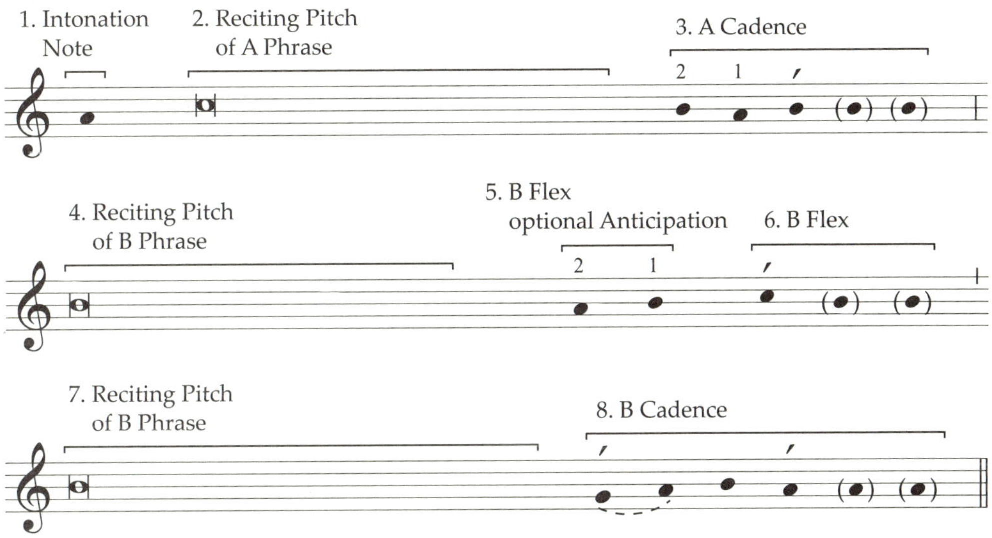

The first line of music above is the A Phrase. It can be repeated many times. The second and third lines of music above are the B Phrase with its cadence, the final cadence of the Simple Preface Tone.

1. The intonation note
   This is always only one pitch (A).

2. The reciting pitch (C) of the A phrase

3. The A cadence
   This simple cadence always has the pitch B on the final accent of the phrase, with additional B pitches if there are additional syllables after the final accent. This final accented syllable is always preceded by the pitch B and A on the preceding two syllables, whatever their accentuation. The 2 and 1 in the chart refer respectively to the second and the first syllable before the final accent.

4. The reciting pitch (B) of the B phrase

5. The B flex optional anticipation
   On rare occasions the simple Preface Tone anticipates the B flex with the pitches A and B on the two syllables preceding the final accent.

6. The B flex
   The B phrase often flexes upward. If the accent falls on the final syllable, there is an "abrupt flex" ending on C. If there are syllables after the accent, the formula returns to B for them.

7. The reciting pitch (C) of B phrase
   If there is a B flex (no. 5), the formula returns to the reciting pitch after it for the next phrase.

8. The B cadence
   The final accent always falls on A, with additional A pitches that follow if needed for syllables after the final accent. The second to last accent falls on G, with the slur used or omitted depending on whether this falls two syllables or three syllables before the final accent.

There are three minor adjustments made to this tone in comparison to the tone of the previous Sacramentary/Missal. These differences are especially relevant here because many priests are so familiar with the previous tone.

First, the intonation note of the A phrase (no. 1) is now always just one note without respect to text accentuation. In the previous *Sacramentary*, the tone always moved to the reciting pitch C on an accented syllable, which sometimes required two or even three preceding intonation notes. Or in many cases, the phrase began on C without an intonation note. This revised treatment is consistent with the new Preface Tone of the English Missal (based on the Latin Solemn Preface Tone) and follows the Latin Simple Preface Tone in this respect.

Second, in the rare case where there are two accents in a row at the A cadence, the new Simple Preface Tone takes the liberty of borrowing from the new Solemn Preface Tone and places a two-note group BA on the second to last accent. Here is an example from the Good Friday intercessions:

Third, the B cadence now follows the Latin model in that it always has only one G pitch. Previously it was possible to sound the G more than once, such as this:

Now this is avoided by putting a "shadow accent" on a light syllable ("to" in this case) closer to the final accent:

3) The Preface Dialogue

The music committee considered and rejected a setting of the Preface Dialogue based on the Latin solemn tone (*Graduale Romanum*, nos. 809-810; *Graduale Simplex*, no. 8):

A new melody such as this would have been difficult for congregations, especially the quilisma; furthermore, it does not fit the English text as well as the already-known setting. The setting of the previous *Sacramentary* was retained, therefore, with necessary adjustments for the new translation:

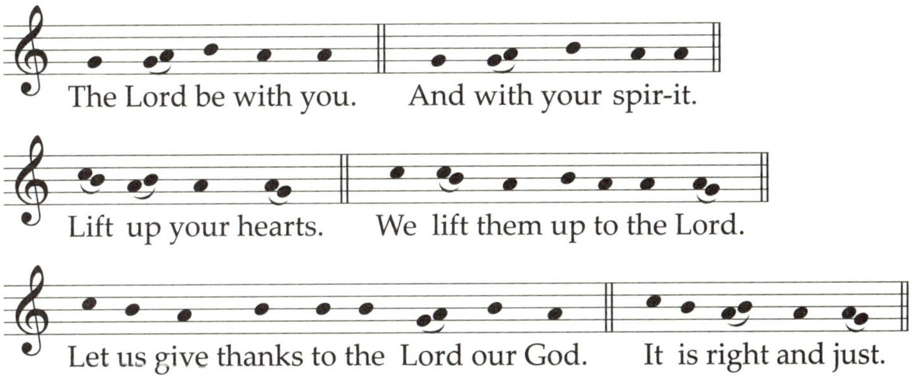

For the congregational response "It is right and just," two other possibilities were considered and rejected:

Opening on two As (left above), as the previous setting did, would not have been consistent with the new Preface tone, which reintroduces the pattern of using only one A in all such cases. Also, it would be unwise to ask congregations to learn a revised setting (right above) with just one note that is different from the familiar opening. The solution was to start on C.

4) Doxology of the Eucharistic Prayer

The opening phrase ("Through him, and with him, and in him") treats the English text as in the cadence formula of the new Preface Tone.

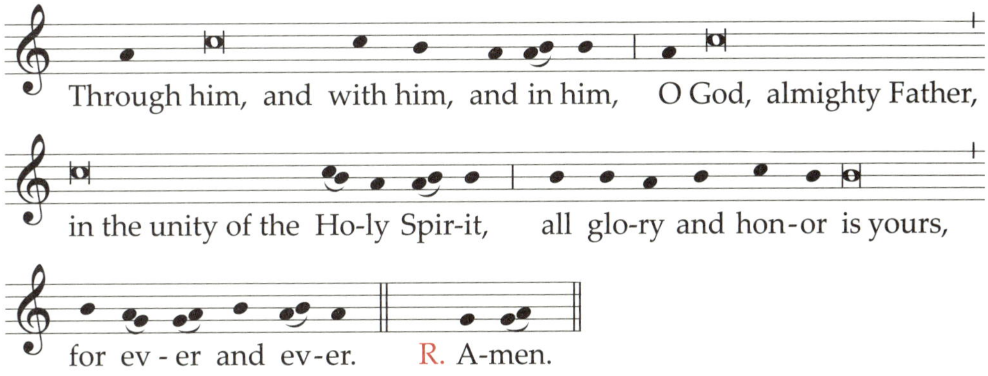

In the judgment of the committee, this was preferable to retaining AC and CB note groups on "through" and "with" as in the previous Sacramentary/Missal, in order to avoid too many repeated notes:

It is felicitous that the full concluding cadence of the new Preface Tone (see V, p. 46 above, no. 10 in the chart) is able to be used for "for ever and ever." By singing the Preface Dialogue and Doxology, the celebrant will become familiar with the new Preface Tone.

5) The *Sanctus*

The *Sanctus* in English begins as follows:

Considering only the accentuation of the English text, it might seem as if placing a single note A on the second syllable of "Holy" is the best solution:

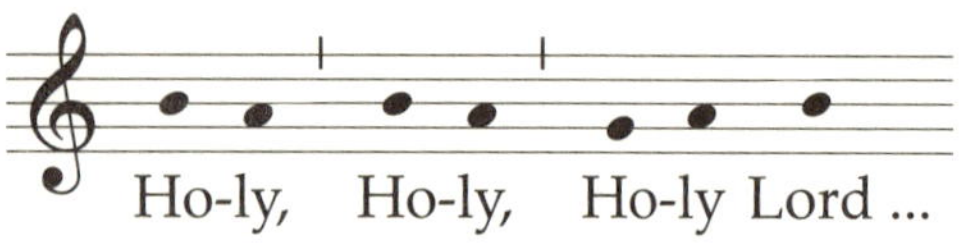

But the committee decided to imitate the Latin chant with its note group on the unaccented final syllable of the word, in part because the Latin setting is likely to be sung with great frequency by congregations in the future. This makes it important that the Latin and English settings be similar.

Because official Vatican editions do not have added rhythmic signs such as the episema or dot—these are found only in chant editions from Solesmes—there are no such rhythmic signs in the *Missale Romanum*. The English chant in the Missal follows the Latin Missal and does not have any rhythmic signs. For purely practical reasons and to help congregations stay together, a double note was placed on "he" in the place where the familiar Solesmes edition has a dotted note:

6) The Lord's Prayer (*Pater noster*)

The new English setting begins as follows:

The first word of the setting, "our" on GA, is admittedly a challenge, for it might come out as a two-syllable "ow-er." Still, it was decided to retain this eminently memorable opening of the Latin setting, rather than simplifying it by remaining on B for the first three syllables, or by shifting the opening notes to be G AB B.

Within each phrase, the new setting employs that part of the respective Latin melody that best fits the English text. "Hallowed be thy name," for example, draws on the corresponding Latin phrase "*sancificetur nomen tuum*":

The new English setting employs the notes from "*sancti - . . . nomen tu -*." This allows for a modally strong beginning on A and G following the preceding phrase, and it makes less likely an incorrect accent on "be," which would result from a setting such as this:

Note groups CB and AB were used for "kingdom," both to avoid a modally unstable run down the scale from C to G, which is uncharacteristic of Latin chant (see below, and see V, p. 43 above), and to balance the emphasis on the important words "kingdom" and "will." Similarly, B rather than G is placed on "Give" so as to avoid a run up the scale from G to C (see below). "Forgive us" is not set with a run up the scale on G AB C (see below), which would overemphasize "us." The result of such careful use of Latin formulas is an English chant that is as redolent as possible of the Latin chant while fitting the English text as naturally as possible.

Rejected possible solutions in the Lord's Prayer:

(see III, p. 22 above for an explanation of how this new chant setting is employed in the Missals of the various English-speaking countries).

7) *Agnus Dei*

The treatment of "have mercy" adds a note not found in the Latin chant in order to correctly stress "mercy" rather than "have." Experimentation has shown that this added note on "have" should be A rather than G.

8) Antiphons and Versicles

In a few cases, the Latin Missal provides proper antiphons or a versicle to be sung on particular days of the year. The chants treated here appear in both Latin and English in the English Missal. The English settings vary in the extent to which they follow the Latin melody or are more freely composed.

a. Hosanna to the Son of David

This chant from the Introductory Rites of Passion (Palm) Sunday appears in both Latin and English in the English Missal (see p. 73). The English setting is inspired by the Latin setting, but also adjusted to suit the English language. Since pitch in the Missal notation is relative and not absolute (see II, pp. 9–11), the English version surely will be printed for singing at a much lower pitch in congregational worship aids.

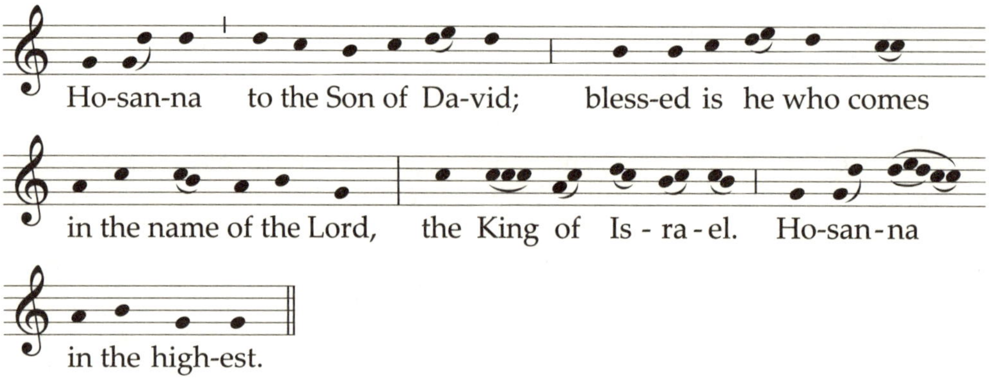

The melody of the English version follows the Latin closely, except that it is simplified, but still very much inspired by the primarily melodic elements of the original, for "in the name of the Lord." This simplification follows the English accentuation better than a more literal adaptation of the Latin chant, in addition to being well suited to the essentially congregational character of this chant in the reformed liturgy. The Latin melody is taken over without any problem for "the King of Israel." Then, as a practical aid to congregations, the melody of the final syllable of "Hosanna" is already familiar, for it is identical to the setting of "he who comes." The committee was not as concerned to follow the Latin chant for "Hosanna" literally, for it is known that the Latin melody is in need of correction according to the earliest medieval manuscripts. It likely will be corrected (as called for by the Second Vatican Council) in future editions of the Latin chant books and the Latin Missal.

b. Behold the Wood

The versicle "Behold the wood" is sung at the Veneration of the Cross on Good Friday. A side-by-side comparison shows that it draws its inspiration closely from the Latin melody and quotes it in full for some passages:

Or:

The Missal clearly says that "all respond," but the setting in the Latin Missal seems to be suited more to a trained schola than a congregation. It is for this reason that the English setting is somewhat simpler.

Because of the importance of this chant for the Liturgy of the Lord's Passion on Good Friday, an even simpler setting is also provided, lest the difficulty of the first setting be prohibitive for some ministers. The simpler setting is designed to be used with the same response as the first setting.

c. Springs of Water, Bless the Lord

This acclamation of the congregation is part of the baptismal liturgy of the Easter Vigil. The melody is nothing more than a psalm tone. The English setting attempts to do justice to the English text with its accented final syllable "Lord."

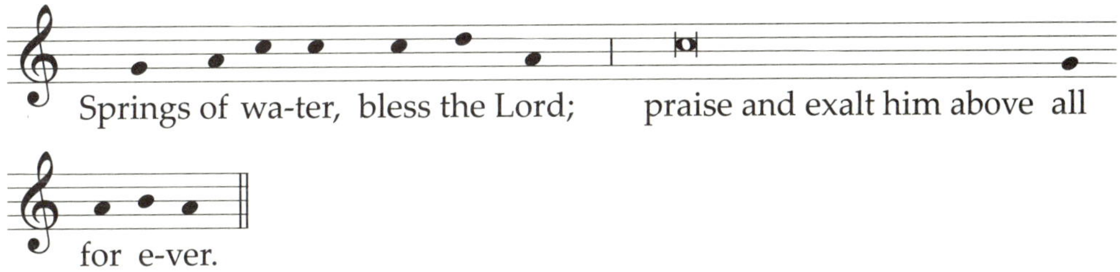

It is based on the setting in the Latin Missal:

An English setting of the first phrase that follows the melody of the Latin at the cadence more literally would also have been possible (see below). However, in addition to overemphasizing "bless" in comparison to "Lord," such a setting fails to establish the modally important reciting note C.

d. I Saw Water

This antiphon from the baptismal liturgy of the Easter Vigil appears in both Latin and English in the Missal. The Latin chant is very beautiful:

But this setting is clearly suited to a trained schola and not the typical congregation. This poses a dilemma, for the Missal clearly instructs that "all sing" this antiphon during the sprinkling. An easier setting for congregation was needed.

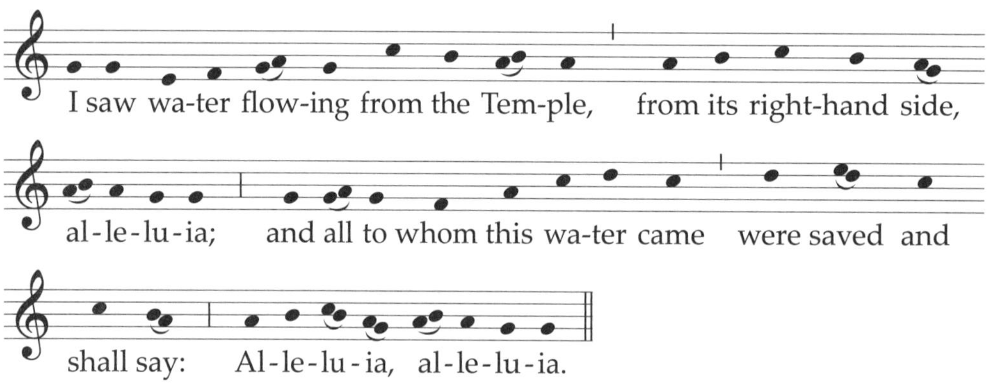

As daunting as it is to presume to compose a chant destined to be part of the official liturgical books, the committee prepared this original chant. This English chant is loosely inspired more by the principal melodic elements of Mode VIII than by the specifics of the original Latin melody. The setting of "to whom this water came" with its FA-LA-DO employs a melodic motif typical of Latin chants in Mode VIII. As befits a congregational setting, the melody of the final alleluias purposely repeats the melody of "from its right-hand side, alleluia" earlier.

e. Behold, Our Lord Will Come

The English setting of this chant for February 2, Presentation of the Lord, is closely modeled on the Latin chant (which also appears in the English Missal), although the English text poses certain challenges. The setting of the first phrase highlights "Lord" and "come," and the melody draws inspiration for the simple psalm tone of Mode III.

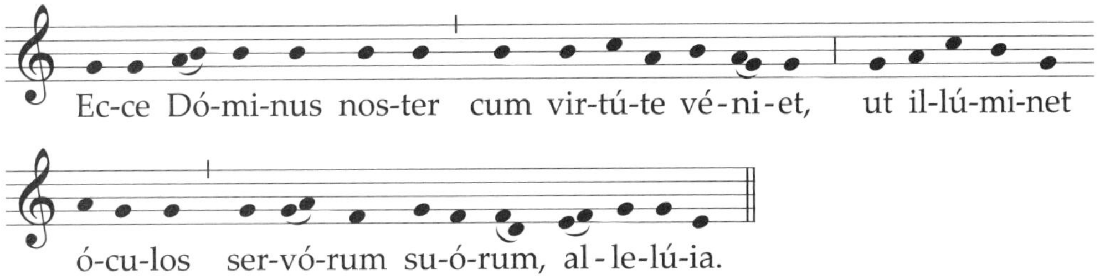

f. A Light for Revelation

This chant during the procession with candles on February 2 appears in both Latin and English in the Missal. After the addition of an initial G as required by the English text, the melody of the English version follows the Latin melody almost exactly. The English setting places the two-note group on "glo-" of "glory."

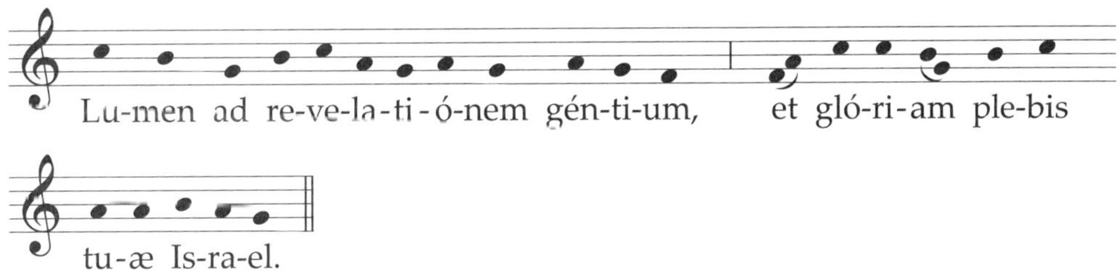

This is a "type melody" that was adapted for several Latin Office antiphon texts already in the first millennium. Based on the various ways the Gregorian composers adapted the type melody, a setting such as the following would also have been possible:

This hypothetical setting gives more modal weight to C on "glory," following the treatment of "*gloriam*" in the Latin. Placing three notes on the final syllable of "Israel" is not as uncharacteristic as it might at first seem, for the Gregorian Mass propers sometimes treat Hebrew words so as to accent the final syllable. See, for example, "*Ierusalem*" in the opening phrase of the Introit *Lætare*, and also the accentuation of Davíd, in *Hosanna filio David* above at V, pp. 55–56.

But the committee agreed that there is good reason to place the note group C-B on "glory," even though it affects the modal stability of the phrase. By happy coincidence, the English word "light" at the beginning of the piece has but one syllable, unlike "*lumen*" in Latin. This requires placing a note group C-B on the single syllable of "light." The note group C-B on "glory," then, lends to the chant a satisfying allusion to the chant's opening phrase.

The discussion of this chant is an appropriate way to end this chapter. It reminds us that the adaptation of Latin chant to the English language involves taking many aspects into consideration, balancing many goods, and making sometimes difficult decisions. Often many good solutions are possible for a given passage. ICEL and the music committee hope that scholarly and pastoral discussion of the issues raised in this chapter will continue in the years to come and, thereby, contribute to the adaptation of chant for future editions of *The Roman Missal*.

VI. RESOURCES

A. Recordings of the Missal Chants

- International Commission on English in the Liturgy Corporation (ICEL)
  - *Become One Body, One Spirit in Christ*. This resource from the translators of the new Missal includes a substantial section on the chants, along with some recordings. For a list of regional distributors see: *www.becomeonebodyonespiritinchrist.org/available_from.html*.
- National Association of Pastoral Musicians (NPM): www.npm.org/Chants/index.html.
- Church Music Association of America (CMAA): www.musicasacra.com/ordinary/#english.
- Bishops' Conference of Scotland: romanmissalscotland.org.uk/music-resources.html.
- New Zealand Catholic Bishops Conference: www.catholic.org.nz.
- The Music Makers: www.themusicmakers.org.
  - *And with Your Spirit: A Guide to Singing the New English Translation of the Mass* (2 CDs)
- Liturgy Training Publications: www.ltp.org.
  - *Learning the Chants of the Missal, Part I: The Order of Mass* (CD)
  - *Learning the Chants of the Mass: Part II: Essential Presidential Prayers* (CD)

B. Worship Aids with Missal Chants

- Australian National Liturgical Music Board: www.catholic.org.au.
  - *A Chant Mass for the Assembly*
- Canadian Conference of Catholic Bishops Publications Service: www.cccpublications.ca.
  - *Celebrate in Song*
- Liturgy Office of England & Wales
  - *Chants from the Roman Missal*: www.liturgyoffice.org.uk/Missal/Music/Chants/index .shtml.
- Liturgical Press: www.litpress.org; www.theromanmissal.org.
  - *Lift Up Your Hearts: Music for the Order of Mass according to the Third Edition of* The Roman Missal (*People's Edition*)
- Liturgy Training Publications: www.ltp.org.
  - *The Order of Mass Worship Aid with Chant*
- The Music Makers: www.themusicmakers.org.
  - *Missa Simplex: Chants of the Roman Missal* (melody part)
- Oregon Catholic Press: www.ocp.org.
  - *Revised Order of Mass with Supplemental Mass Settings*
- Sunday Missal Service: www.sundaymissal.com.
  - *The Order of Mass Worship Aid with Chant*
- World Library Publications: www.wlpmusic.com.
  - *The Order of Mass* (with chant)

C. Missal Chant Accompaniments

- International Commission on English in the Liturgy (ICEL)
  - *Accompaniments for the Chants of the Roman Missal*: www.icelweb.org/musicfolder/openmusic.php.
- Australian National Liturgical Music Board: www.catholic.org.au.
  - *A Chant Mass for the Assembly* (accompaniment edition)
- Canadian Conference of Catholic Bishops Publications Service: www.cccbpublications.ca.
  - *Celebrate in Song: Accompaniments for Hymns and Mass Settings*
- Decani Music, Ltd.: www.decanimusic.co.uk.
  - *ICEL Chants with Accompaniment*
- Diocese of Leeds Music Department
  - *Accompanying the Missal Tones*: dioceseofleedsmusic.org.uk/advice_materials.
- Liturgical Press: www.litpress.org.
  - *Lift Up Your Hearts: Music for the Order of Mass according to the Third Edition of* The Roman Missal (Accompaniment Book)
- Missal Bulletin Publications
  - *Music for English Speaking Churches*
- The Music Makers: www.themusicmakers.org.
  - *Missa Simplex: Chants of the Roman Missal* (accompaniment part)

D. Other Resources for Singing the Missal Chants

- Liturgy Training Publications: www.ltp.org.
  - Michael Driscoll and J. Michael Joncas. *The Order of Mass: A Roman Missal Study Edition and Workbook*. This book provides instructions on singing the chant.
  - Daniel Merz and Abbot Marcel Rooney. *Essential Presidential Prayers and Texts*. This book provides instructions on singing the chant.
  - *The Roman Missal, Study Edition*. This edition includes the presidential prayers pointed for singing.
- Oregon Catholic Press: www.ocp.org.
  - Ricky Manalo. *Chanting On Our Behalf: A Pastoral Guide to Presidential Chanting and Musical Leadership (Revised Edition).*
- Charles Gardner. "Chanting the Simple Dialogues at Mass: Not Just for Priests Who 'Like to Sing'." *Pastoral Music* 34.6 (September 2010): 39–41.
- Anthony Ruff, OSB
  - "Do Priests Need to Sing?" *Pastoral Music* 28.3 (March 2004): 41-43. Online: http://www.npm.org/pastoral_music/issues/PM%20Vol%2028-3.pdf.
  - "The Value of Unaccompanied Vernacular Chant in the Liturgy." *Pastoral Liturgy* 42.2 (March–April 2011): 9-11.

E. Other Useful Resources

Graduale Romanum. Tournai, Belgium: Desclée, 1974.

Graduale Simplex, editio typica altera. Libreria Editrice Vaticana, 1975.

Collegeville Composers Group. *Psallite: Sacred Song for Liturgy and Life*. Collegeville: Liturgical Press, 2008.

Foley, Edward, ed. *Worship Music: A Concise Dictionary*. Collegeville: Liturgical Press, 2000.

Ford, Paul F. *By Flowing Waters: Chants for the Liturgy*. Collegeville: Liturgical Press, 1999.

Harmon, Kathleen. *The Mystery We Celebrate, the Song We Sing: A Theology of Liturgical Music*. Collegeville: Liturgical Press, 2008.

International Committee on English in the Liturgy. *Resource Collection of Hymns and Service Music for the Liturgy*. Chicago: GIA Publications, 1981.

———. *The Simple Gradual: An English Translation of the Antiphons and Responsories of the Graduale Simplex for Use in English-speaking Countries*. Washington, DC: ICEL Secretariat, 1968.

Joncas, J. Michael. *From Sacred Song to Ritual Music: Twentieth-century Understandings of Roman Catholic Worship Music*. Collegeville: Liturgical Press, 1997.

Kroeker, Charlotte, ed. *Music in Christian Worship*. Collegeville: Liturgical Press, 2005.

McFarland, Jason J. *Announcing the Feast: The Entrance Song in the Mass of the Roman Rite*. Collegeville: Liturgical Press, 2012.

Ruff, Anthony. *Responsorial Psalms for Weekday Mass: Advent, Christmas, Lent, and Easter*. Collegeville: Liturgical Press, 2008.

———. *Sacred Music and Liturgical Reform: Treasures and Transformations*. Chicago: Liturgy Training Publications, 2007.

Tietze, Christoph. *Hymn Introits for the Liturgical Year*. Chicago: Liturgy Training Publications, 2005.

United States Conference of Catholic Bishops. *Sing to the Lord: Music in Divine Worship*. Washington, DC: USCCB Publishing, 2007.

PROPER OF TIME

CHRISTMAS TIME

The Baptism of the Lord

Preface: The Baptism of the Lord.

LENT

First Sunday of Lent

Preface: The Temptation of the Lord.

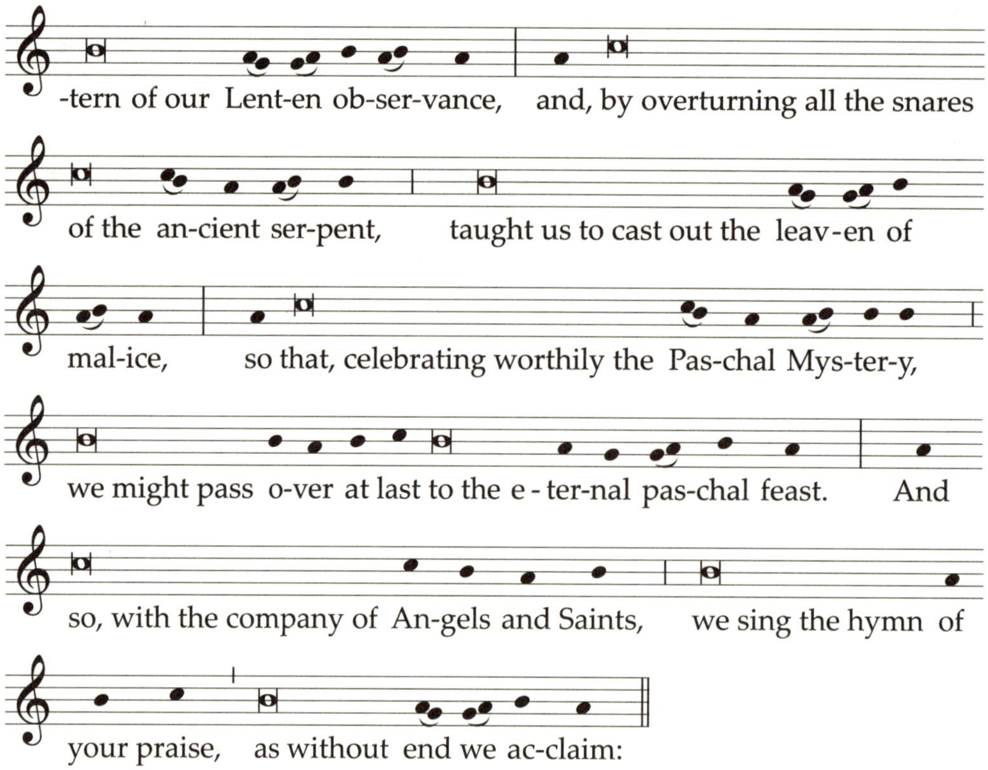

Second Sunday of Lent

Preface: The Transfiguration of the Lord.

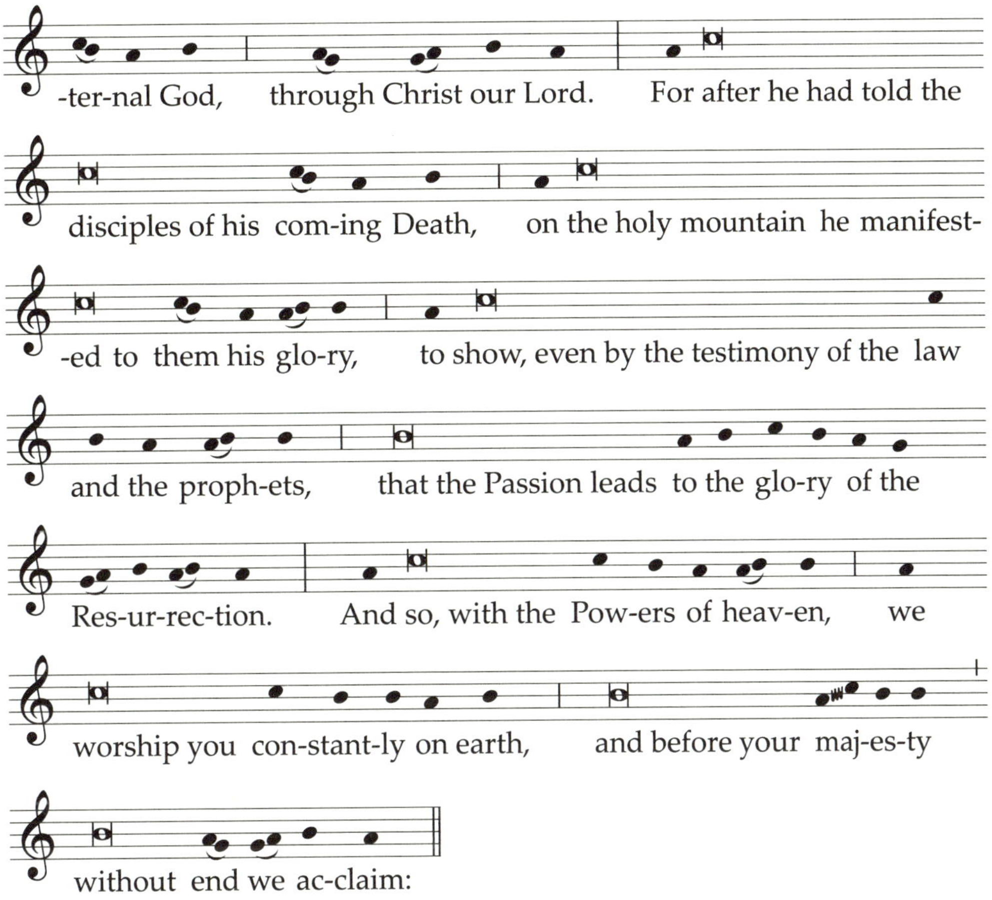

Third Sunday of Lent

Preface: The Samaritan Woman.

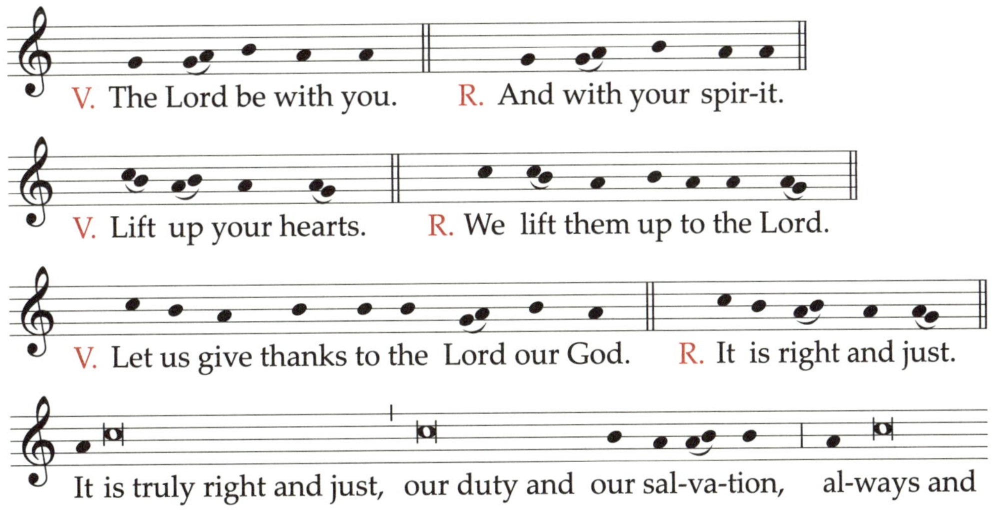

Fourth Sunday of Lent

Preface: The Man Born Blind.

Fifth Sunday of Lent

Preface: Lazarus.

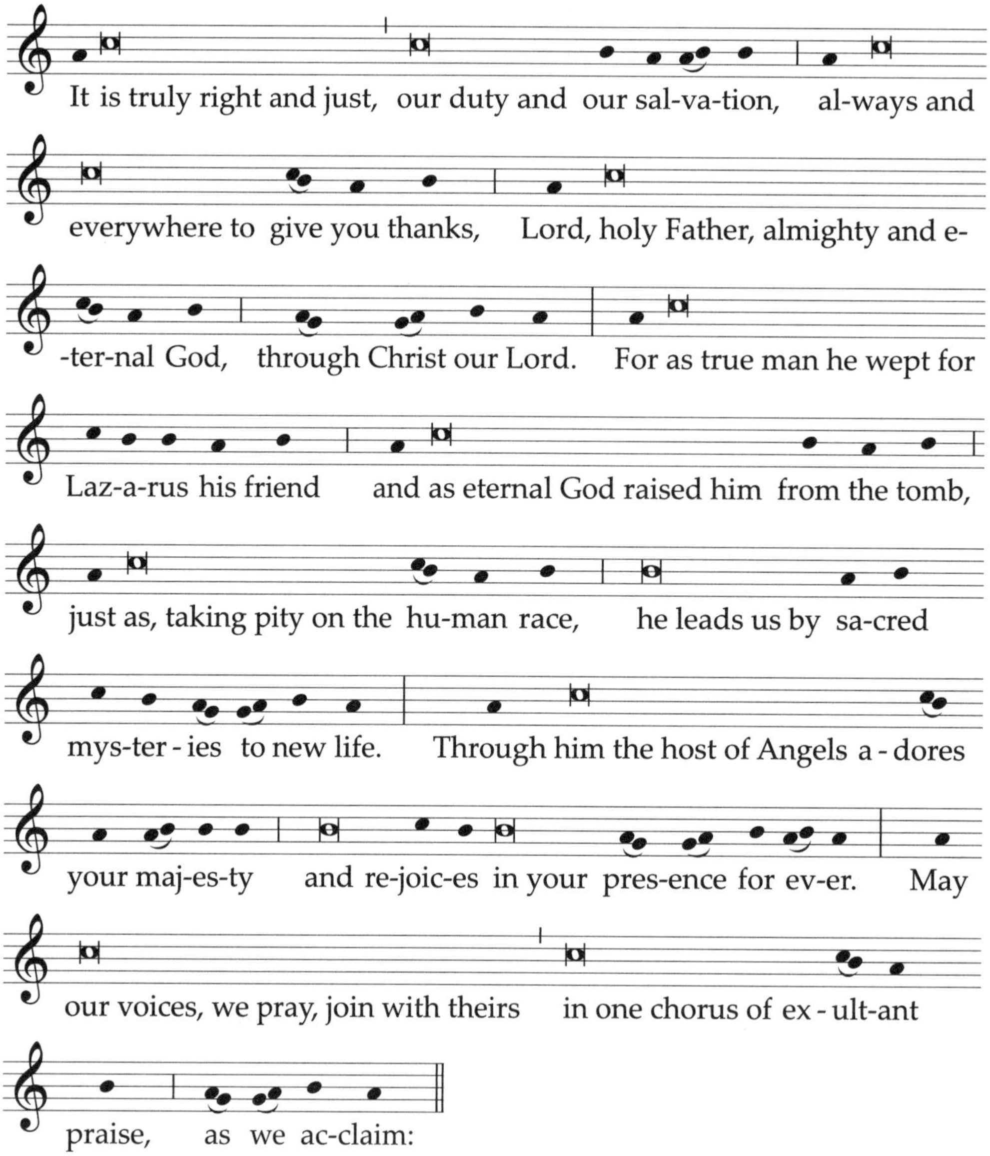
It is truly right and just, our duty and our sal-va-tion, al-ways and
everywhere to give you thanks, Lord, holy Father, almighty and e-
-ter-nal God, through Christ our Lord. For as true man he wept for
Laz-a-rus his friend and as eternal God raised him from the tomb,
just as, taking pity on the hu-man race, he leads us by sa-cred
mys-ter - ies to new life. Through him the host of Angels a - dores
your maj-es-ty and re-joic-es in your pres-ence for ev-er. May
our voices, we pray, join with theirs in one chorus of ex - ult-ant
praise, as we ac-claim:

HOLY WEEK

Palm Sunday of the Passion of the Lord

The Commemoration of the Lord's Entrance into Jerusalem

4. Antiphon Mt 21: 9

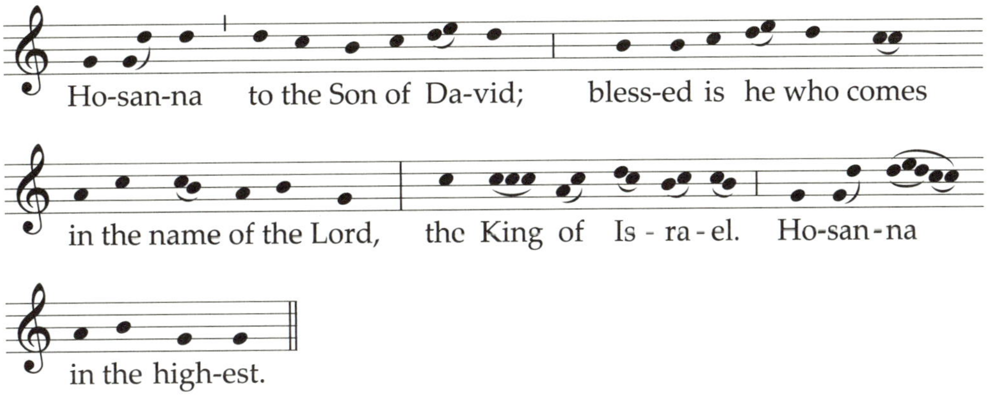

Or:

8.

Priest, Deacon, or lay minister:

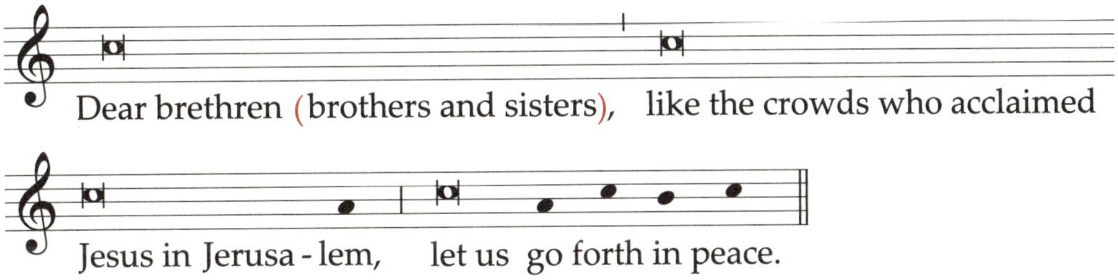

Or:

In this latter case, all respond:

In the name of Christ. A-men.

9. Hymn to Christ the King *(Gloria, laus et honor)*

Refrain

Glo-ry and hon-or and praise be to you, Christ, King and Re-deem-er,

to whom young chil-dren cried out lov-ing Ho-san-nas with joy.

1. Is - ra - el's King are you, King Da - vid's mag-
2. Heav - en - ly hosts on high u - nite in
3. Bear - ing branch - es of palm, He-brews came

4. They of - fered gifts of praise to you, so
5. Those you were pleased to ac - cept; now ac - cept our

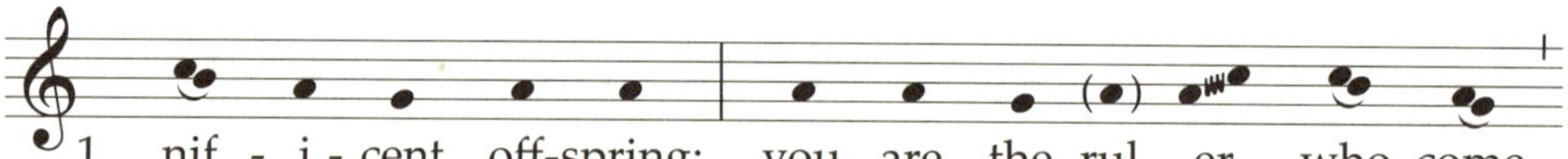

1. nif - i - cent off-spring; you are the rul - er who come
2. sing - ing your prais - es; men and wom - en on earth
3. crowd-ing to greet you; see how with prayers and hymns

4. near to your Pas - sion; see how we sing this song now
5. gifts of de - vo - tion, good and mer - ci - ful King,

1. blest in the name of the Lord.
2. and all cre - a - tion join in.
3. we come to pay you our vows.

4. to you reign-ing on high.
5. lov - er of all that is good.

24. Preface: The Passion of the Lord.

Thursday of Holy Week [Holy Thursday]

The Chrism Mass

12. Preface: The Priesthood of Christ and the Ministry of Priests.

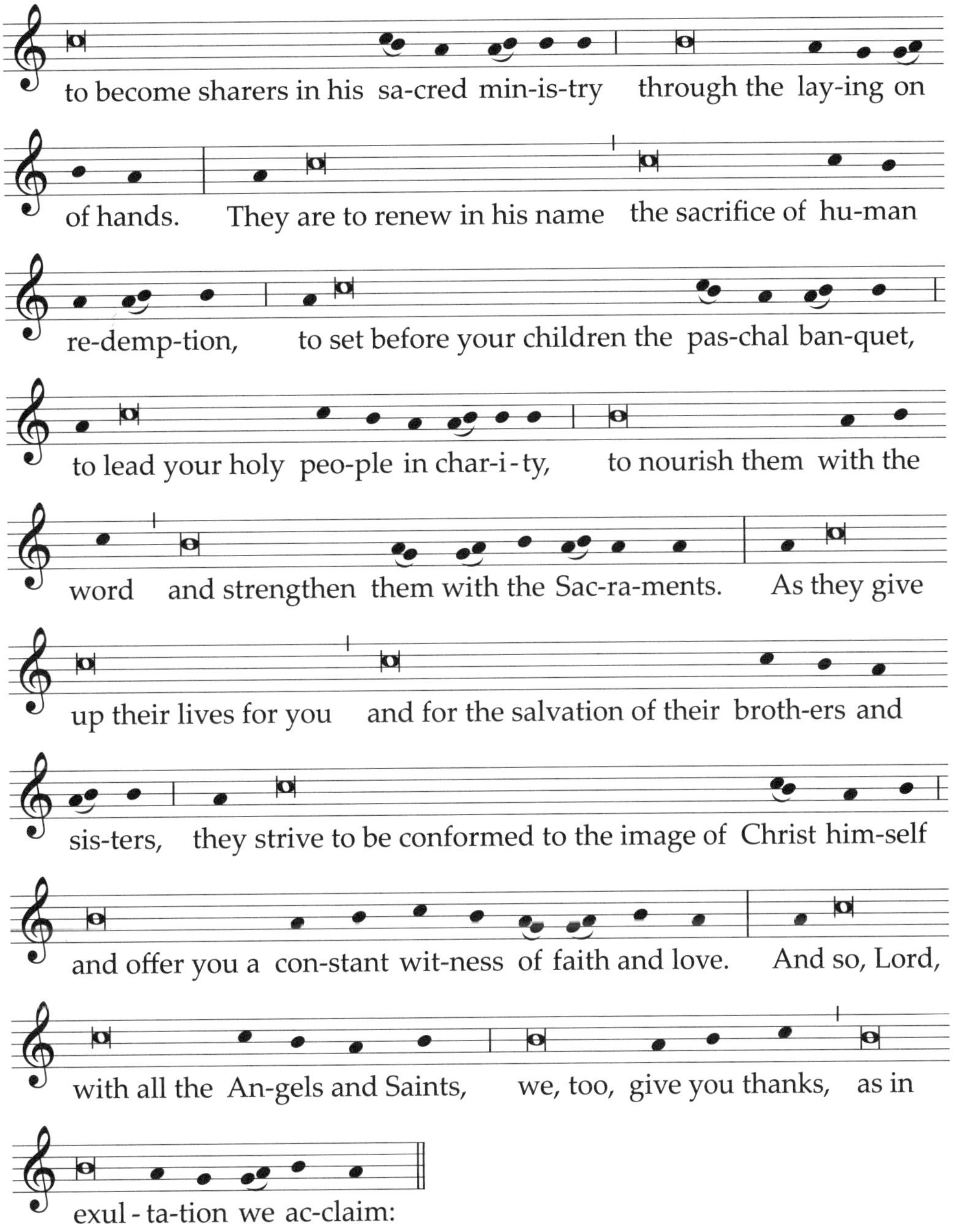
to become sharers in his sa-cred min-is-try through the lay-ing on
of hands. They are to renew in his name the sacrifice of hu-man
re-demp-tion, to set before your children the pas-chal ban-quet,
to lead your holy peo-ple in char-i-ty, to nourish them with the
word and strengthen them with the Sac-ra-ments. As they give
up their lives for you and for the salvation of their broth-ers and
sis-ters, they strive to be conformed to the image of Christ him-self
and offer you a con-stant wit-ness of faith and love. And so, Lord,
with all the An-gels and Saints, we, too, give you thanks, as in
exul-ta-tion we ac-claim:

THE SACRED PASCHAL TRIDUUM

Thursday of The Lord's Supper

At the Evening Mass

14. *Ubi Caritas*

16. Preface: The Sacrifice and the Sacrament of Christ.

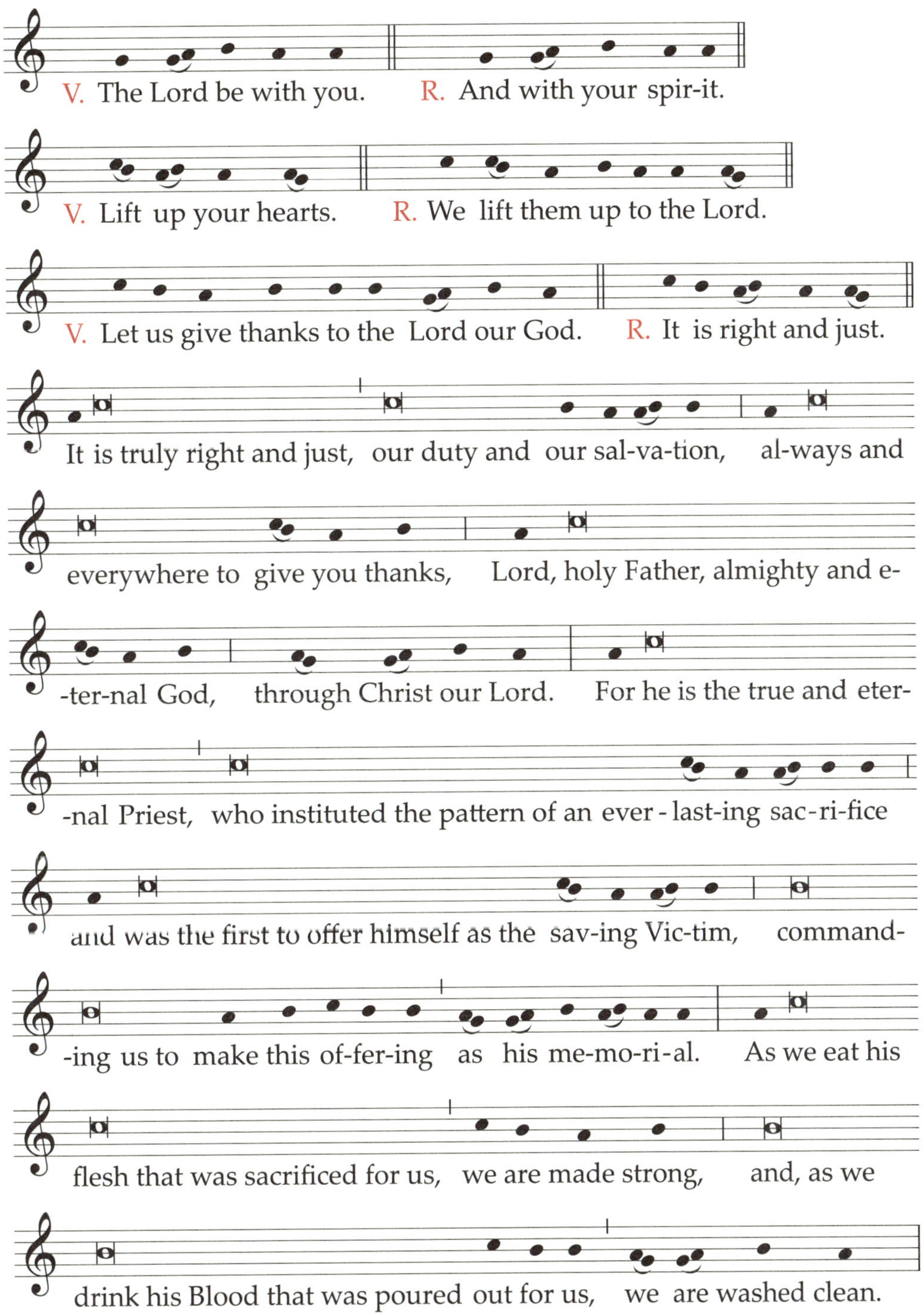

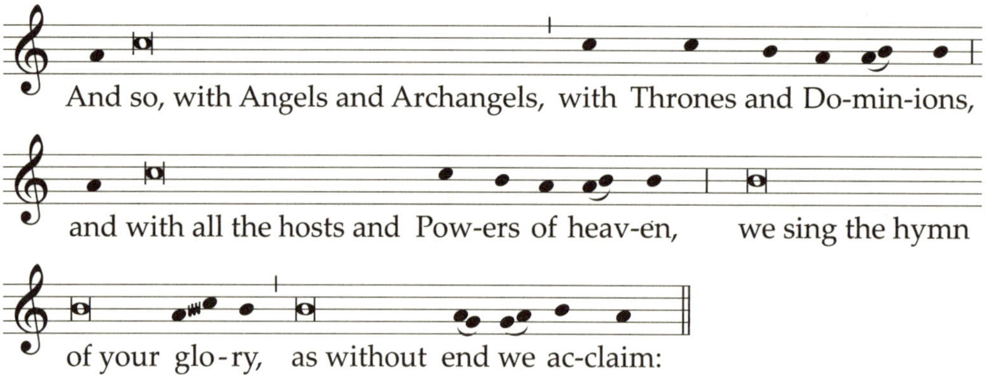

Friday of the Passion of the Lord

[Good Friday]

The Solemn Intercessions

12. Before the Priest's prayer, in accord with tradition, it is permissible to use the Deacon's invitations Let us kneel — Let us stand, with all kneeling for silent prayer.

13.

I. For Holy Church

Deacon or lay minister:

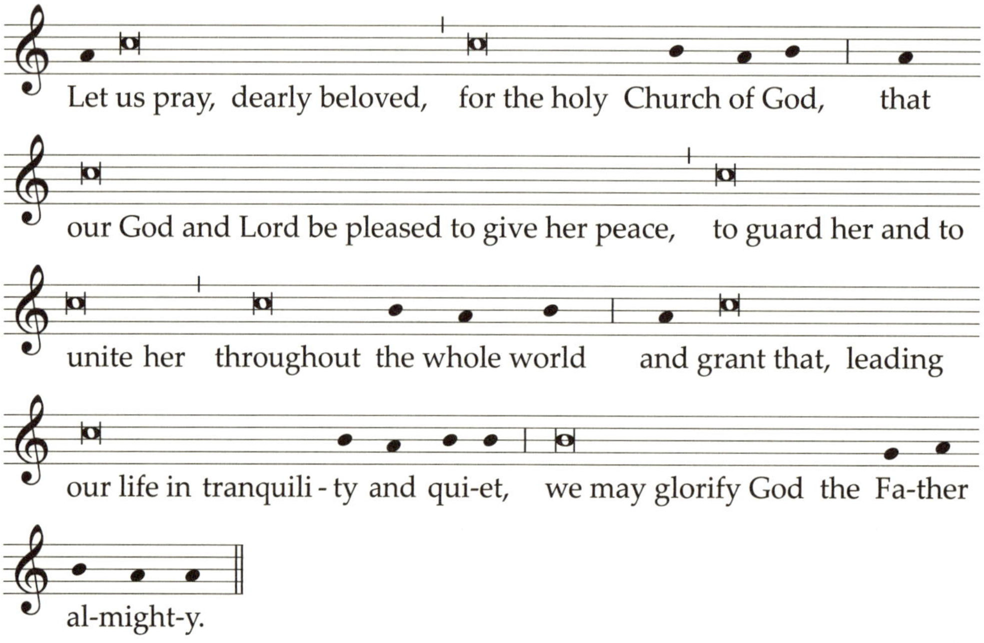

Priest:

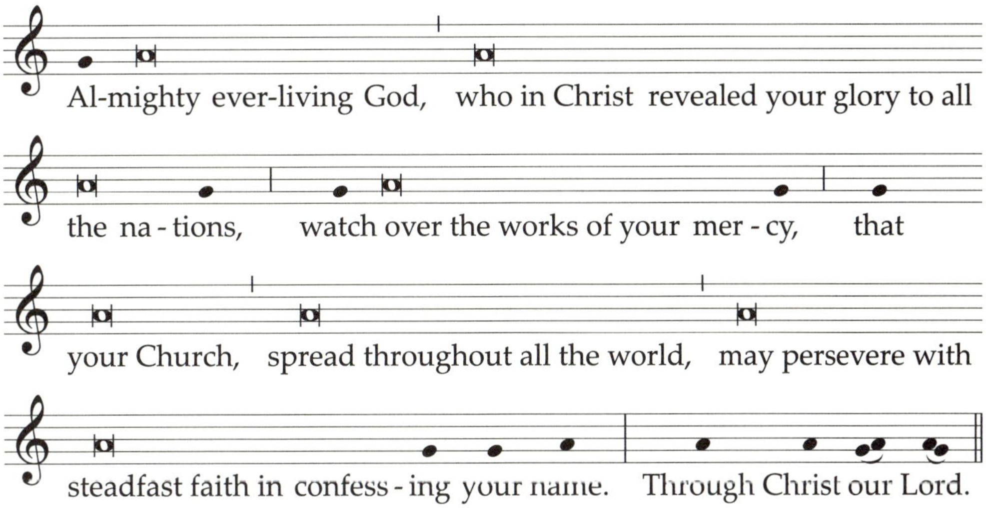

II. For the Pope

Deacon or lay minister:

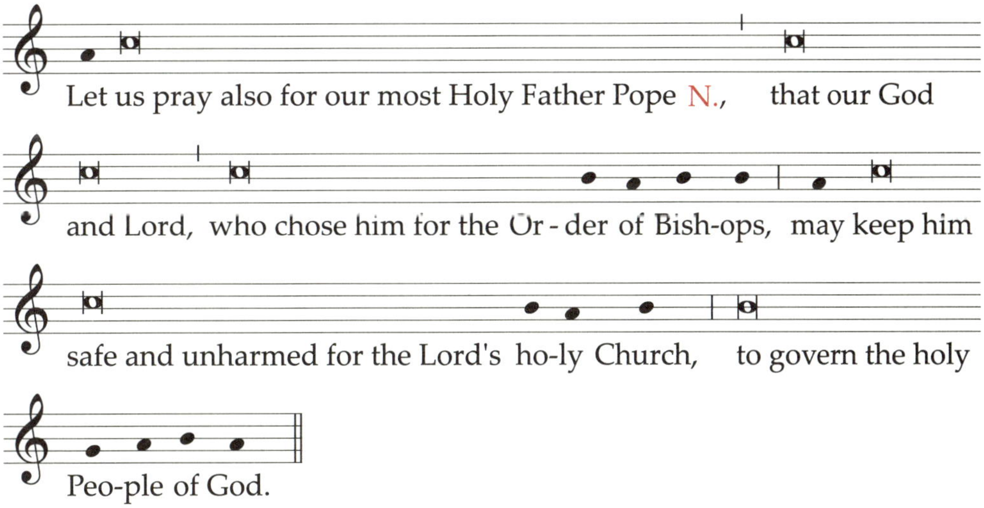

Priest:

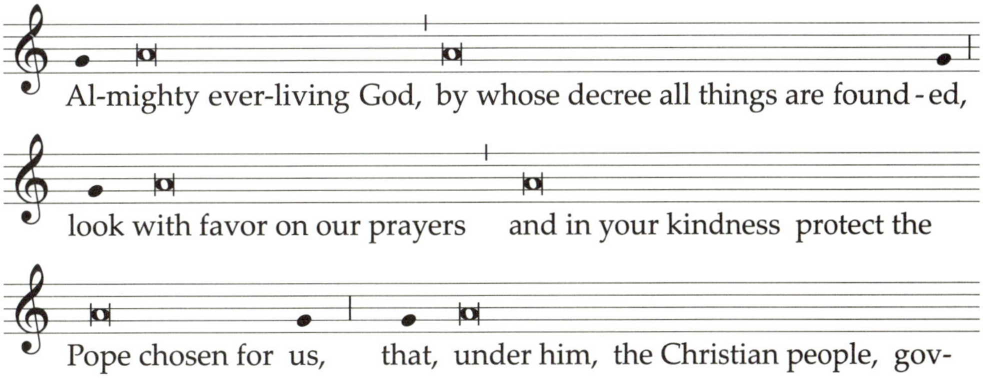

-erned by you their maker, may grow in merit by reason of their faith.

Through Christ our Lord. R. A-men.

III. For all orders and degrees of the faithful

Deacon or lay minister:

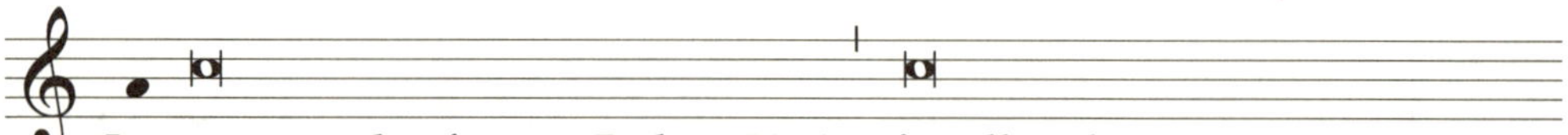
Let us pray also for our Bishop N.,* for all Bishops, Priests, and

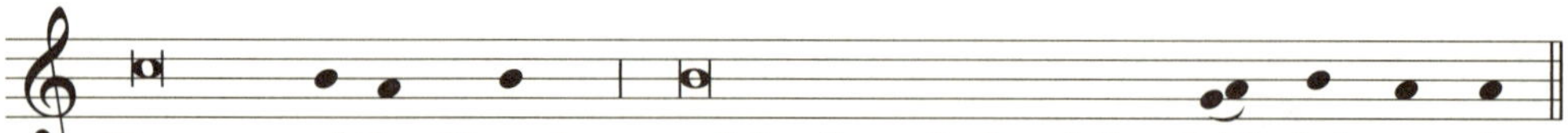
Deacons of the Church and for the whole of the faith-ful peo-ple.

Priest:

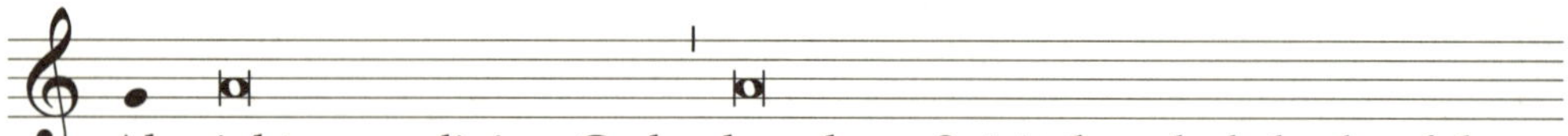
Al-mighty ever-living God, by whose Spirit the whole body of the

Church is sanctified and gov-erned, hear our humble prayer for

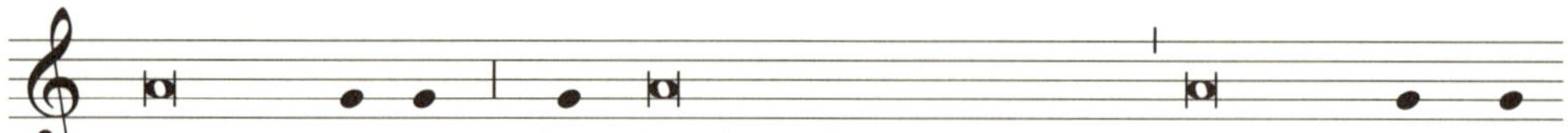
your min-is-ters, that, by the gift of your grace, all may serve you

faith-ful-ly. Through Christ our Lord. R. A-men.

IV. For catechumens

Deacon or lay minister:

Let us pray also for (our) cat-e-chu-mens, that our God and Lord

may open wide the ears of their inmost hearts and unlock the gates

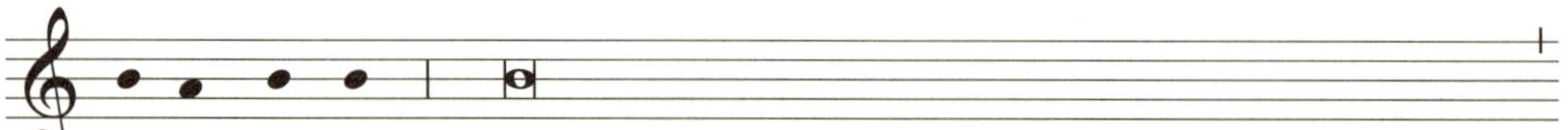
of his mer-cy, that, having received forgiveness of all their sins

Priest:

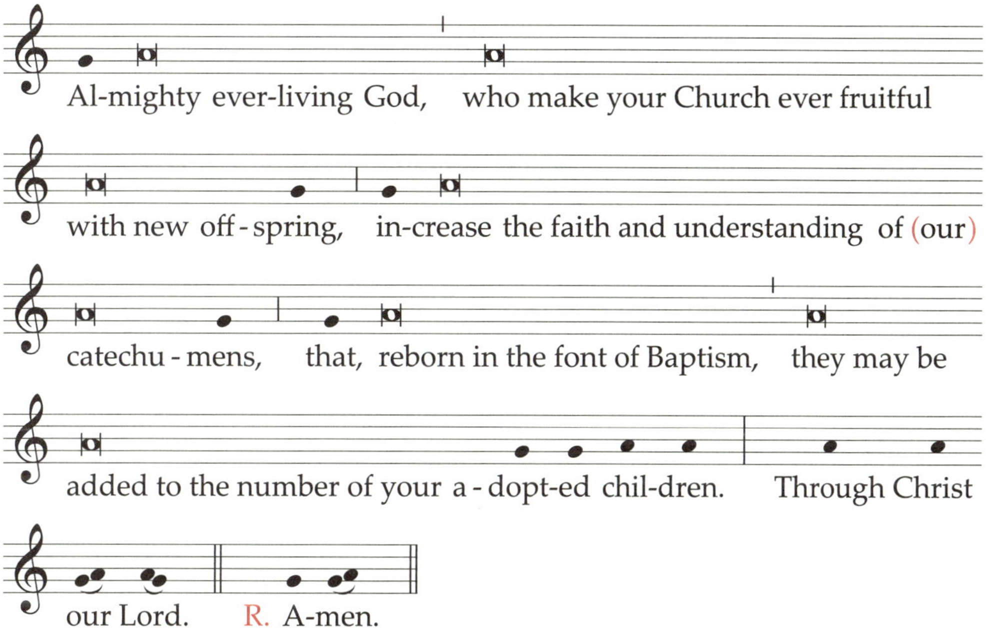

V. For the unity of Christians

Deacon or lay minister:

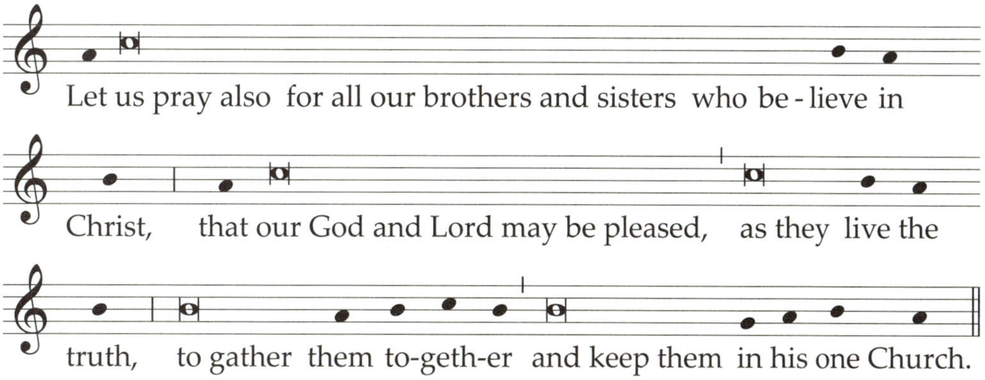

Priest:

Al-mighty ever-living God, who gather what is scattered and keep together what you have gath-ered, look kindly on the flock of your Son, that those whom one Baptism has consecrated may be joined together by integrity of faith and united in the bond of char-i-ty.

Through Christ our Lord. R. A-men.

VI. For the Jewish people

Deacon or lay minister:

Let us pray also for the Jew-ish peo-ple, to whom the Lord our God spoke first, that he may grant them to advance in love of his name and in faithfulness to his cov-e-nant.

Priest:

Al-mighty ever-living God, who bestowed your promises on Abra--ham and his descend-ants, gra-ciously hear the prayers of your Church, that the people you first made your own may attain the fullness of re-demp-tion. Through Christ our Lord. R. A-men.

VII. For those who do not believe in Christ

Deacon or lay minister:

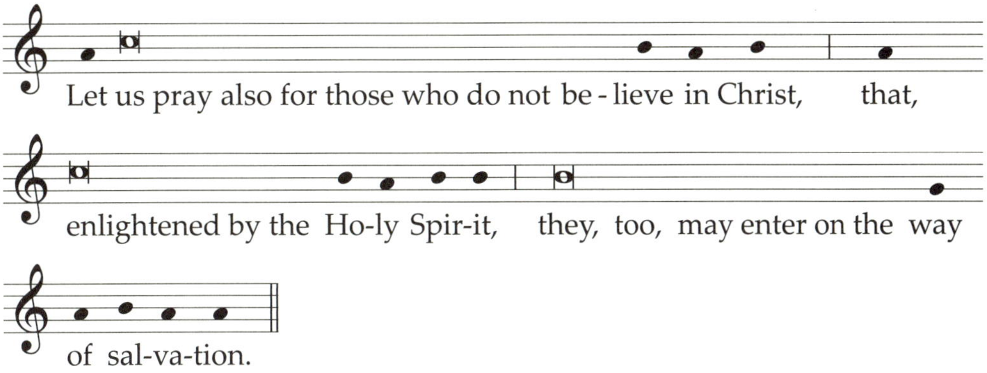

Priest:

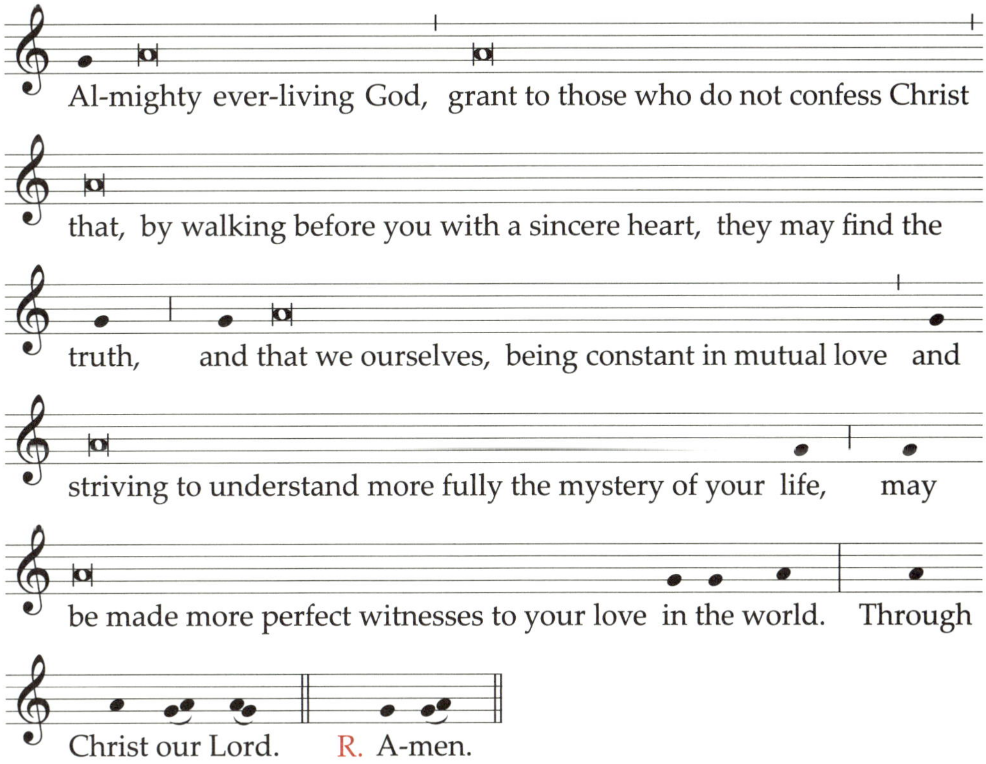

VIII. For those who do not believe in God

Deacon or lay minister:

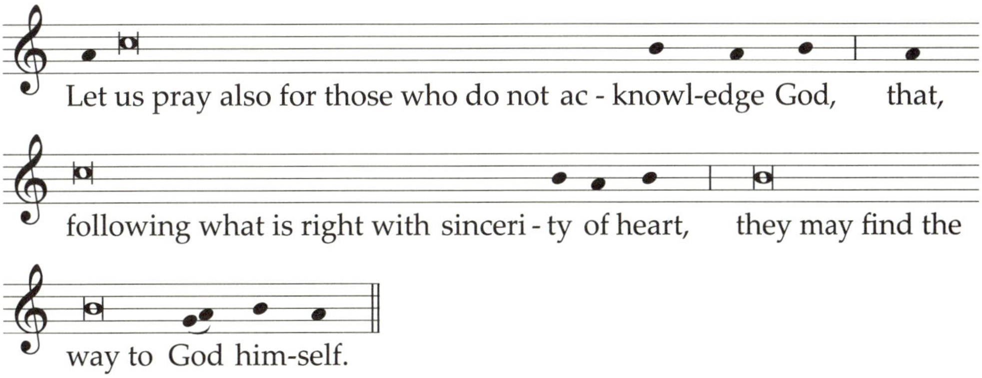

Priest:

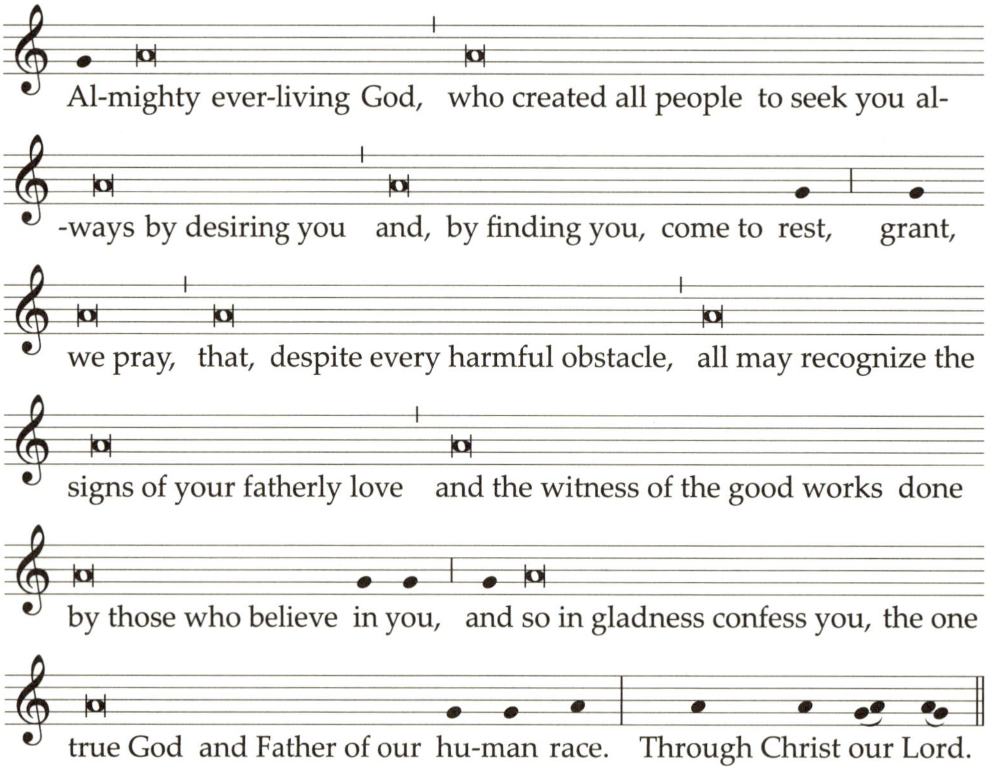

IX. For those in public office

Deacon or lay minister:

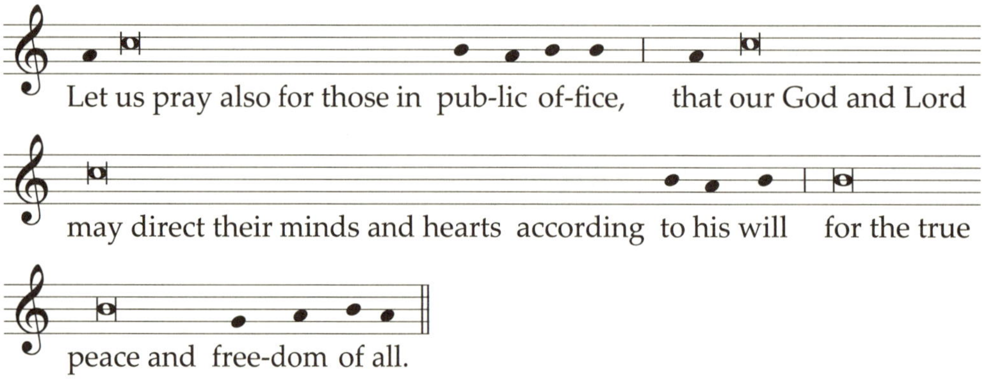

Priest:

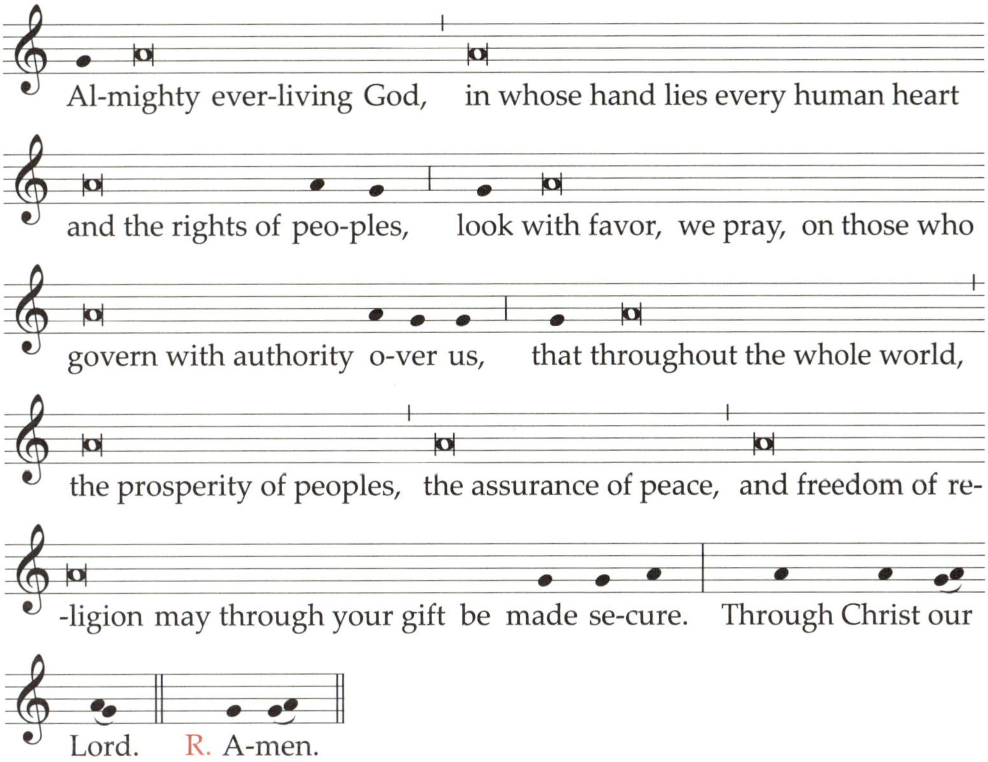

X. For those in tribulation

Deacon or lay minister:

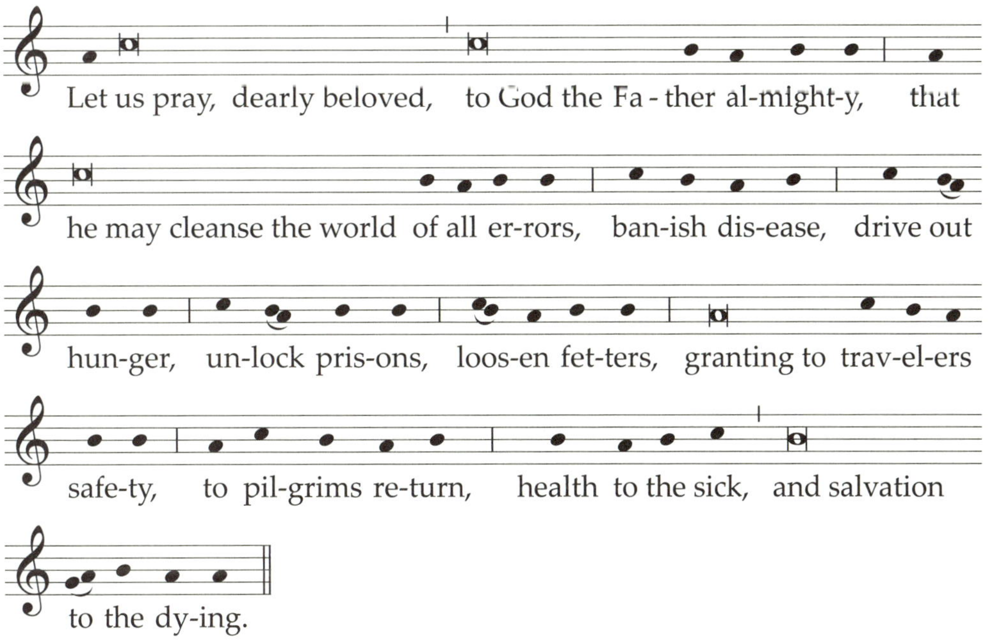

Priest:

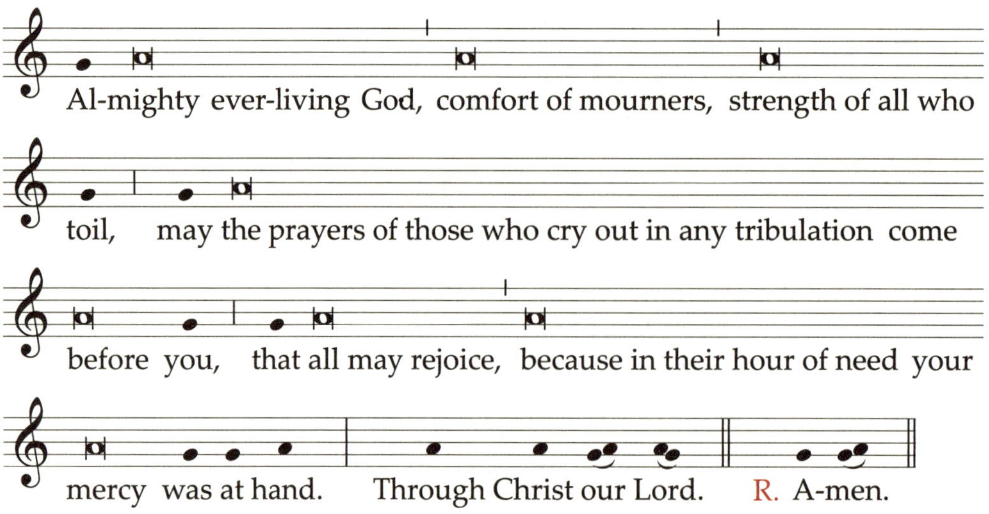

The Showing of the Holy Cross

15. *Ecce lignum*

The Priest, standing before the altar and facing the people, receives the Cross, uncovers a little of its upper part and elevates it while beginning the Ecce lignum Crucis (Behold the wood of the Cross). He is assisted in singing by the Deacon or, if need be, by the choir. All respond, Come, let us adore.

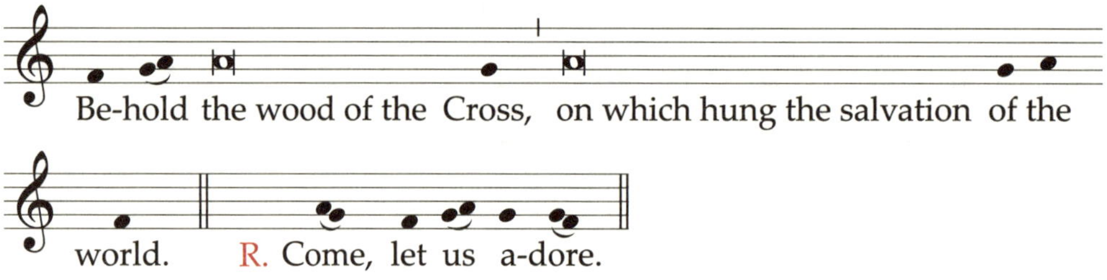

Or:

Or:

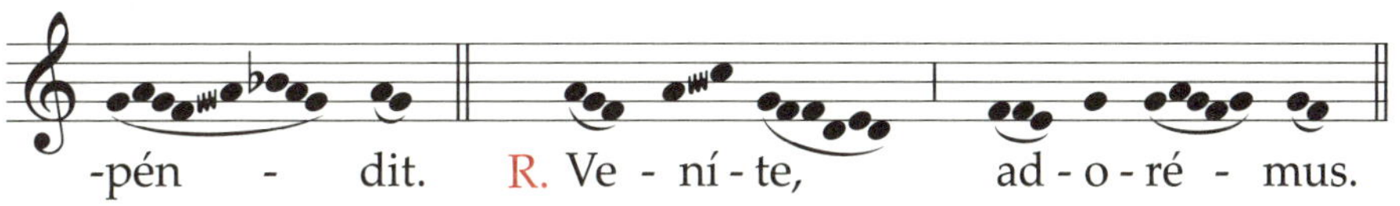

The Adoration of the Holy Cross

20. *Crux fidelis*

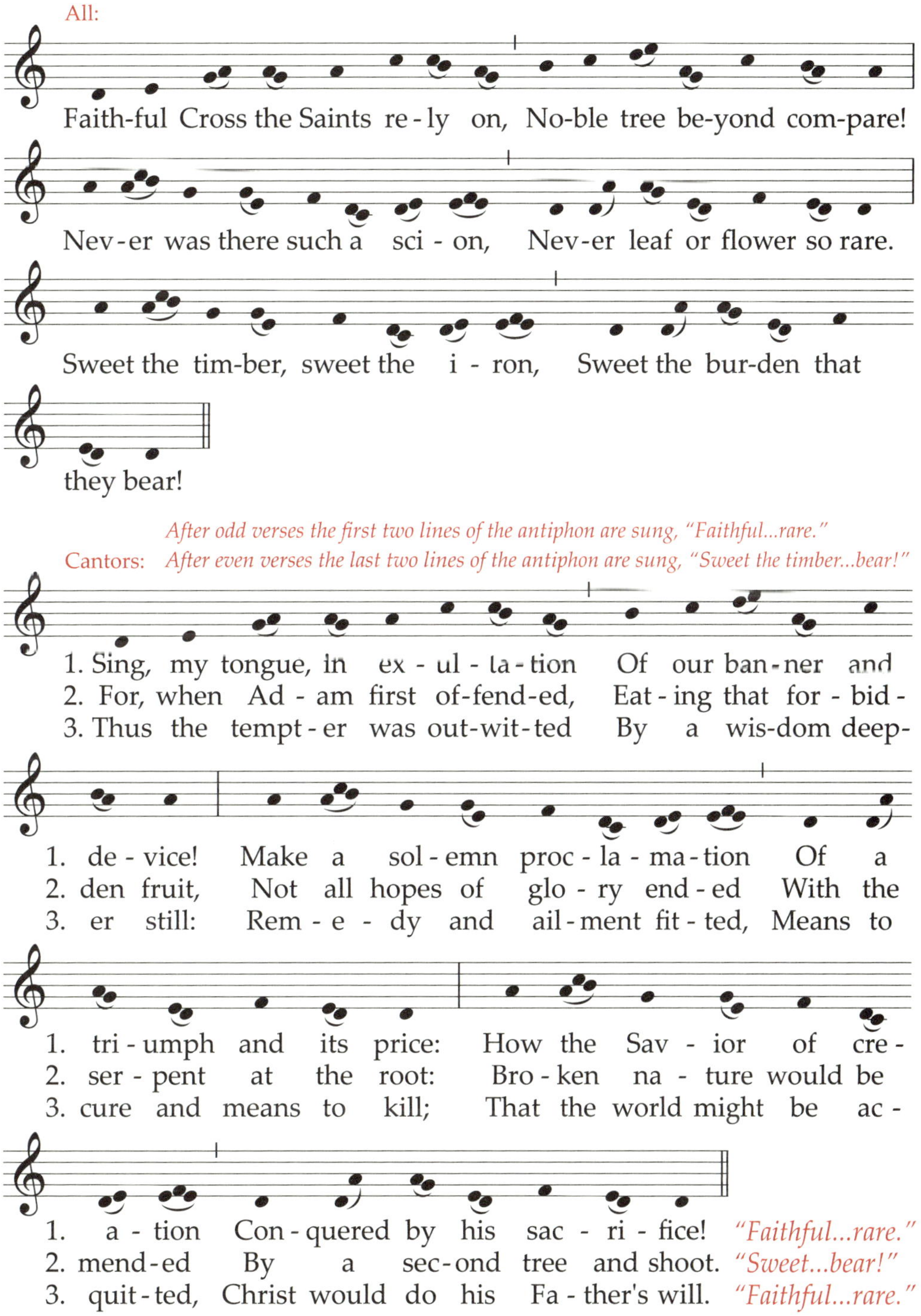

All:
Faith-ful Cross the Saints re-ly on, No-ble tree be-yond com-pare!
Nev-er was there such a sci-on, Nev-er leaf or flower so rare.
Sweet the tim-ber, sweet the i-ron, Sweet the bur-den that they bear!
Cantors:
4. So the Fa-ther, out of pit-y For our self in-flict-ed doom, Sent him from the heaven-ly cit-y When the ho-ly time had come: He, the Son and the Al-might-y, Took our flesh in Mar-y's womb. "Sweet...bear!"
5. Hear a ti-ny ba-by cry-ing, Found-er of the seas and strands; See his vir-gin Moth-er ty-ing Cloth a-round his feet and hands; Find him in a man-ger ly-ing Tight-ly wrapped in swaddl-ing bands! "Faithful...rare."
6. So he came, the long ex-pect-ed, Not in glo-ry, not to reign; On-ly born to be re-ject-ed, Choos-ing hun-ger, toil and pain, Till the scaf-fold was e-rect-ed And the Pas-chal Lamb was slain. "Sweet...bear!"

Cantors:
7. No dis - grace was too ab - hor - rent: Nailed and
8. Loft - y tim - ber, smooth your rough-ness, Flex your
9. Nobl - est tree of all cre - at - ed, Rich - ly
10. Wis-dom, power, and ad - o - ra - tion To the
7. mocked and parched he died; Blood and wa - ter, dou-
8. boughs for blos - som - ing; Let your fi - bers lose
9. jew - eled and em-bossed: Post by Lamb's blood con-
10. bless - ed Trin - i - ty For re - demp - tion and
7. ble war - rant, Is - sue from his wound-ed side,
8. their tough-ness, Gen - tly let your ten - drils cling;
9. se - crat - ed; Spar that saves the tem - pest tossed;
10. sal - va - tion Through the Pas - chal Mys - ter - y,
7. Wash-ing in a might-y tor - rent Earth and stars and
8. Lay a - side your na - tive gruff-ness, Clasp the bod - y
9. Scaf-fold beam which, el - e - vat - ed, Car - ries what the
10. Now, in eve - ry gen - er - a - tion, And for all e -
7. o - cean tide. "Faithful...rare."
8. of your King! "Sweet...bear!"
9. world has cost! "Faithful...rare."
10. ter - ni - ty. "Sweet...bear!"

EASTER TIME

The Easter Vigil in the Holy Night

The Blessing of the Fire and Preparation of the Candle

14.

Priest:

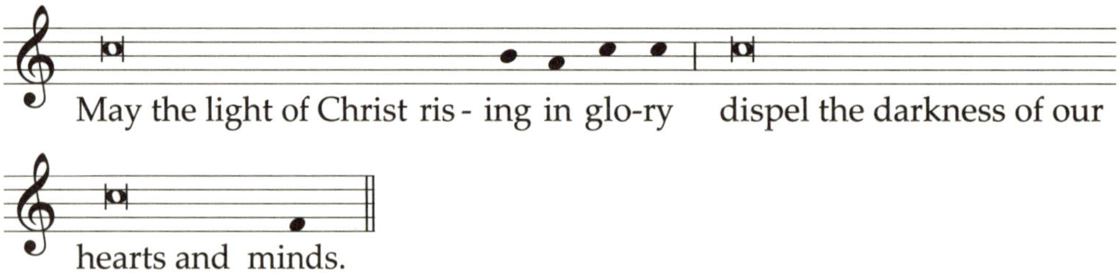

Procession

15.

Deacon:

Or:

All reply:

Or:

The Easter Proclamation (*Exsultet*)

19. Longer Form of the Easter Proclamation

The Deacon, after incensing the book and the candle, proclaims the Easter Proclamation (Exsultet) at the ambo or at a lectern, with all standing and holding lighted candles in their hands.

The Easter Proclamation may be made, in the absence of a Deacon, by the Priest himself or by another concelebrating Priest. If, however, because of necessity, a lay cantor sings the Proclamation, the words Therefore, dearest friends up to the end of the invitation are omitted, along with the greeting The Lord be with you.

The Proclamation may also be sung in the shorter form (pp. 98–101).

a - mong the Le-vites, may pour into me his light un-shad-owed,
that I may sing this can-dle's per-fect prais-es.)
(V. The Lord be with you. R. And with your spir-it.)
V. Lift up your hearts. R. We lift them up to the Lord.
V. Let us give thanks to the Lord our God. R. It is right and just.
It is truly right and just, with ardent love of mind and heart and
with devoted service of our voice, to acclaim our God in-vis-i-ble,
the al - might-y Fa-ther, and Jesus Christ, our Lord, his Son, his
On - ly Be-got-ten. Who for our sake paid Adam's debt to the e-
-ter-nal Fa-ther, and, pouring out his own dear Blood, wiped clean
the re-cord of our an-cient sin-ful-ness. These then are the feasts
of Pass-o-ver, in which is slain the Lamb, the one true Lamb,
whose Blood anoints the door - posts of be-liev-ers. This is the

night, when once you led our fore-bears, Is-ra-el's chil-dren,
from slaver-y in E-gypt and made them pass dry-shod through
the Red Sea. This is the night that with a pil-lar of fire
banished the dark-ness of sin. This is the night that even now,
throughout the world, sets Christian believers apart from world-ly
vic-es and from the gloom of sin, lead-ing them to grace and
join-ing them to his ho-ly ones. This is the night, when
Christ broke the prison-bars of death and rose vic-to-ri-ous
from the un-der-world. Our birth would have been no gain,
had we not been re-deemed. O wonder of your hum-ble care
for us! O love, O char-i-ty be-yond all tell-ing, to ran-som
a slave you gave a-way your Son! O tru-ly nec-es-sar-y sin of
Ad-am, de-stroyed com-plete-ly by the Death of Christ! O

hap-py fault that earned so great, so glo-ri - ous a Re-deem-er!
O truly bless-ed night, wor-thy alone to know the time and
hour when Christ rose from the un-der-world! This is the night
of which it is writ-ten: The night shall be as bright as day,
dazzling is the night for me, and full of glad-ness. The sanctifying
power of this night dis - pels wick-ed-ness, washes faults a-way,
re-stores innocence to the fall-en, and joy to mourn-ers, drives
out ha-tred, fos-ters con-cord, and brings down the might-y.
On this, your night of grace, O ho-ly Fa-ther, accept this candle, a
sol-emn of-fer-ing, the work of bees and of your serv-ants' hands,
an evening sacri - fice of praise, this gift from your most ho-ly
Church. But now we know the praises of this pil-lar, which glow-
-ing fire ig - nites for God's hon-or, a fire into many flames

di-vid-ed, yet nev-er dimmed by shar - ing of its light, for it is
fed by melt-ing wax, drawn out by moth-er bees to build a torch
so pre-cious. O truly bless-ed night, when things of heaven
are wed to those of earth, and di - vine to the hu-man.
There-fore, O Lord, we pray you that this candle, hallowed to the
honor of your name, may perse - vere un-dimmed, to overcome
the dark - ness of this night. Re-ceive it as a pleas-ing fra-grance,
and let it min-gle with the lights of heav-en. May this flame
be found still burn - ing by the Morn-ing Star: the one Morning
Star who nev-er sets, Christ your Son, who, coming back from
death's do-main, has shed his peaceful light on hu-man-i-ty, and
lives and reigns for ev - er and ev-er. R. A - men.

Shorter Form of the Easter Proclamation

the al - might-y Fa-ther, and Jesus Christ, our Lord, his Son, his
On - ly Be-got-ten. Who for our sake paid Adam's debt to the e-
-ter-nal Fa-ther, and, pouring out his own dear Blood, wiped clean
the re-cord of our an-cient sin-ful-ness. These then are the feasts
of Pass-o-ver, in which is slain the Lamb, the one true Lamb,
whose Blood anoints the door - posts of be-liev-ers. This is the
night, when once you led our fore-bears, Is-ra-el's chil-dren,
from slaver - y in E-gypt and made them pass dry - shod through
the Red Sea. This is the night that with a pil-lar of fire
banished the dark-ness of sin. This is the night that even now,
throughout the world, sets Christian believers apart from world-ly
vic-es and from the gloom of sin, lead-ing them to grace and
join-ing them to his ho-ly ones. This is the night, when

Christ broke the prison - bars of death and rose vic-to-ri - ous
from the un-der-world. O wonder of your hum-ble care for us!
O love, O char-i-ty be - yond all tell-ing, to ran - som a slave
you gave a-way your Son! O tru-ly nec-es-sar-y sin of Ad-am,
de - stroyed com-plete-ly by the Death of Christ! O hap-py fault
that earned so great, so glo-ri - ous a Re-deem-er! The sanctifying
power of this night dis - pels wick-ed-ness, washes faults a-way,
re-stores innocence to the fall-en, and joy to mourn-ers. O truly
bless-ed night, when things of heaven are wed to those of earth,
and di - vine to the hu-man.
On this, your night of grace, O ho-ly Fa-ther, accept this candle, a
sol-emn of-fer-ing, the work of bees and of your serv-ants' hands,
an evening sacri - fice of praise, this gift from your most ho-ly

The Liturgy of the Word

31.

Priest:

34.

Priest or Psalmist:

Baptismal Liturgy

40.

Priest:

If there are candidates to be baptized:

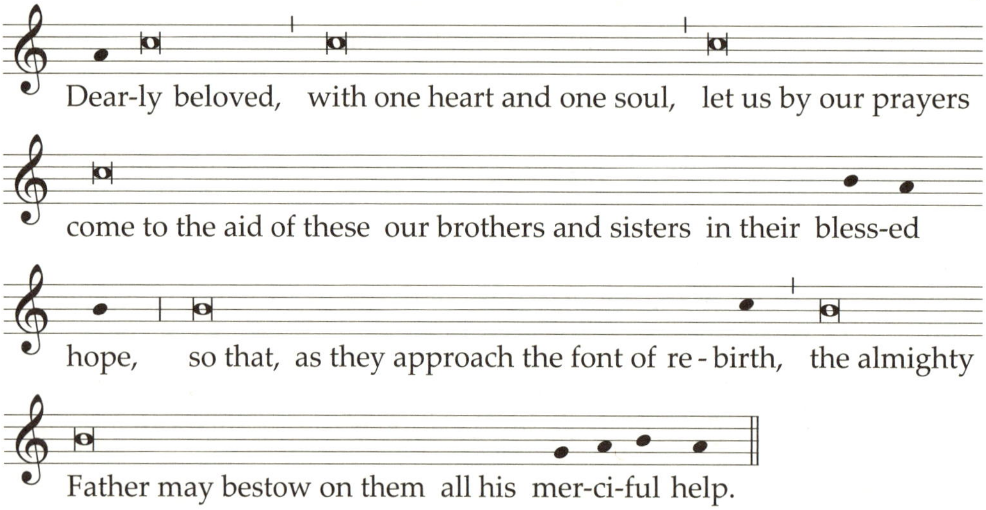

If the font is to be blessed, but no one is to be baptized:

43. The Litany of Saints

Cantors: All:

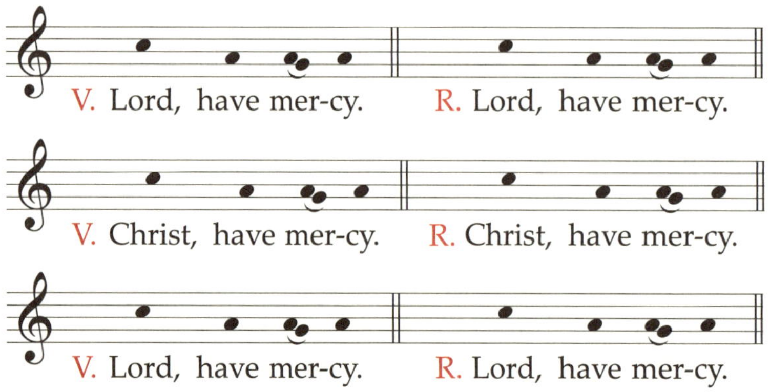

Holy Mary, Mother of God, [ ] R. pray for us.
Saint Mich - ael,
Holy Angels of God, [ ]
Saint John the Bap - tist,
Saint Jo - seph,
Saint Peter and Saint Paul, [ ]
Saint An - drew,
Saint John, [ ]
Saint Mary Mag - da - lene,
Saint Ste - phen,
Saint Ignatius of An - ti - och,
Saint Law - rence,
Saint Perpetua and Saint Fe - li - ci - ty,
Saint Ag - nes,
Saint Gre - go - ry,
Saint Au - gus - tine,
Saint Atha - na - sius,
Saint Bas - il,
Saint Mar - tin,
Saint Ben - e - dict,
Saint Francis and Saint Dom - i - nic,
Saint Francis Xa - vi - er,
Saint John Vi - an - ney,
Saint Catherine of Si - e - na,
Saint Teresa of Je - sus,
All holy men
and women, Saints of God, [ ]

Lord, be mer-ci-ful, R. Lord, de-liv-er us, we pray.

From all e - vil, R. Lord, de-liv-er us, we pray.
From eve - ry sin,
From ever - last-ing death,
By your In - car - na - tion,
By your
Death and Res - ur - rec - tion,
By the out-
-pouring
of the Ho - ly Spir - it,

Be merciful to us sin-ners, R. Lord, we ask you, hear our prayer.

If there are candidates to be baptized:

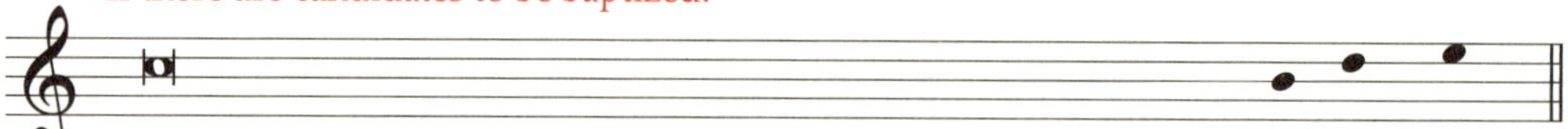

Bring these chosen ones to new birth through the grace of Bap-tism,

R. Lord, we ask you, hear our prayer.

If there is no one to be baptized:

Make this font holy by your grace for the new birth of your child-ren,

R. Lord, we ask you, hear our prayer.

Jesus, Son of the liv-ing God, R. Lord, we ask you, hear our prayer.

Christ, hear us. R. Christ, hear us.

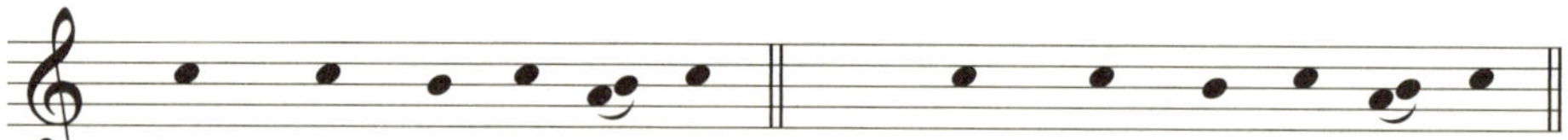

Christ, gra-cious-ly hear us. R. Christ, gra-cious-ly hear us.

44. Blessing of Baptismal Water

Priest:

O God, who by invisible power accomplish a wondrous effect

through sacra - men-tal signs and who in many ways have pre-

-pared water, your cre - a-tion, to show forth the grace of Bap-tism;

O God, whose Spirit in the first moments of the world's creation

hovered o-ver the wa-ters, so that the very substance of wa-ter
would even then take to itself the pow-er to sanc-ti-fy; O God, who
by the outpouring of the flood foreshadowed re - gen-er - a-tion,
so that from the mystery of one and the same ele - ment of wa-ter
would come an end to vice and a be - gin-ning of vir-tue; O
God, who caused the children of Abraham to pass dry-shod
through the Red Sea, so that the chosen people, set free from slav-
-ery to Phar aoh, would prefigure the people of the bap-tized; O
God, whose Son, baptized by John in the waters of the Jordan, was a-
-nointed with the Ho-ly Spir-it, and, as he hung upon the Cross,
gave forth water from his side a - long with blood, and after his Res-
-urrection, commanded his dis-ci-ples: "Go forth, teach all na-tions,
baptizing them in the name of the Father and of the Son and of the

Lowering the paschal candle into the water:

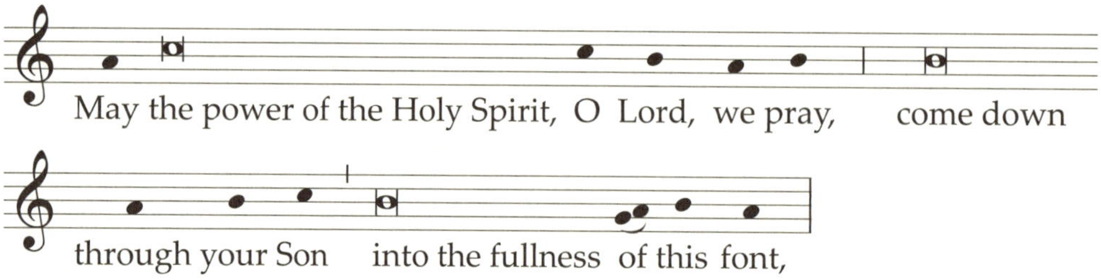

and, holding the candle in the water, he continues:

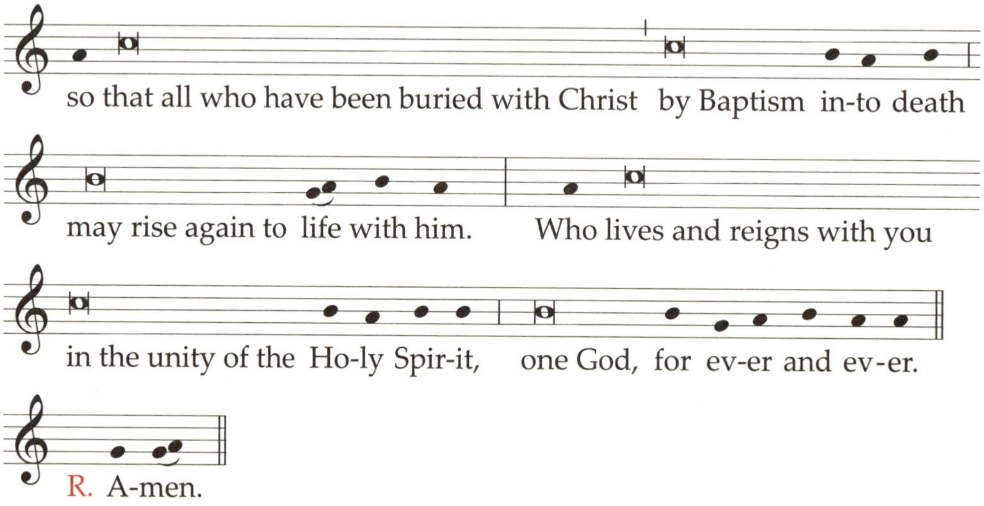

45. Then the candle is lifted out of the water, as the people acclaim:

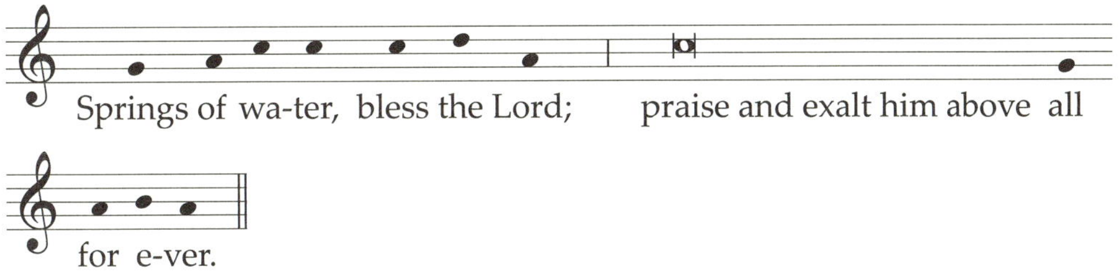

54. The Blessing of Water (If no one is to be baptized and the font is not to be blessed.)

Priest:

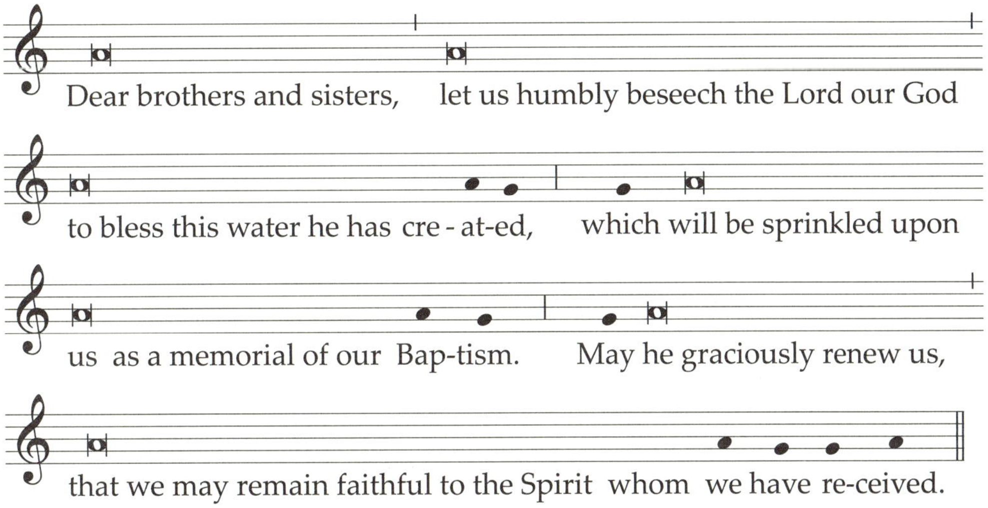

And after a brief pause in silence, he proclaims the following prayer with hands extended:

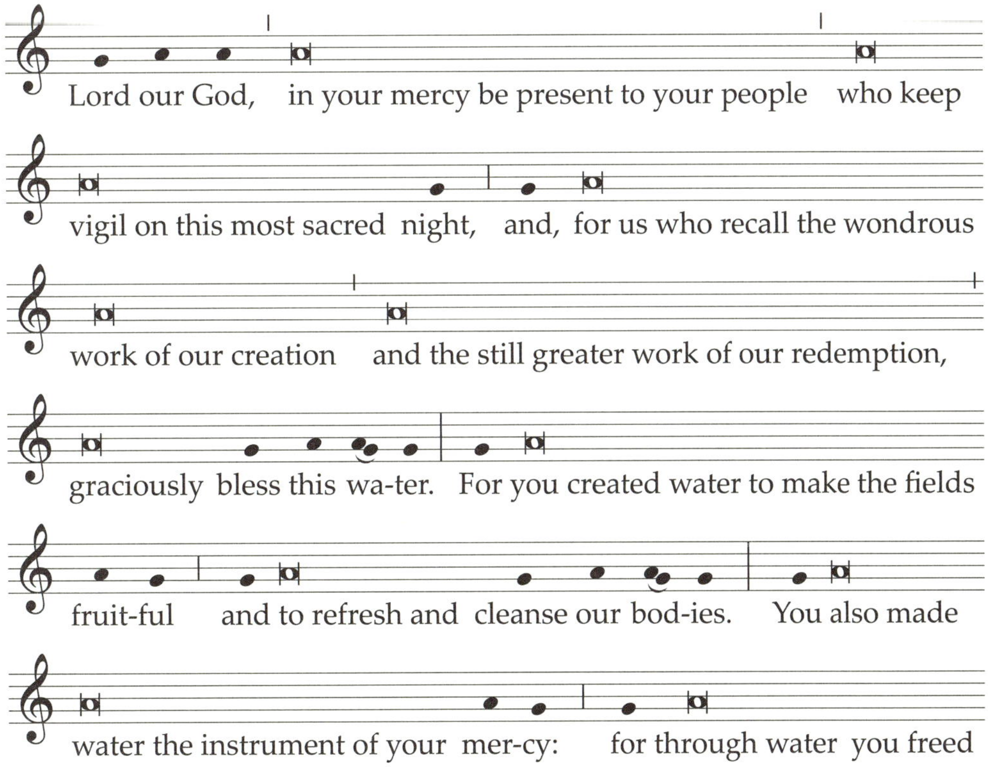

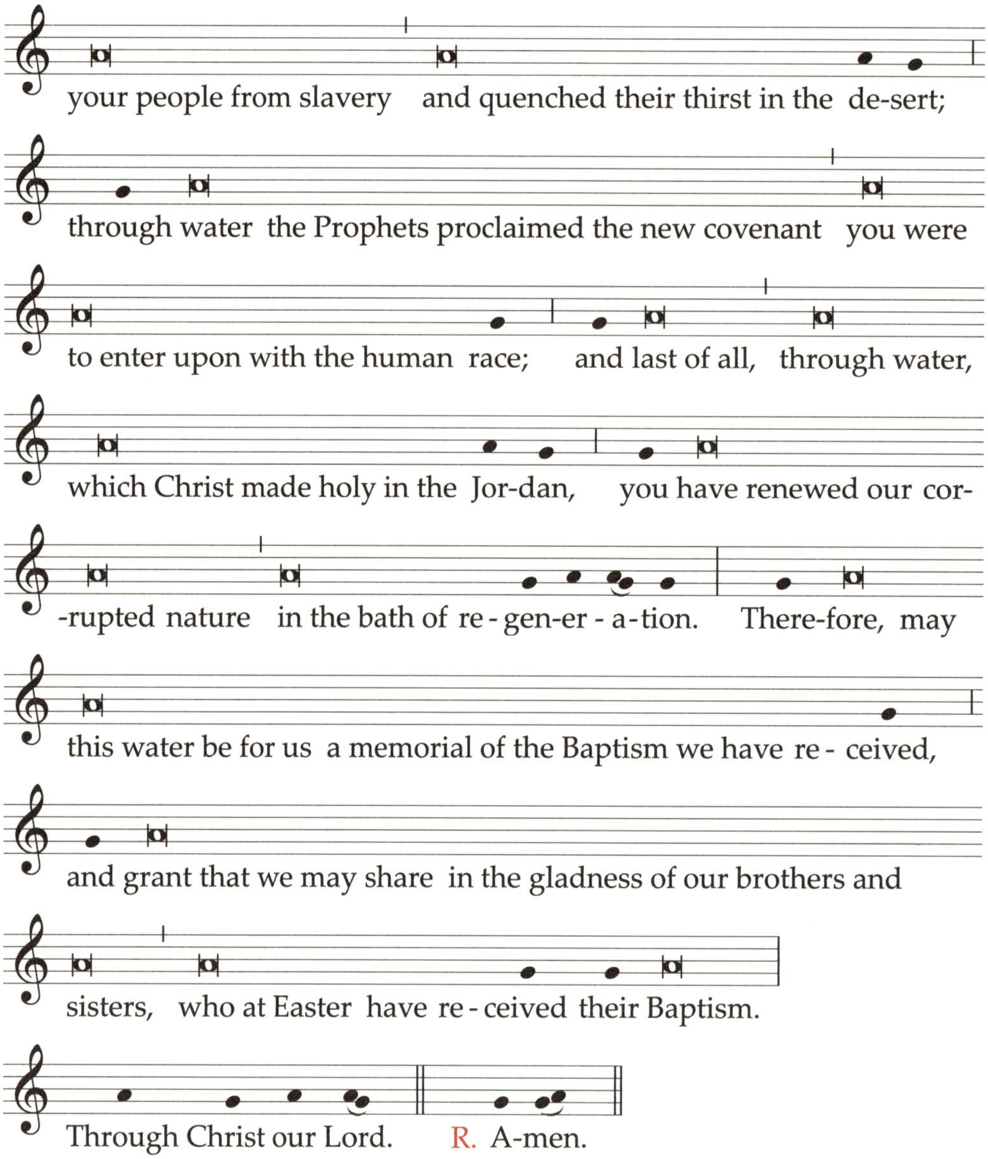

The Renewal of Baptismal Promises

56. Antiphon

Or:

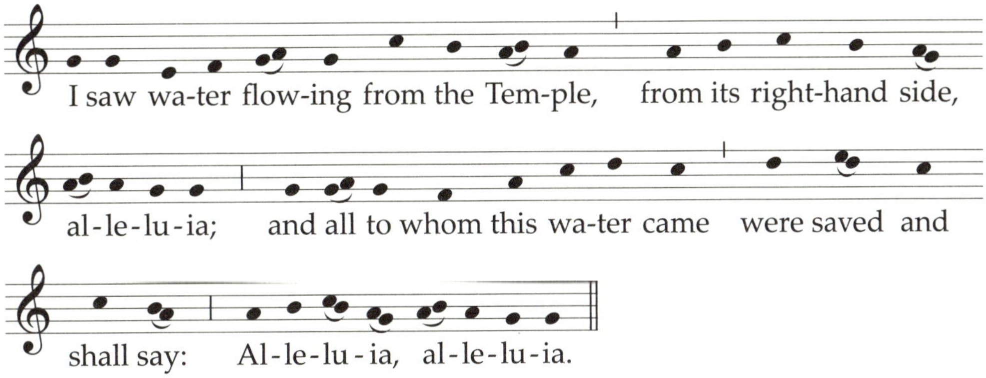

Dismissal

69.

Deacon or, if there is no Deacon, the Priest:

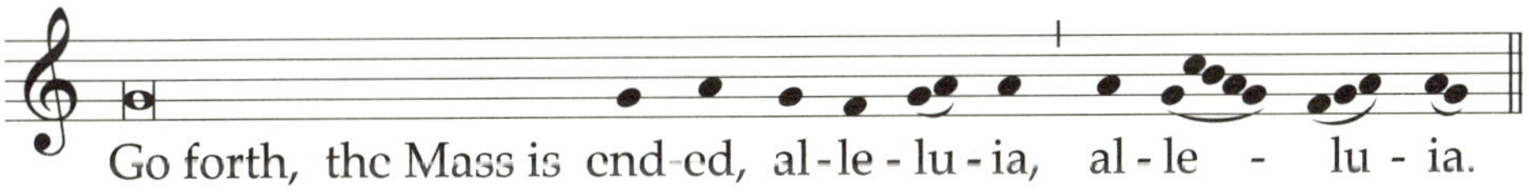

Or:

All reply:

Pentecost Sunday

Preface: The mystery of Pentecost.

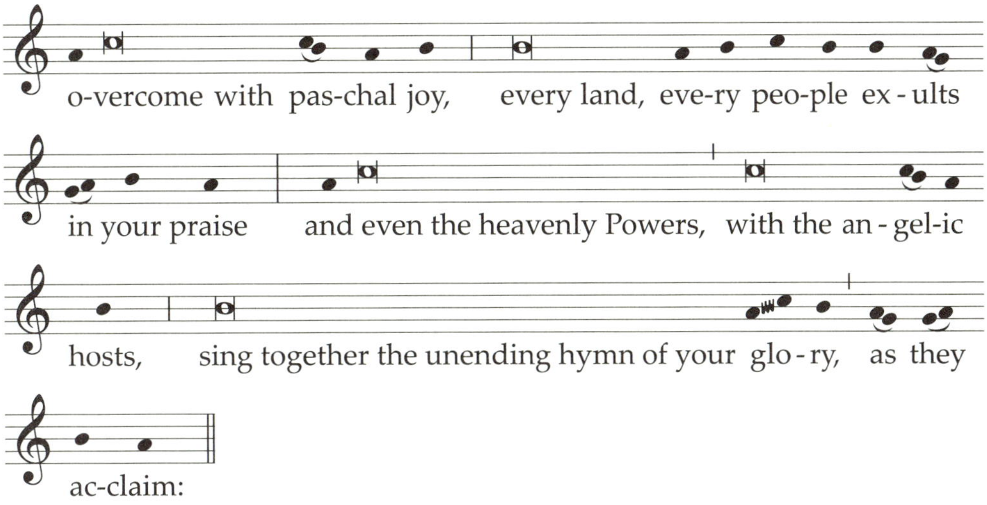

Dismissal

Deacon, or if there is no Deacon, the Priest:

Or:

All reply:

THE SOLEMNITIES OF THE LORD DURING ORDINARY TIME

The Most Holy Trinity

Preface: The mystery of the Most Holy Trinity.

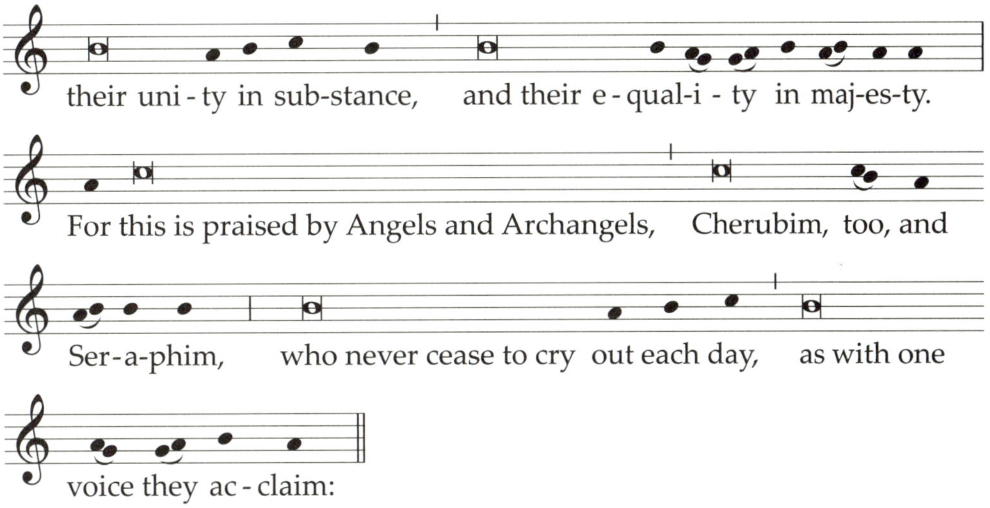

The Most Holy Body and Blood of Christ
(Corpus Christi)

Preface: The fruits of the Most Holy Eucharist.

his A-pos-tles, es-tablishing for the ages to come the saving memo-
-rial of the Cross, he offered himself to you as the un - blem-ished
Lamb, the acceptable gift of per-fect praise. Nour-ishing your
faithful by this sa-cred mys-ter-y, you make them holy, so that the
human race, bounded by one world, may be enlightened by one
faith and united by one bond of char-i - ty. And so, we approach
the table of this won-drous Sac-ra-ment, so that, bathed in the
sweetness of your grace, we may pass o - ver to the heavenly
reali - ties here fore-shad-owed. There-fore, all creatures of heav-
-en and earth sing a new song in ad - o - ra-tion, and we, with all the
host of An-gels, cry out, and without end we ac-claim:

The Most Sacred Heart of Jesus

Preface: The boundless charity of Christ.

Our Lord Jesus Christ, King of the Universe

Preface: Christ, King of the Universe.

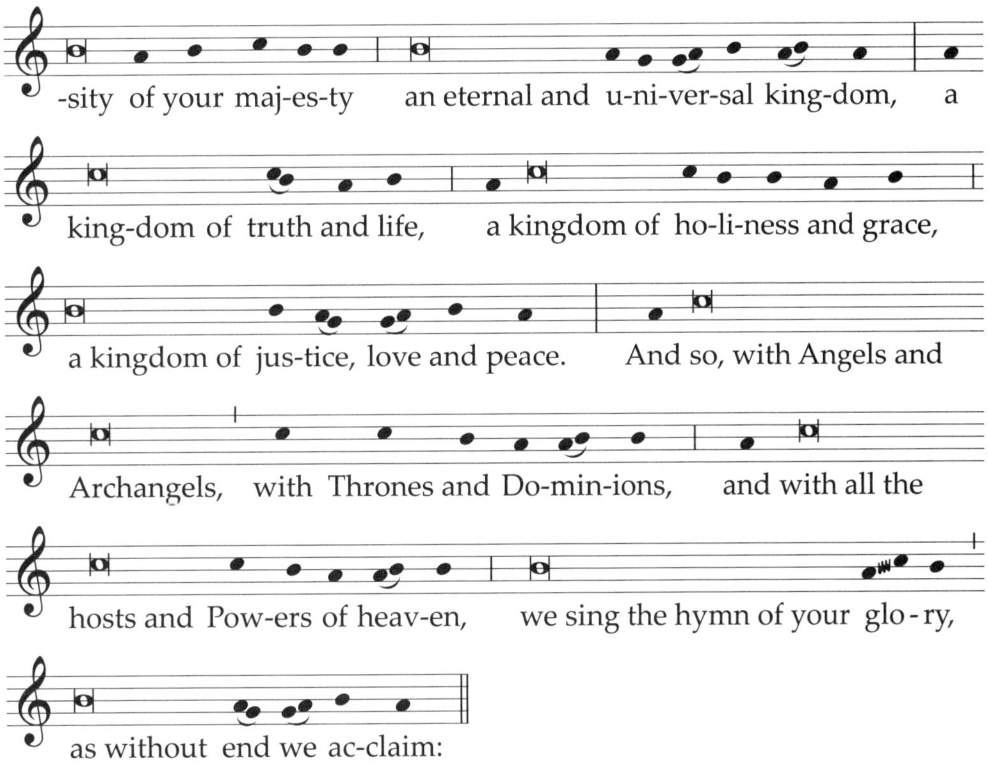
-sity of your maj-es-ty an eternal and u-ni-ver-sal king-dom, a
king-dom of truth and life, a kingdom of ho-li-ness and grace,
a kingdom of jus-tice, love and peace. And so, with Angels and
Archangels, with Thrones and Do-min-ions, and with all the
hosts and Pow-ers of heav-en, we sing the hymn of your glo-ry,
as without end we ac-claim:

THE ORDER OF MASS

THE INTRODUCTORY RITES

Greeting

1.

Priest:

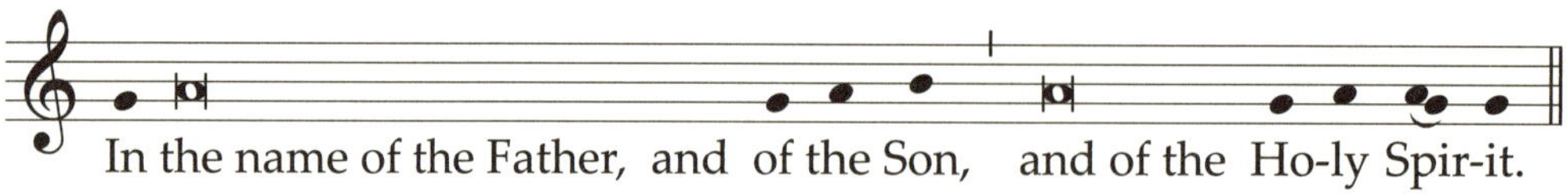

The people reply:

2.

Priest:

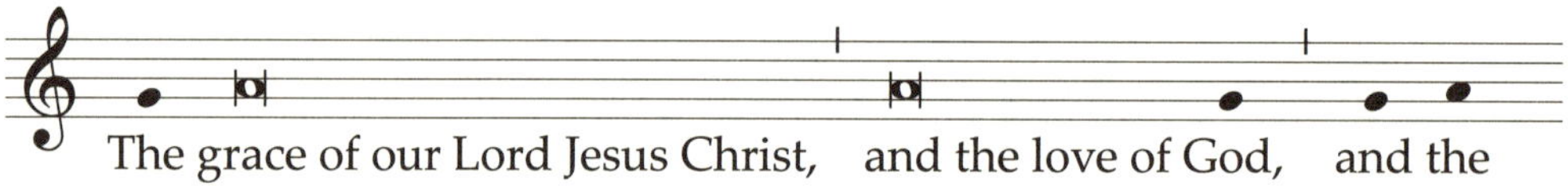

Or:

Or:

The people reply:

In this first greeting a Bishop, instead of The Lord be with you, says:

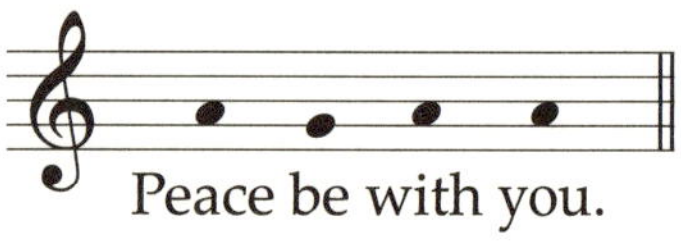

Penitential Act

4/5/6. Invitation

Priest:

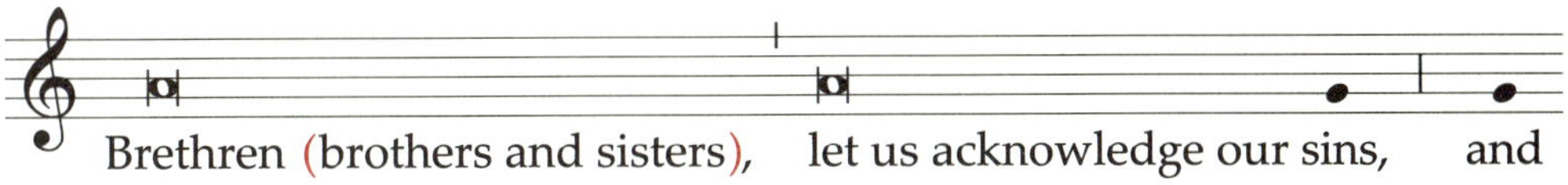

5.

Priest:

People:

Priest:

People:

Or:

6.

Priest, Deacon, or another minister:

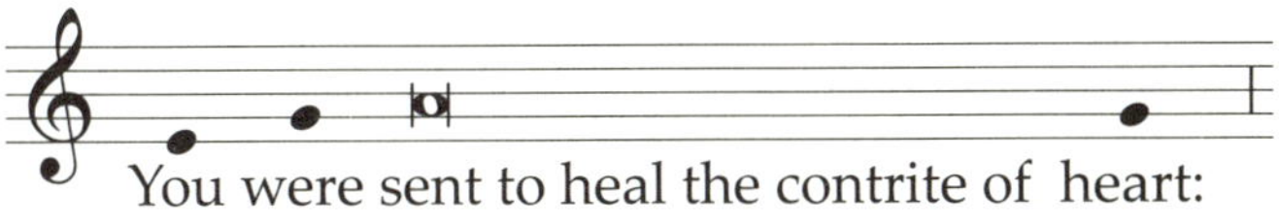

Or:

The people reply:

Or:

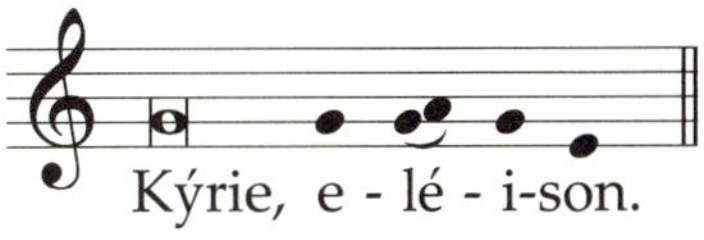

Priest, Deacon, or another minister:

Or:

The people reply:

Or:

Priest, Deacon, or another minister:

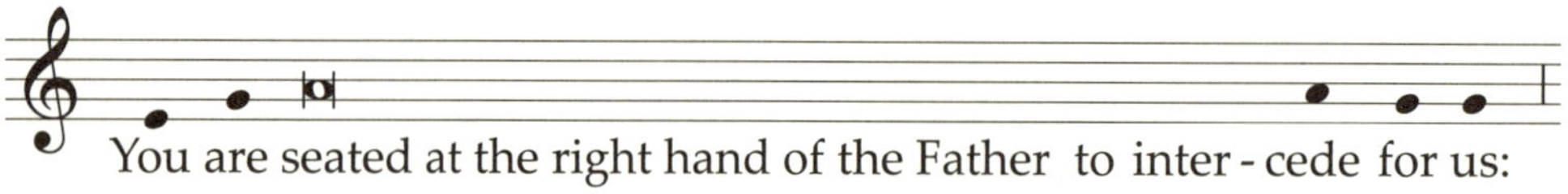

Or:

The people reply:

Or:

4/5/6. Absolution

Priest:

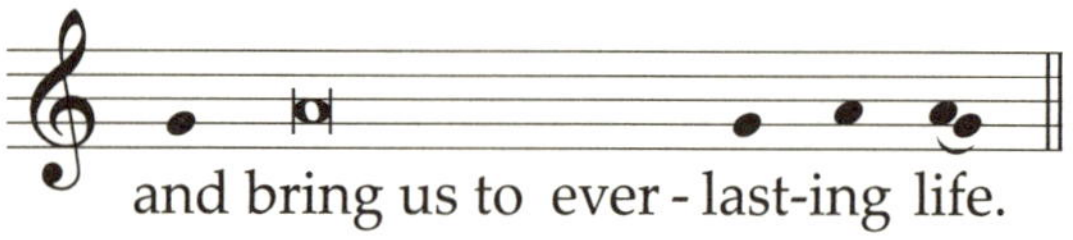

Kyrie

7.

V. Lord, have mer-cy.
R. Lord, have mer-cy.
V. Christ, have mer-cy.
R. Christ, have mer-cy.
V. Lord, have mer-cy.
R. Lord, have mer-cy.

Or:

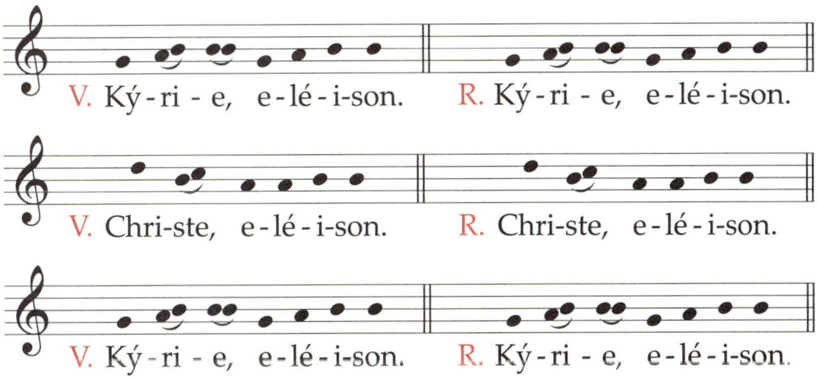
V. Ký-ri - e, e-lé-i-son.
R. Ký-ri - e, e-lé-i-son.
V. Chri-ste, e-lé-i-son.
R. Chri-ste, e-lé-i-son.
V. Ký-ri - e, e-lé-i-son.
R. Ký-ri - e, e-lé-i-son.

Or:

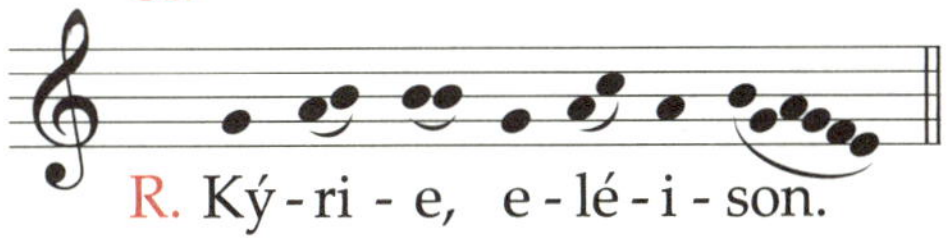
R. Ký-ri - e, e-lé-i - son.

Gloria

8.

Glo-ry to God in the high-est,
and on earth peace to peo-ple of good will.
We praise you, we bless you, we a-dore you, we glo-ri-fy you,
we give you thanks for your great glo-ry,
Lord God, heav-en-ly King, O God, al - might-y Fa-ther.
Lord Je-sus Christ, On-ly Be-got-ten Son,
Lord God, Lamb of God, Son of the Fa-ther,
you take a-way the sins of the world, have mer-cy on us;
you take a-way the sins of the world, re-ceive our prayer;
you are seat-ed at the right hand of the Fa-ther, have mer-cy on us.

THE LITURGY OF THE WORD

First Reading

10.

Reader:

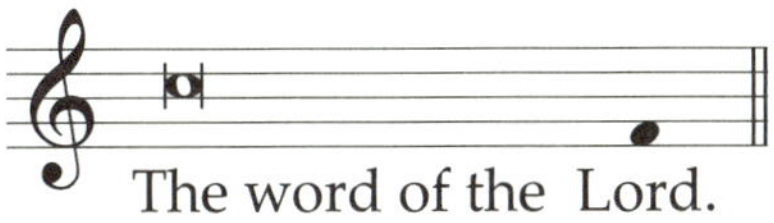

All reply:

Second Reading

12.

Reader:

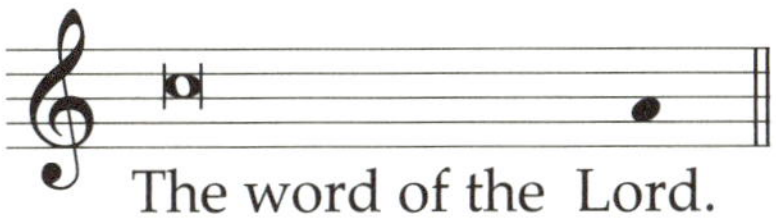

All reply:

Gospel Reading

15.

Deacon, or if there is no Deacon, the Priest:

The Lord be with you.

The people reply:

And with your spir-it.

Deacon, or the Priest:

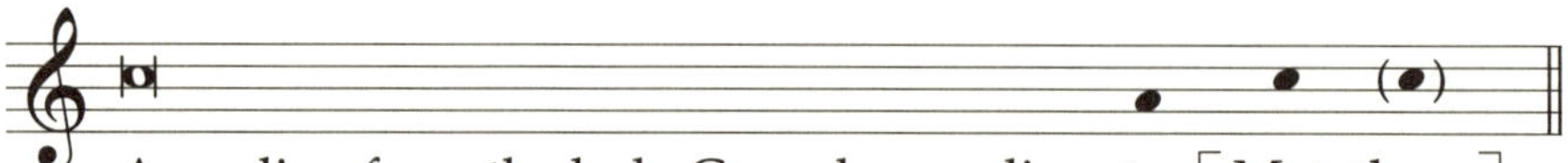

A reading from the holy Gospel according to [Mat-thew. / Mark. / Luke. / John.]

The people acclaim:

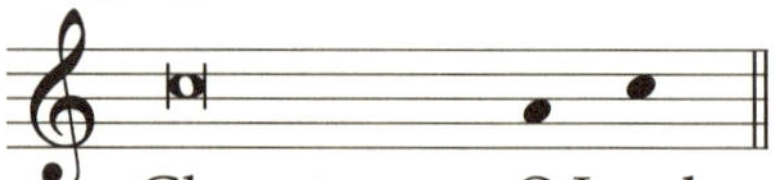

Glory to you, O Lord.

16.

Deacon, or the Priest:

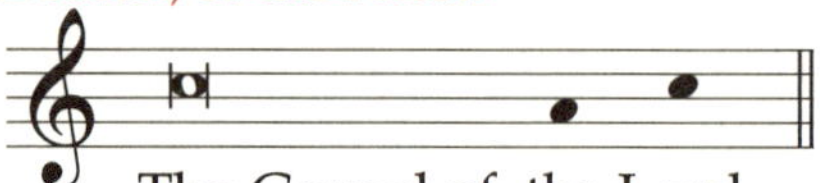

The Gospel of the Lord.

All reply:

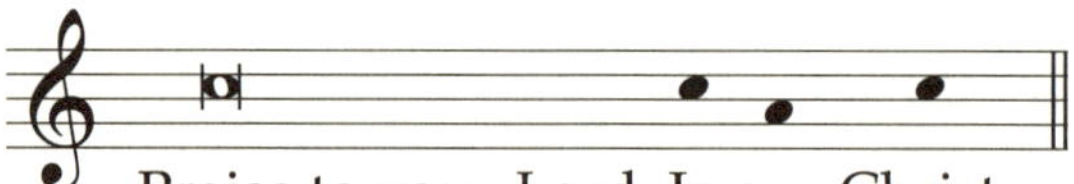

Praise to you, Lord Je-sus Christ.

The Creed

Credo I

18.

For our sake he was cru-ci-fied un-der Pon-tius Pi-late, he
suffered death and was bur-ied, and rose a-gain on the third day
in accordance with the Scrip-tures. He as-cend-ed in-to heav-en
and is seated at the right hand of the Fa-ther. He will come a-gain
in glo-ry to judge the living and the dead and his kingdom will
have no end.
I be-lieve in the Ho-ly Spir-it, the Lord, the giv-er of life, who
pro-ceeds from the Father and the Son, who with the Fa-ther and
the Son is adored and glo-ri-fied, who has spoken through the
proph-ets. I be-lieve in one, ho-ly, ca-tho-lic and a-pos-tol-ic
Church. I con-fess one Bap-tism for the for-give-ness of sins
and I look for-ward to the res-ur-rec-tion of the dead and the life
of the world to come. A - men.

THE LITURGY OF THE EUCHARIST

Invitation to Prayer

29.

Priest:

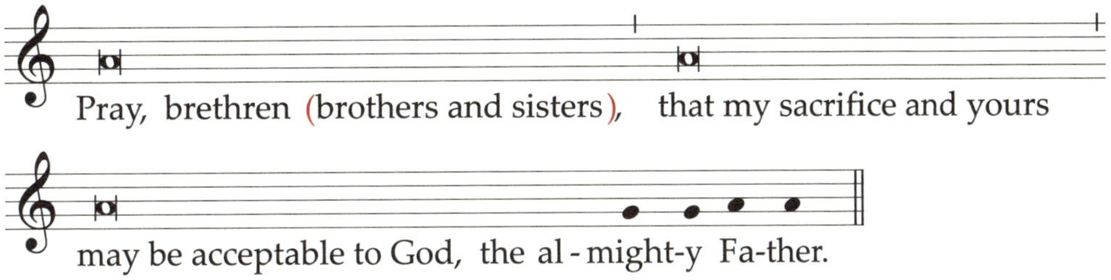

People:

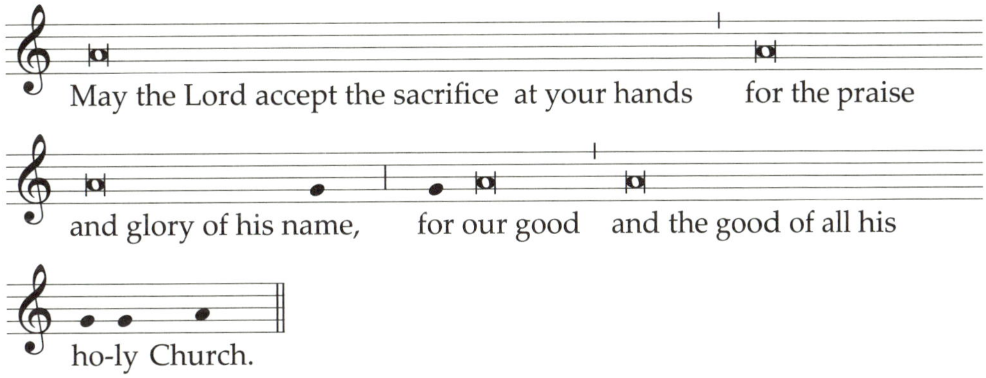

The Eucharistic Prayer

31. Preface Dialogue

Preface Acclamation

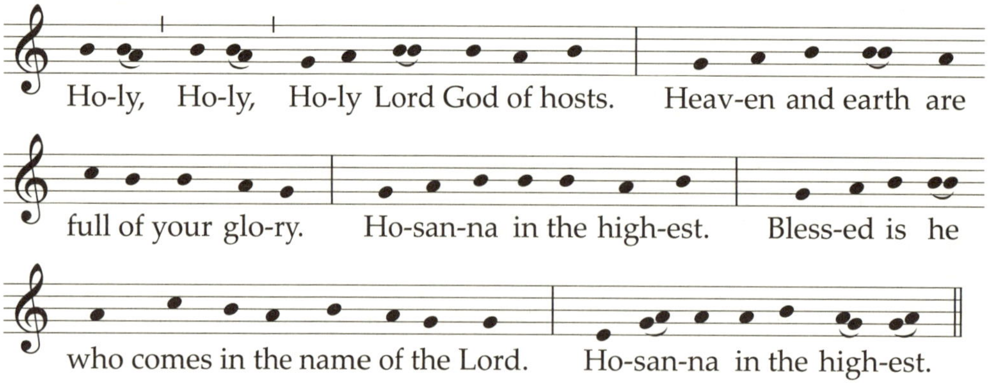

Or:

91/104/112/121. Memorial Acclamation

Priest:

Or:

People:

Or:

Or:

98/106/114/123. Concluding Doxology

Priest:

Preface I of Advent

The two comings of Christ

33.

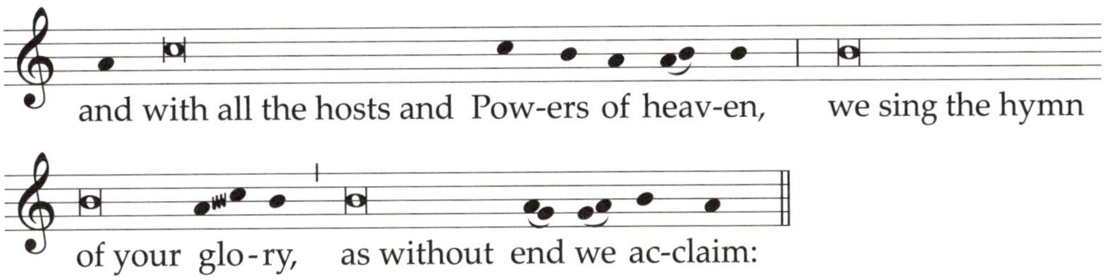

Preface II of Advent

The twofold expectation of Christ

34.

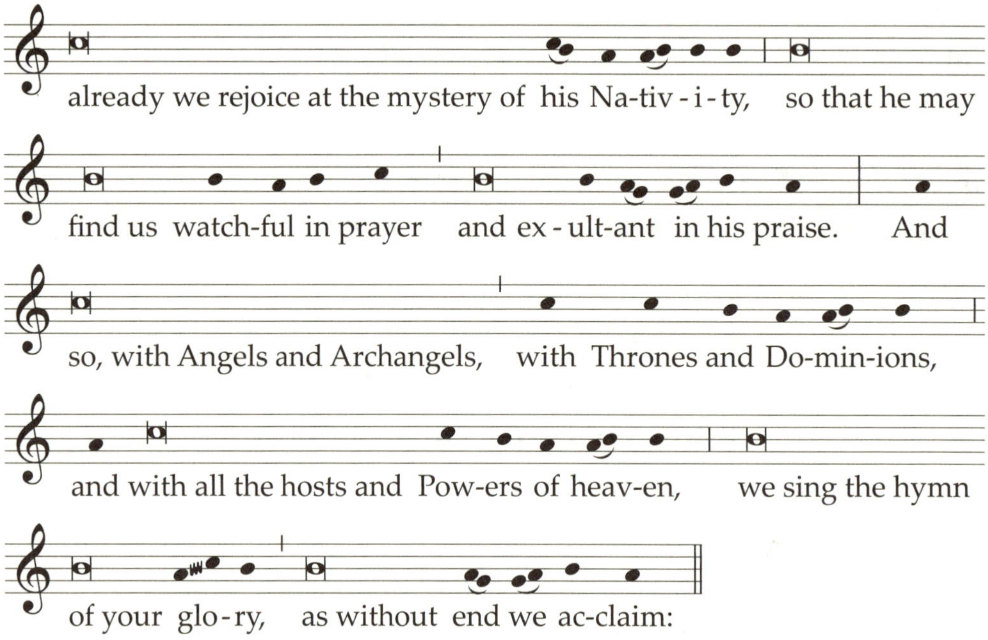

Preface I of the Nativity of the Lord

Christ the Light

35.

Preface II of the Nativity of the Lord

The restoration of all things in the Incarnation

36.

-filled mystery, though invisible in his own di - vine na-ture, he

has appeared visi - bly in ours; and begotten be - fore all ag-es,

he has begun to ex - ist in time; so that, raising up in himself

all that was cast down, he might restore unity to all cre - a-tion

and call stray-ing hu-man-i - ty back to the heav-en - ly King-dom.

And so, with all the An - gels, we praise you, as in joyful cele-

-bra-tion we ac-claim:

Preface III of the Nativity of the Lord

The exchange in the Incarnation of the Word

37.

V. The Lord be with you. R. And with your spir-it.

V. Lift up your hearts. R. We lift them up to the Lord.

V. Let us give thanks to the Lord our God. R. It is right and just.

It is truly right and just, our duty and our sal-va-tion, al-ways and

everywhere to give you thanks, Lord, holy Father, almighty and e-

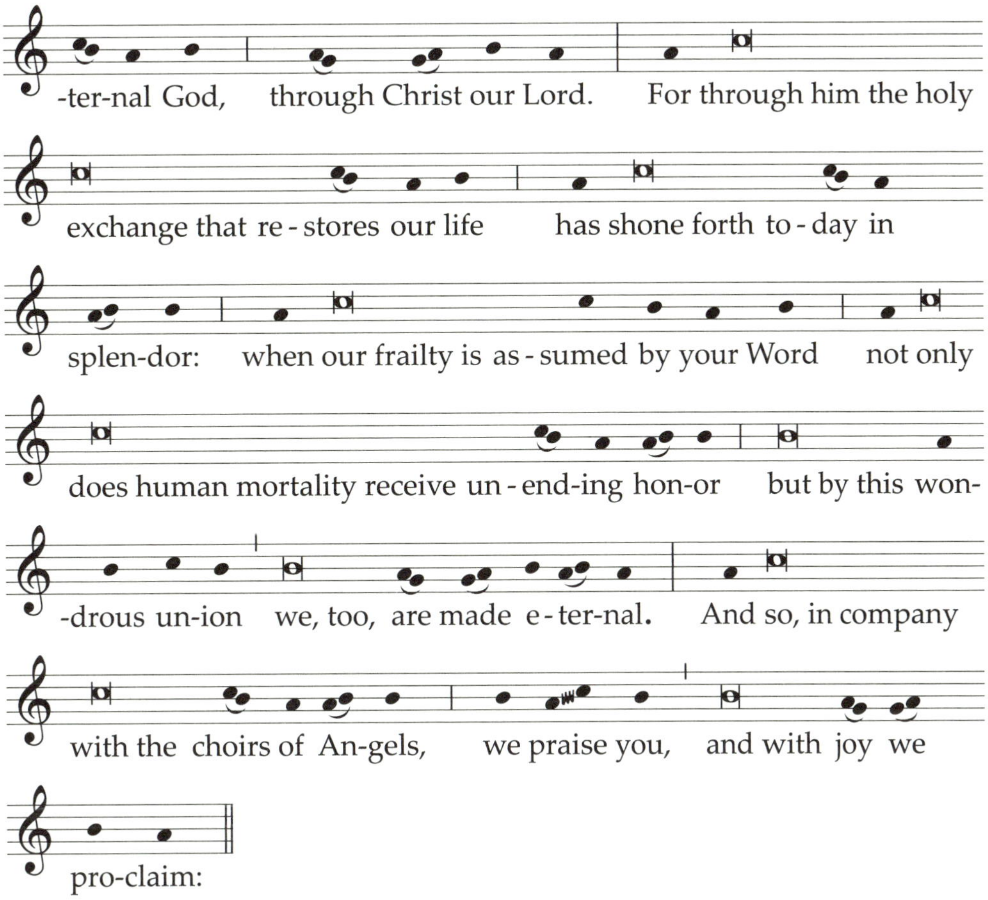

Preface of the Epiphany of the Lord

Christ the light of the nations

38.

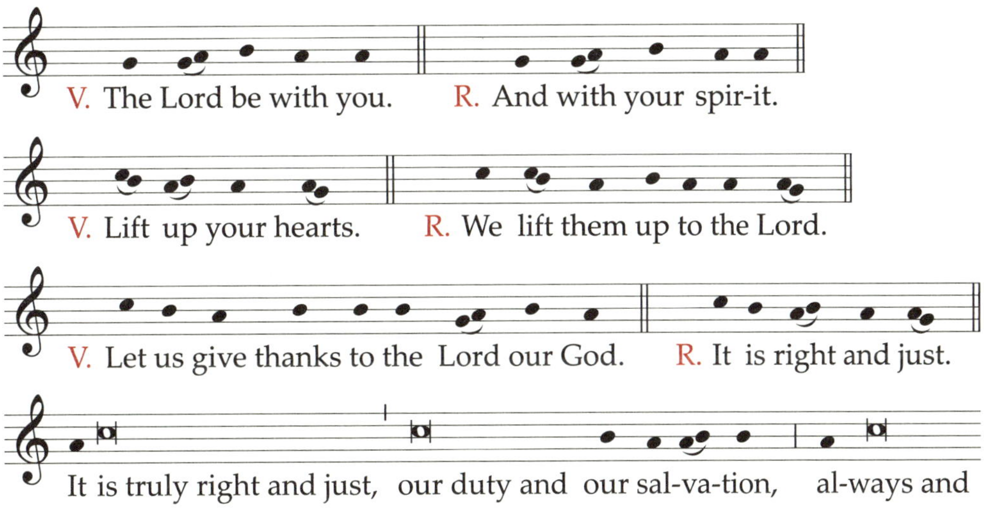

Preface I of Lent

The spiritual meaning of Lent

39.

Preface II of Lent

Spiritual penance

40.

Preface III of Lent

The fruits of abstinence

41.

Preface IV of Lent

The fruits of fasting

42.

Preface I of the Passion of the Lord

The power of the Cross

43.

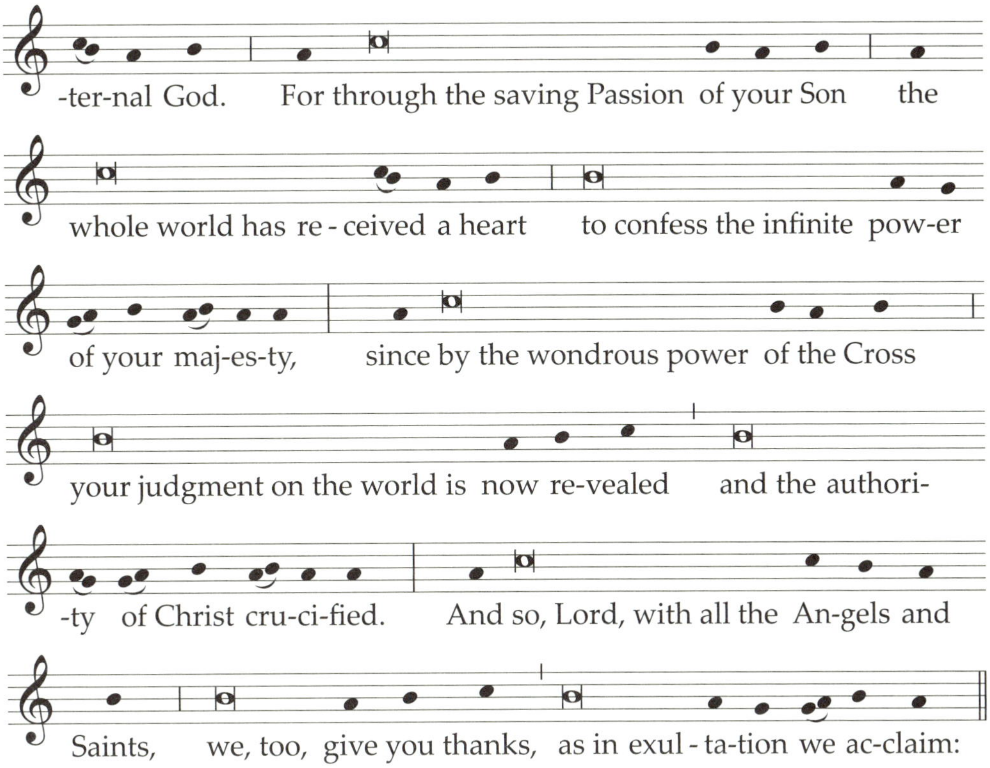

Preface II of the Passion of the Lord

The victory of the Passion

44.

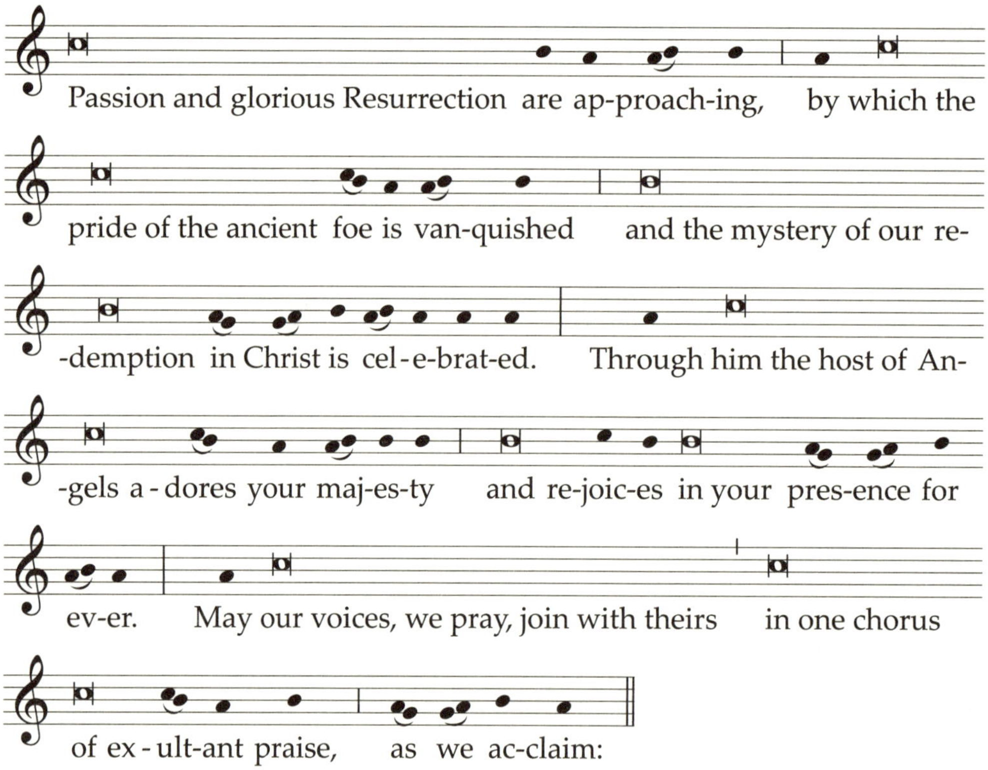

Preface I of Easter

The Paschal Mystery

45.

Preface II of Easter

New life in Christ

46.

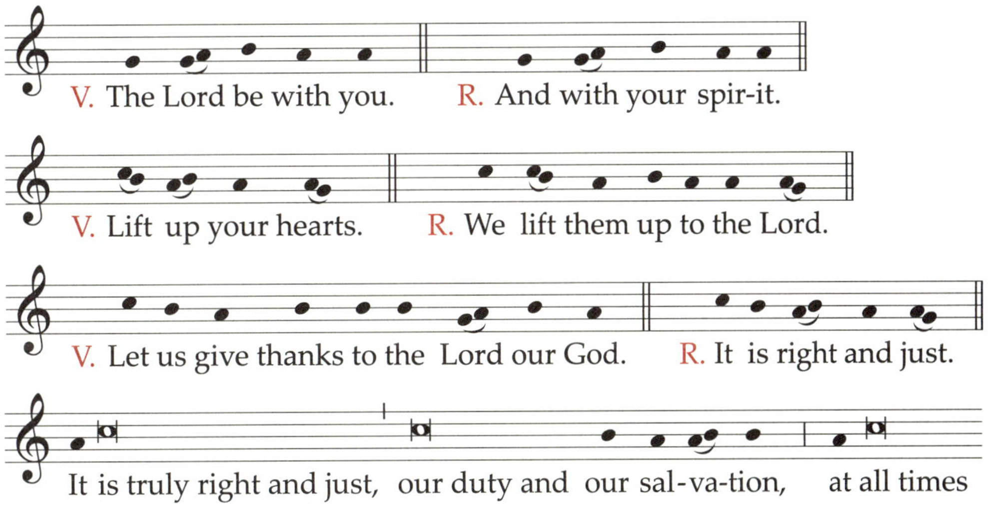

Preface III of Easter

Christ living and always interceding for us

47.

Preface IV of Easter

The restoration of the universe through the Paschal Mystery

48.

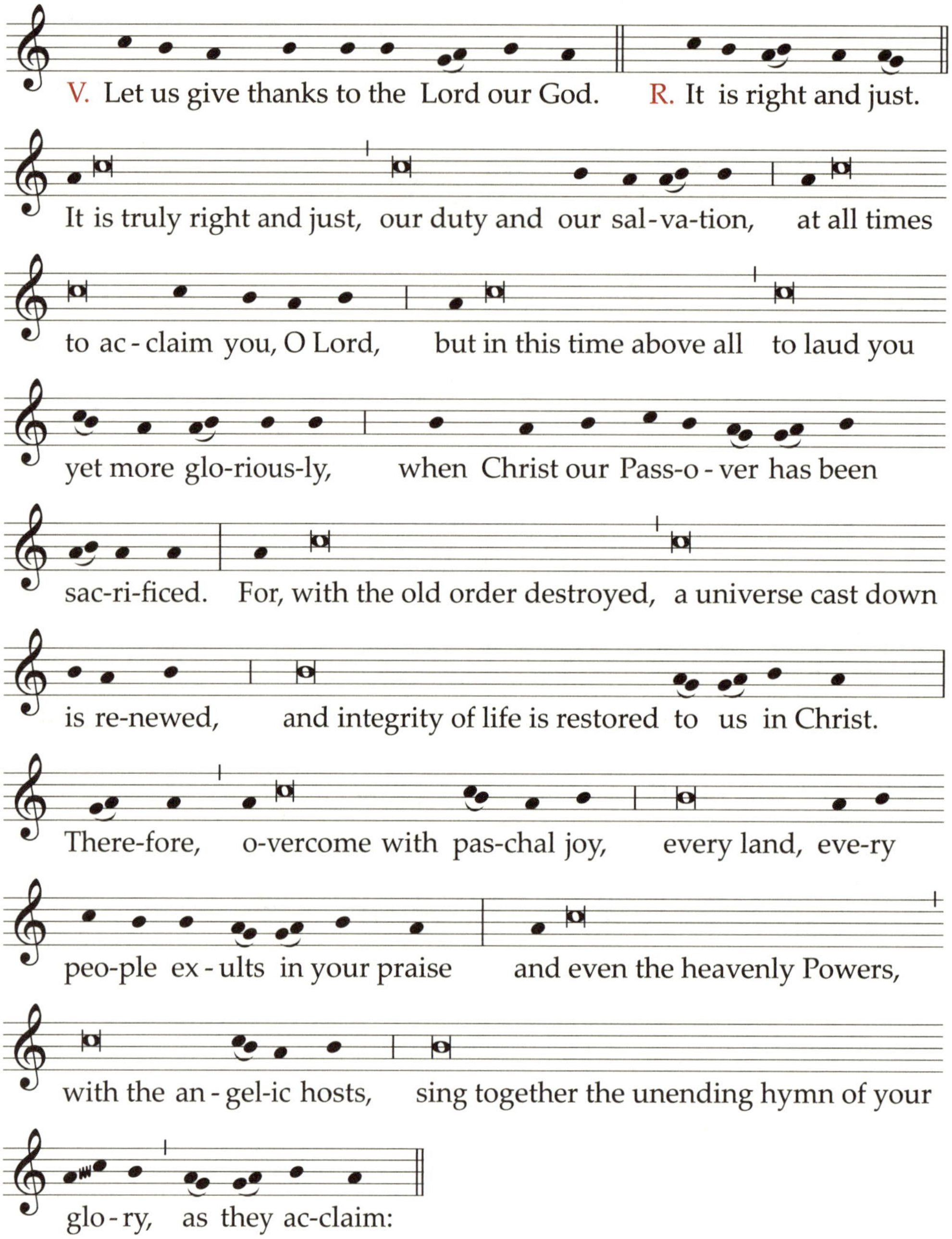

Preface V of Easter

Christ, Priest and Victim

49.

V. Let us give thanks to the Lord our God. R. It is right and just.
It is truly right and just, our duty and our sal-va-tion, at all times
to ac - claim you, O Lord, but in this time above all to laud you
yet more glo-rious-ly, when Christ our Pass-o - ver has been
sac-ri-ficed. By the oblation of his Body, he brought the sacrifices
of old to fulfillment in the reality of the Cross and, by commend-
-ing himself to you for our sal-va-tion, showed him - self the Priest,
the Altar, and the Lamb of sac-ri-fice. There-fore, o-vercome with
pas-chal joy, every land, eve-ry peo-ple ex - ults in your praise
and even the heavenly Powers, with the an - gel-ic hosts, sing to-
-gether the unending hymn of your glo - ry, as they ac-claim:

Preface I of the Ascension of the Lord

The mystery of the Ascension

50.

Preface II of the Ascension of the Lord

The mystery of the Ascension

51.

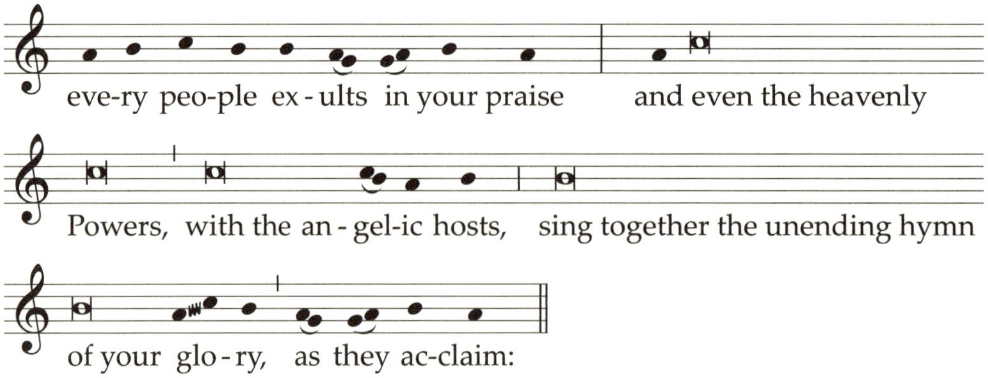

Preface I of the Sundays in Ordinary Time

The Paschal Mystery and the People of God

52.

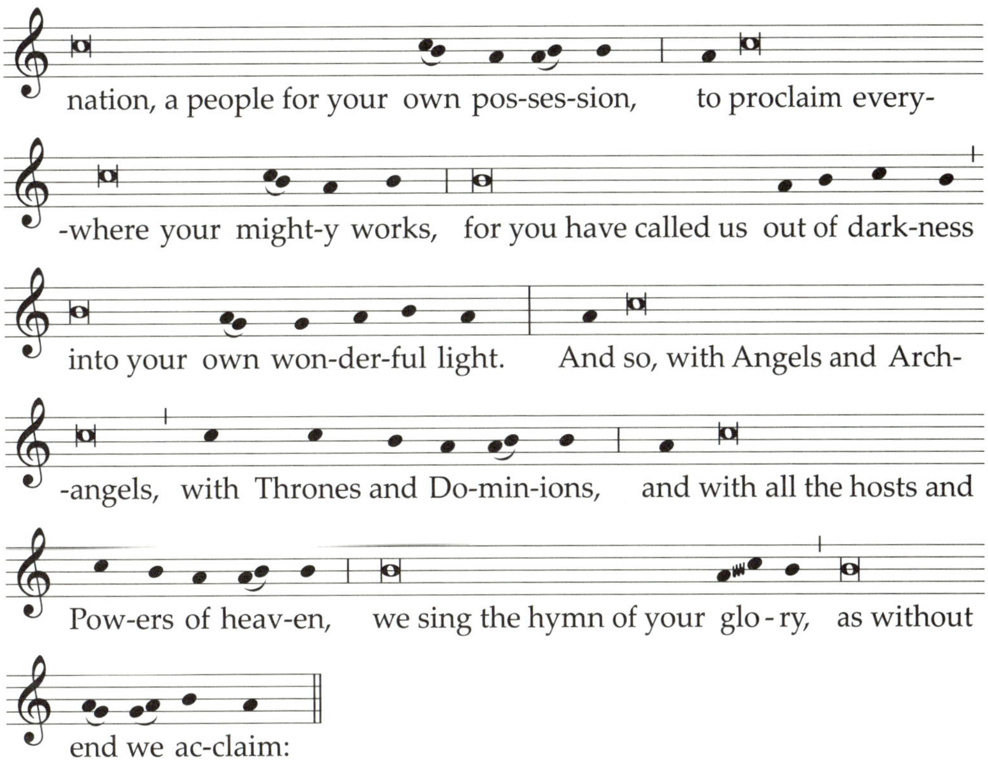

Preface II of the Sundays in Ordinary Time

The mystery of salvation

53.

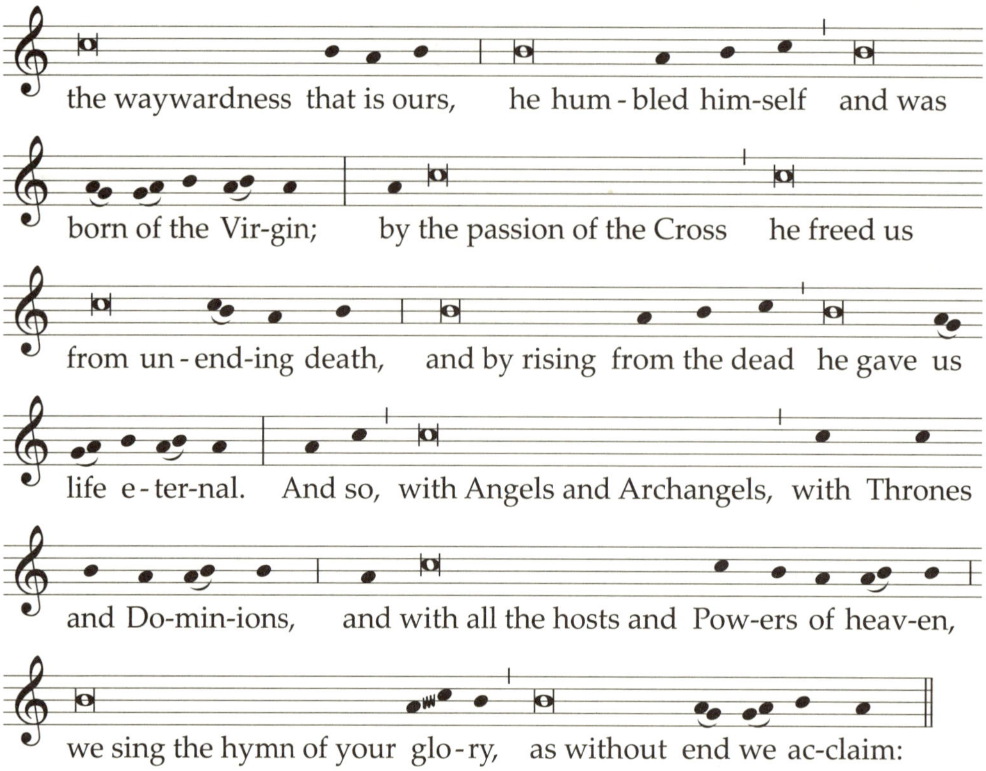

Preface III of the Sundays in Ordinary Time

The salvation of man by a man

54.

Preface IV of the Sundays in Ordinary Time

The history of salvation

55.

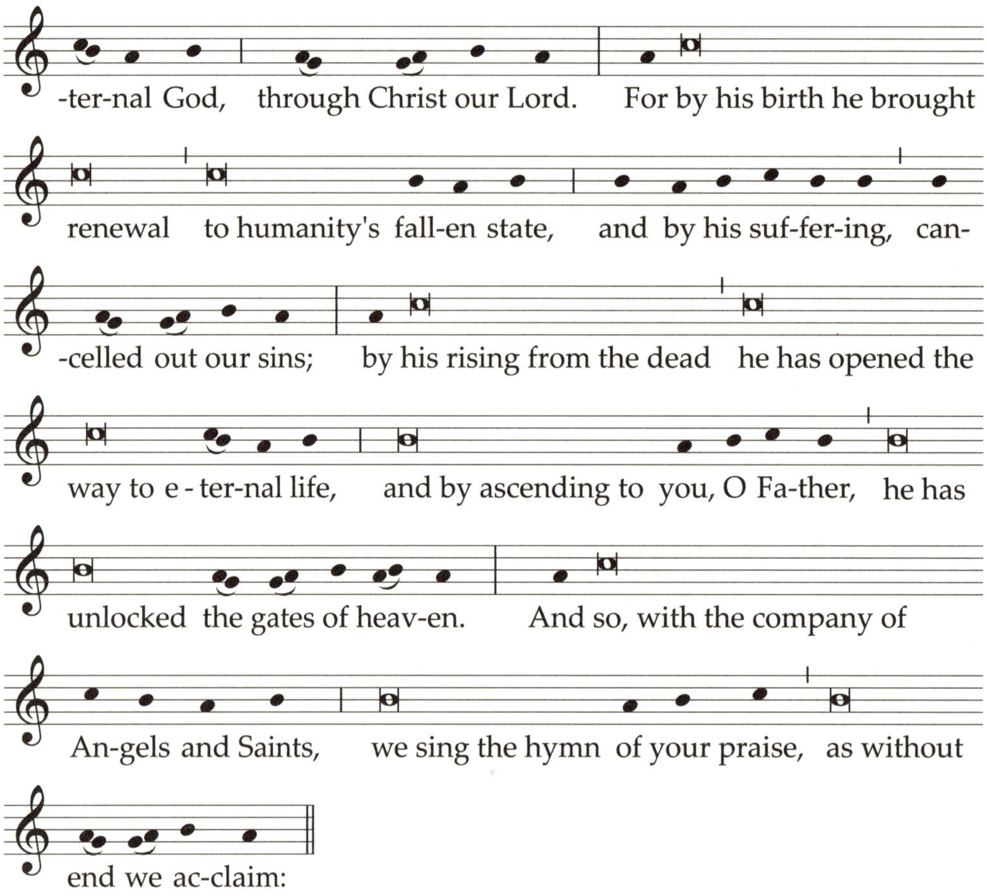

Preface V of the Sundays in Ordinary Time

Creation

56.

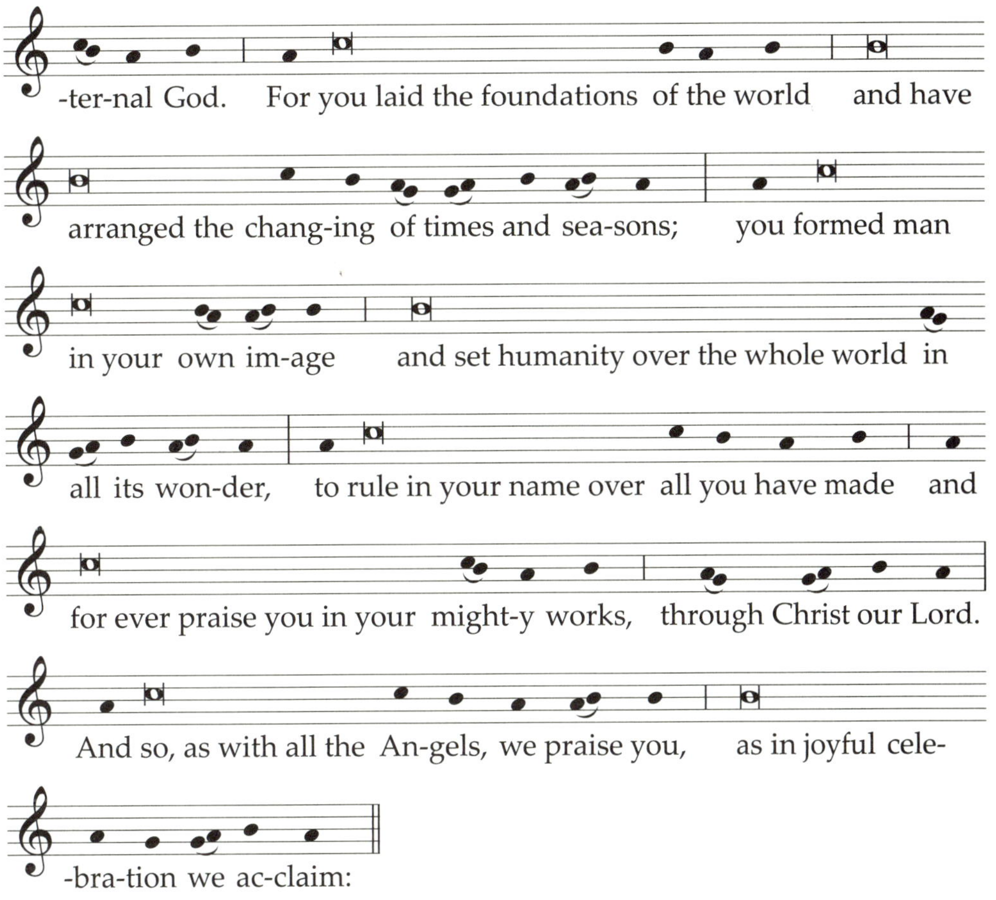

Preface VI of the Sundays in Ordinary Time

The pledge of the eternal Passover

57.

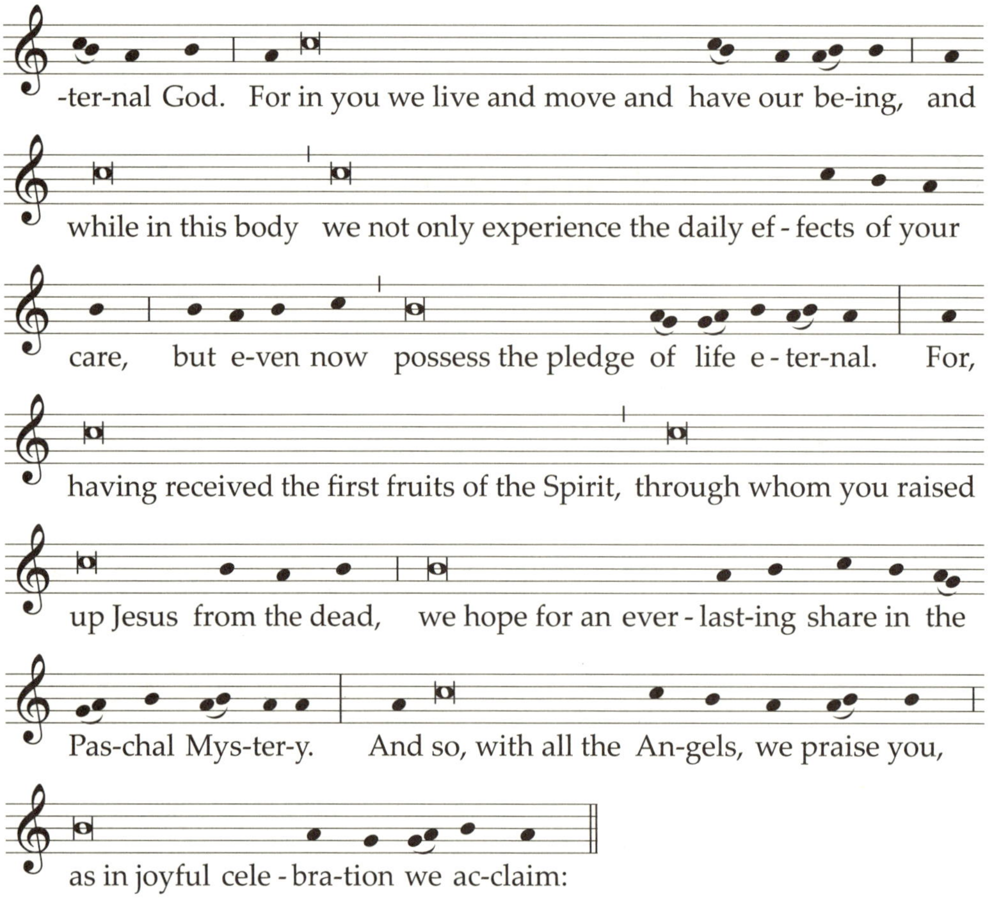

Preface VII of the Sundays in Ordinary Time

Salvation through the obedience of Christ

58.

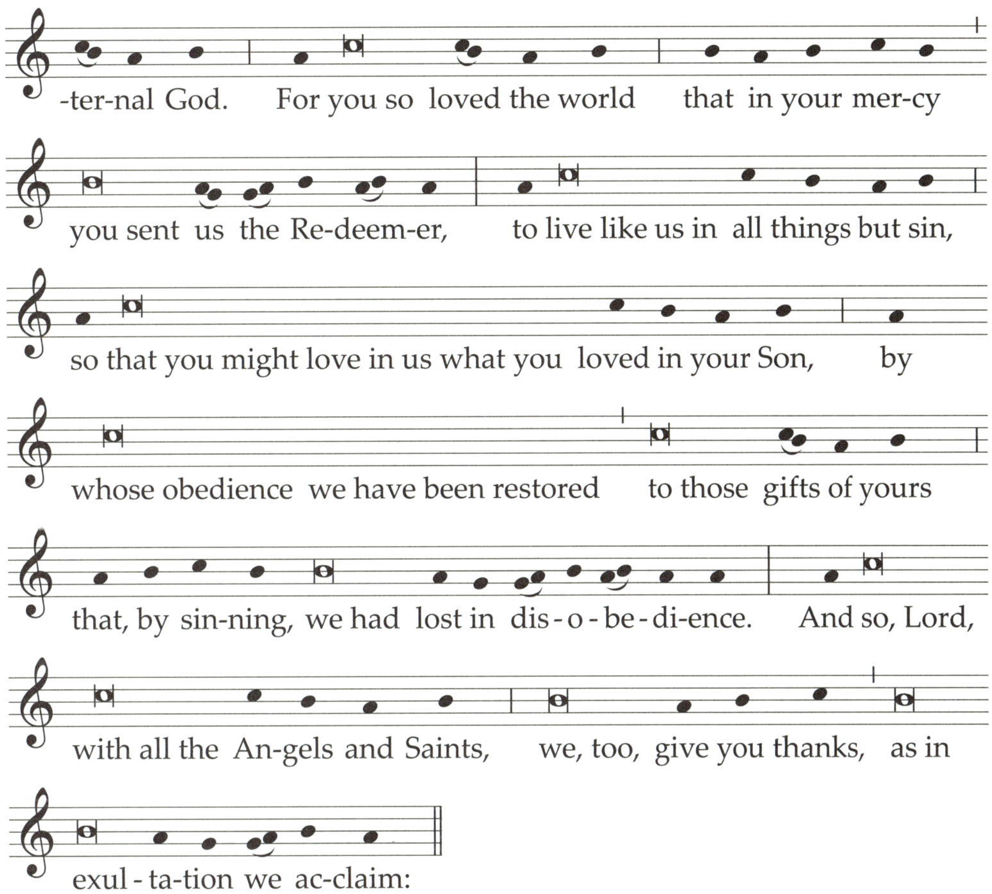

Preface VIII of the Sundays in Ordinary Time

The Church united by the unity of the Trinity

59.

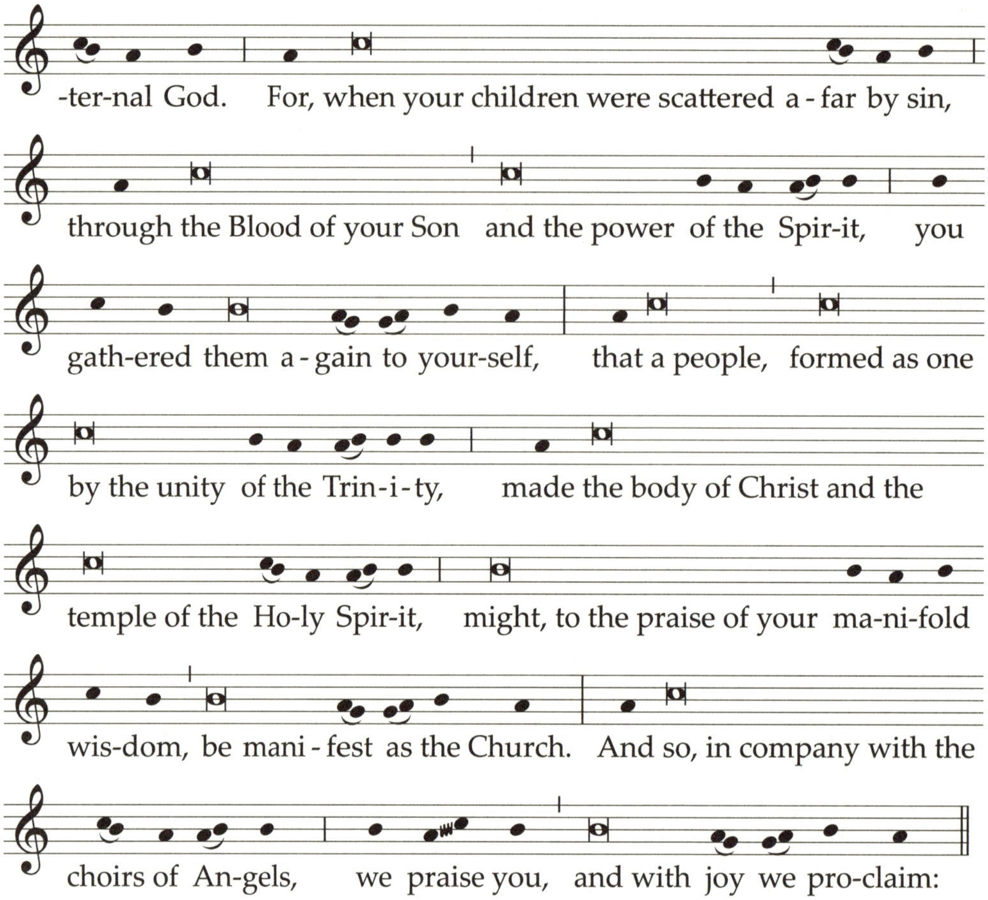

Preface I of the Most Holy Eucharist

60. **(See Thursday of the Lord's Supper, pp. 79–80)**

Preface II of the Most Holy Eucharist

61. **(See The Most Holy Body and Blood of Christ, pp. 113–14)**

Preface I of the Blessed Virgin Mary

The Motherhood of the Blessed Virgin Mary

62.

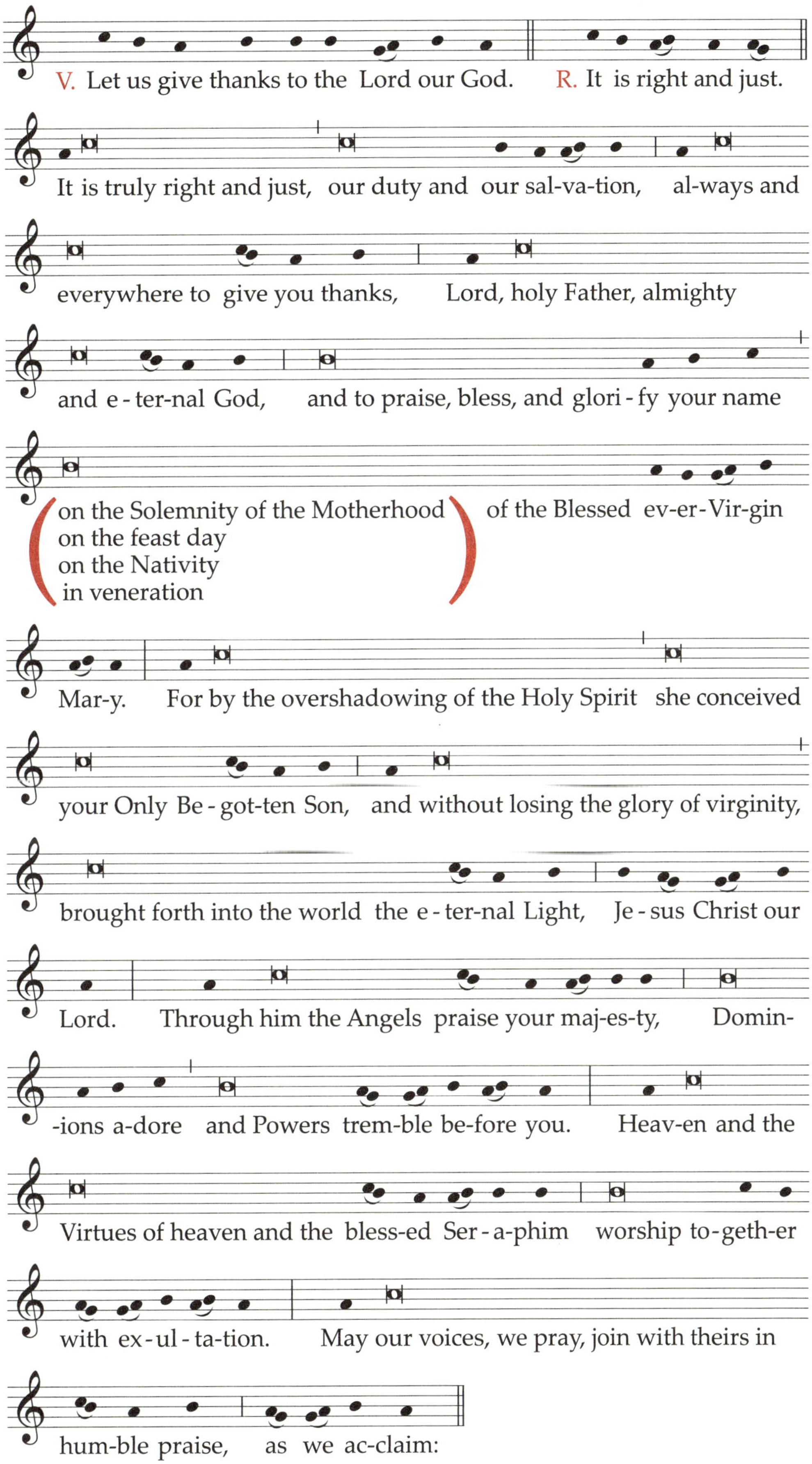
V. Let us give thanks to the Lord our God. R. It is right and just.
It is truly right and just, our duty and our sal-va-tion, al-ways and
everywhere to give you thanks, Lord, holy Father, almighty
and e - ter-nal God, and to praise, bless, and glori - fy your name
on the Solemnity of the Motherhood
on the feast day
on the Nativity
in veneration
of the Blessed ev-er-Vir-gin
Mar-y. For by the overshadowing of the Holy Spirit she conceived
your Only Be - got-ten Son, and without losing the glory of virginity,
brought forth into the world the e - ter-nal Light, Je - sus Christ our
Lord. Through him the Angels praise your maj-es-ty, Domin-
-ions a-dore and Powers trem-ble be-fore you. Heav-en and the
Virtues of heaven and the bless-ed Ser - a-phim worship to-geth-er
with ex - ul - ta-tion. May our voices, we pray, join with theirs in
hum-ble praise, as we ac-claim:

Preface II of the Blessed Virgin Mary

The Church praises God with the words of Mary

63.

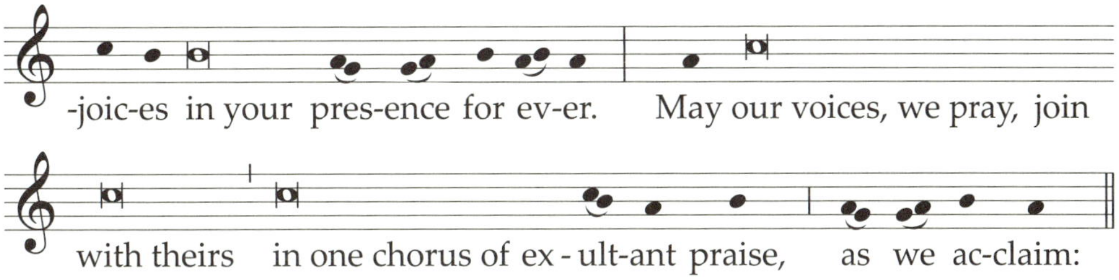

Preface I of Apostles

The Apostles, shepherds of God's people

64.

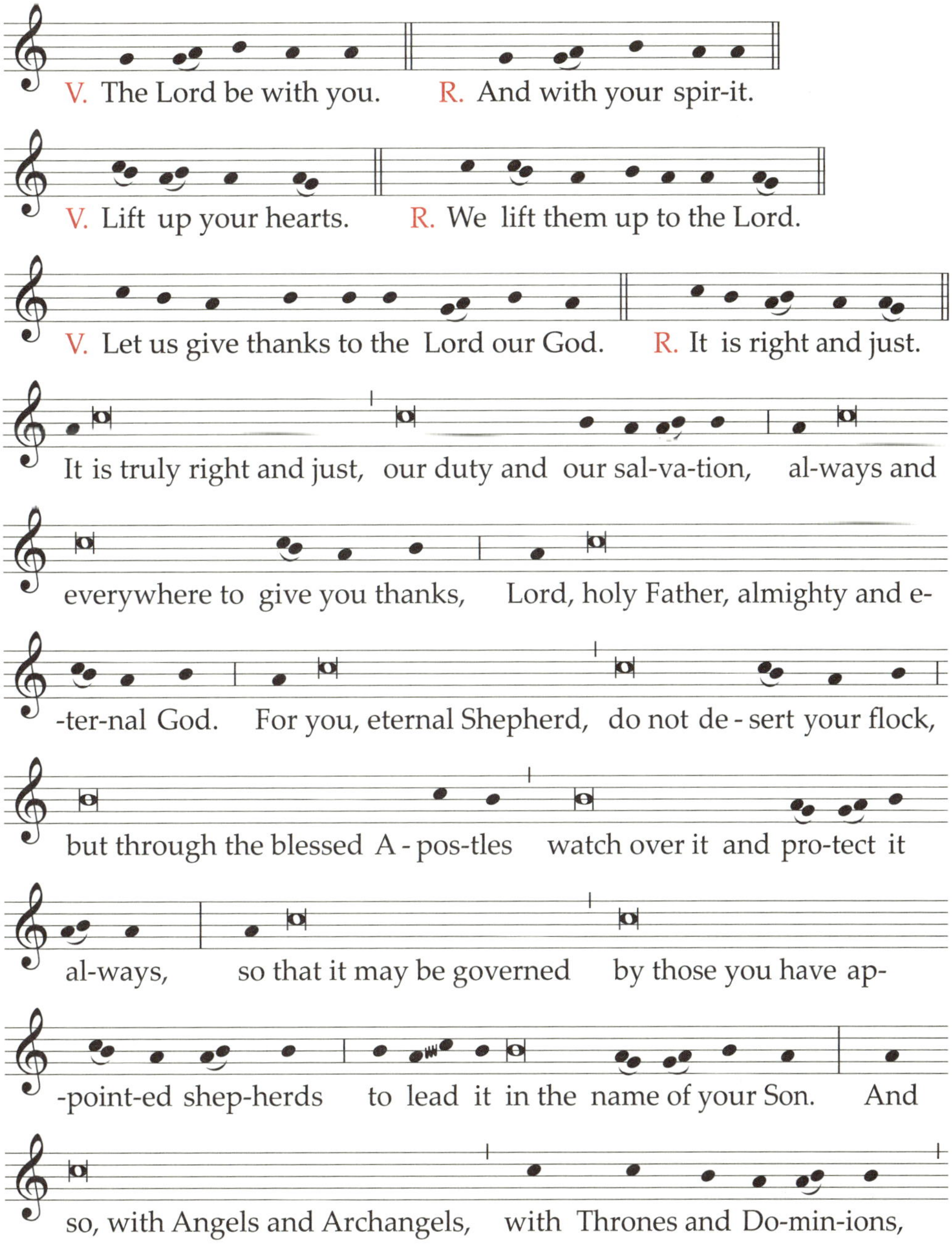

Preface II of Apostles

The apostolic foundation and witness

65.

with all the host of An-gels, we sing to you with all our hearts,

crying out as we ac-claim:

Preface I of Saints

The glory of the Saints

66.

V. The Lord be with you. R. And with your spir-it.

V. Lift up your hearts. R. We lift them up to the Lord.

V. Let us give thanks to the Lord our God. R. It is right and just.

It is truly right and just, our duty and our sal-va-tion, al-ways and

everywhere to give you thanks, Lord, holy Father, almighty and e-

-ter-nal God. For you are praised in the company of your Saints

and, in crown-ing their mer-its, you crown your own gifts. By

their way of life you offer us an ex-am-ple, by communion

with them you gave us com-pan-ion-ship, by their inter-ces-sion,

sure sup-port, so that, encouraged by so great a cloud of

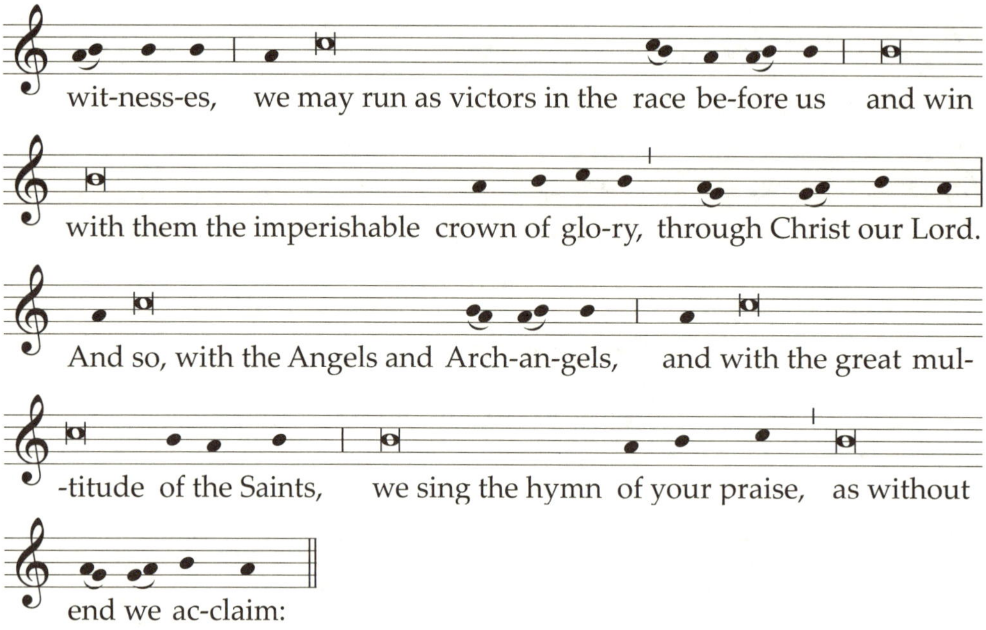

Preface II of Saints

The action of the Saints

67.

ev-er new and offer us sure signs of your love. And that your
saving mysteries may be ful-filled, their great example lends us
cour-age, their fer-vent prayers sus-tain us in all we do. And
so, Lord, with all the An-gels and Saints, we, too, give you thanks,
as in exul - ta-tion we ac-claim:

Preface I of Holy Martyrs

The sign and example of martyrdom

68.

V. The Lord be with you. R. And with your spir-it.

V. Lift up your hearts. R. We lift them up to the Lord.

V. Let us give thanks to the Lord our God. R. It is right and just.

It is truly right and just, our duty and our sal-va-tion, al-ways and
everywhere to give you thanks, Lord, holy Father, almighty and e-
-ter-nal God. For the blood of your blessed Martyr N., poured out
like Christ's to glo-ri-fy your name, shows forth your mar-vel-ous

Preface II of Holy Martyrs

The wonders of God in the victory of the Martyrs

69.

Preface of Holy Pastors

The presence of holy Pastors in the Church

70.

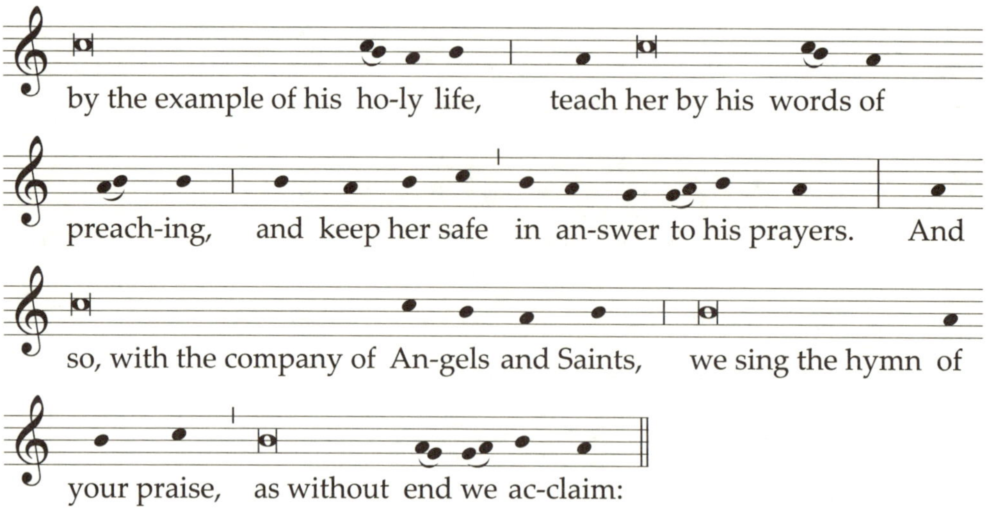

Preface of Holy Virgins and Religious

The sign of a life consecrated to God

71.

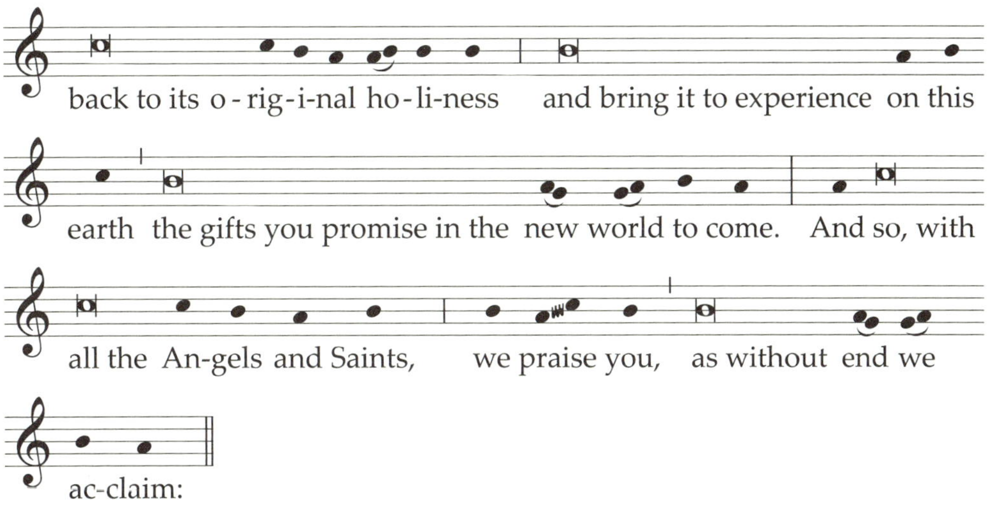

Common Preface I

The renewal of all things in Christ

72.

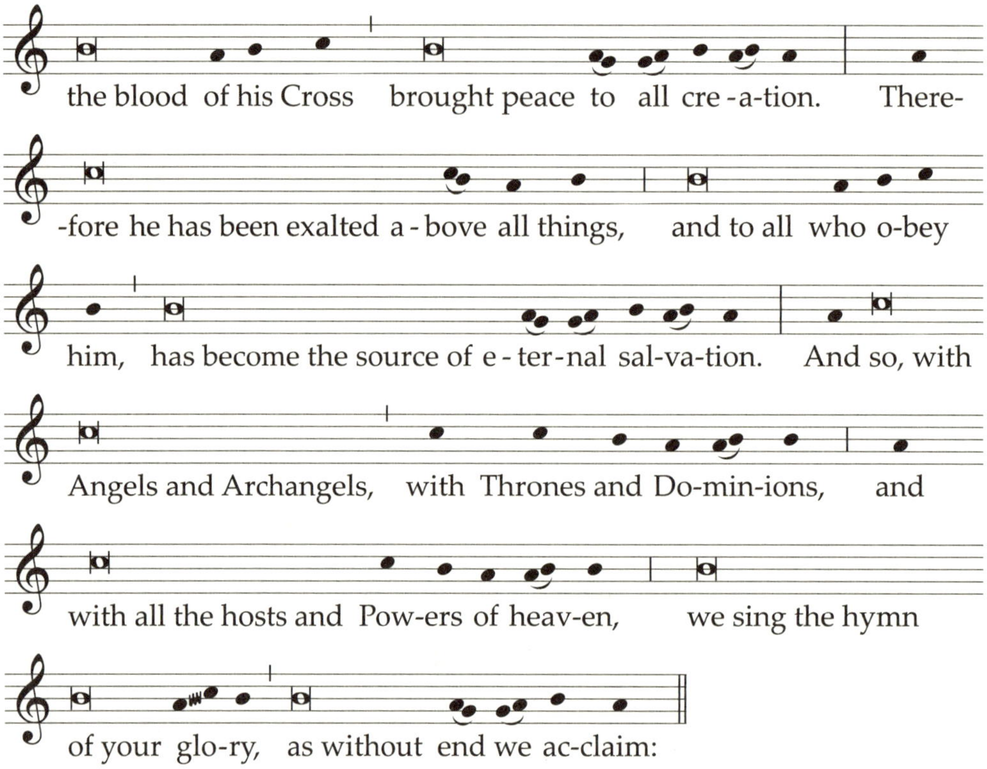

Common Preface II

Salvation through Christ

73.

Common Preface III

Praise to God for the creation and restoration of the human race

74.

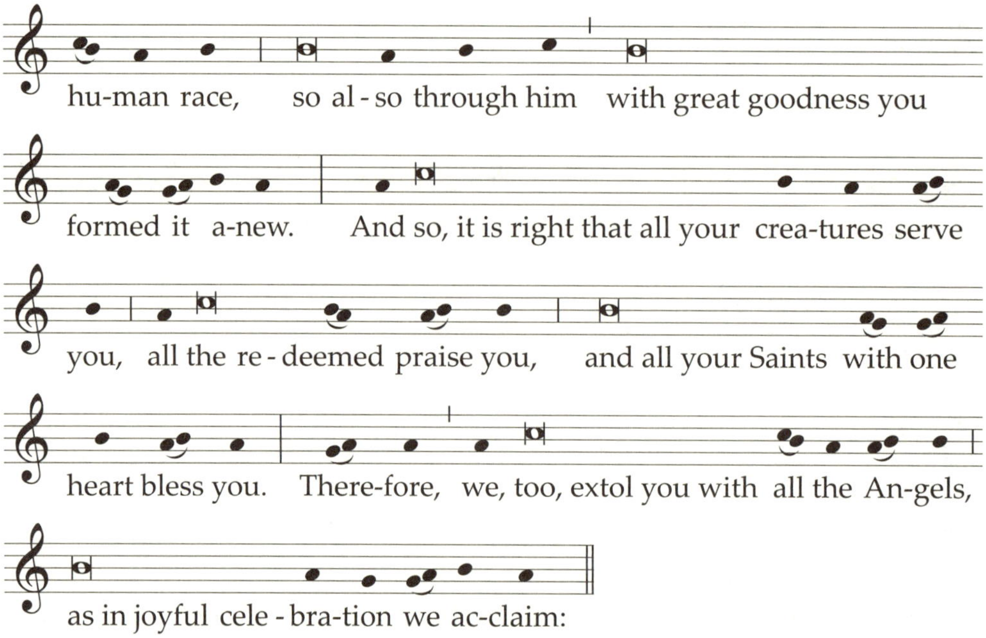

Common Preface IV

Praise, the gift of God

75.

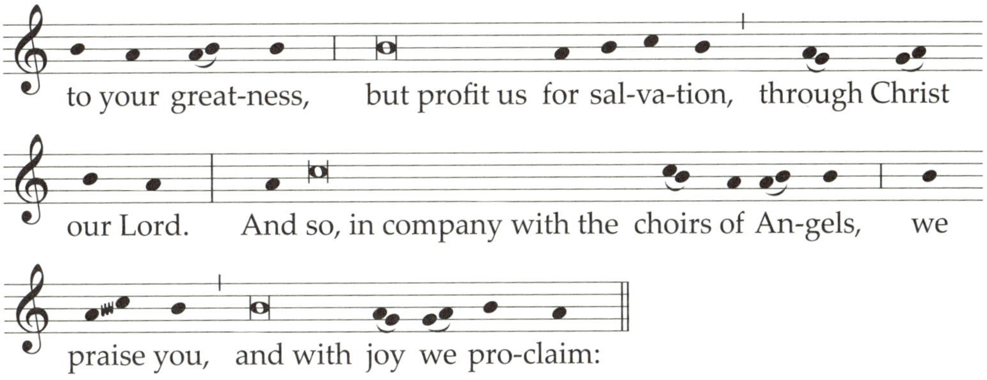

Common Preface V

The proclamation of the mystery of Christ

76.

Common Preface VI

The mystery of salvation in Christ

77.

and manifest the res-ur-rec-tion. And so, with the Angels and all
the Saints, we declare your glo-ry, as with one voice we ac-claim:

Preface I for the Dead

The hope of resurrection in Christ

78.

V. The Lord be with you. R. And with your spir-it.

V. Lift up your hearts. R. We lift them up to the Lord.

V. Let us give thanks to the Lord our God. R. It is right and just.

It is truly right and just, our duty and our sal-va-tion, al-ways and
everywhere to give you thanks, Lord, holy Father, almighty and e-
-ter-nal God, through Christ our Lord. In him the hope of blessed
resur-rec-tion has dawned, that those saddened by the certain-ty
of dy-ing might be consoled by the prom-ise of immor-tal-i-ty
to come. In-deed for your faithful, Lord, life is changed not end-ed,
and, when this earthly dwelling turns to dust, an e-ter-nal

Preface II for the Dead

Christ died so that we might live

79.

Preface III for the Dead

Christ, the salvation and the life

80.

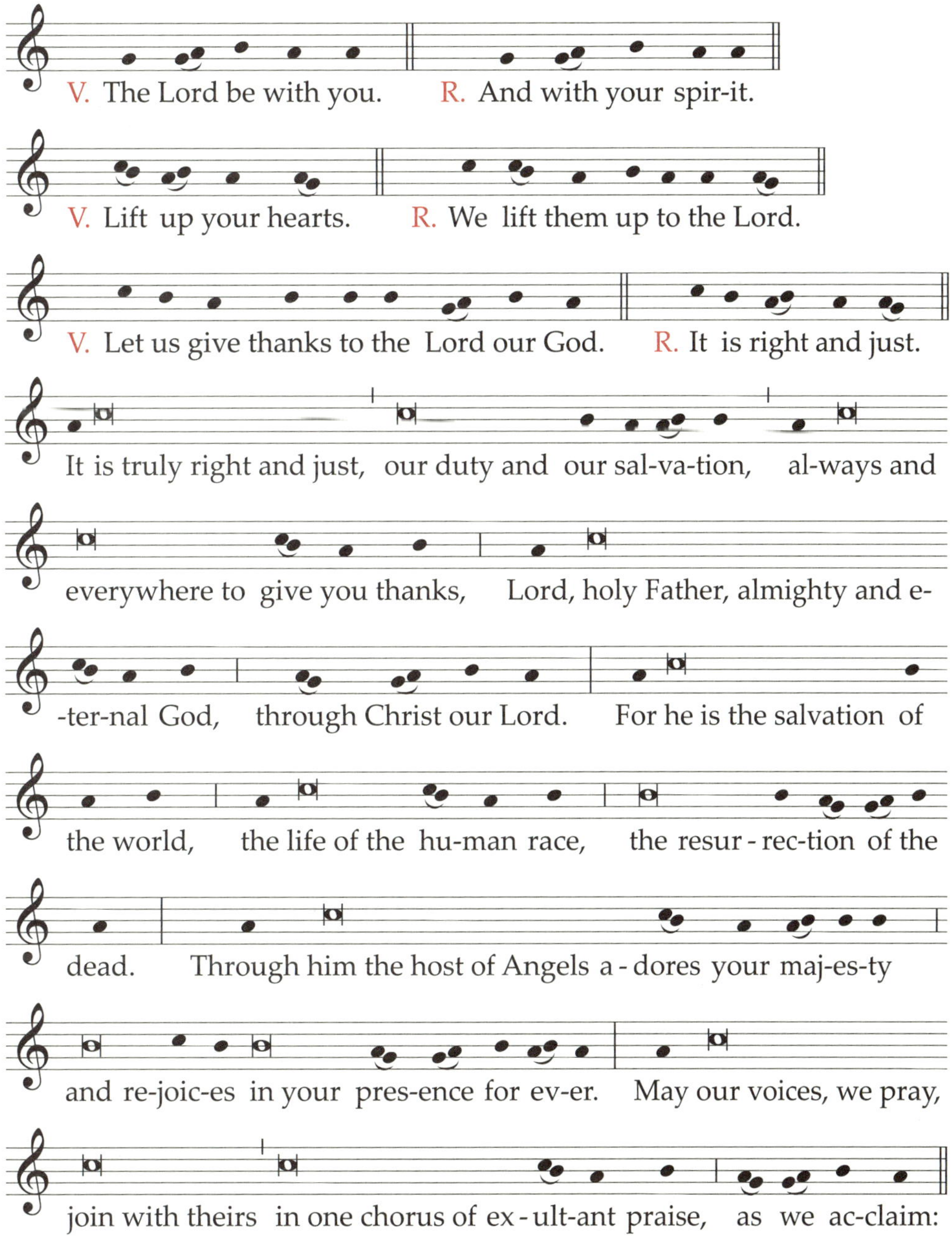

Preface IV for the Dead

From earthly life to heavenly glory

81.

Preface V for the Dead

Our resurrection through the victory of Christ

82.

CHANTS FOR THE EUCHARISTIC PRAYER

Eucharistic Prayer I (or the Roman Canon)

The Priest, with hands extended, sings:

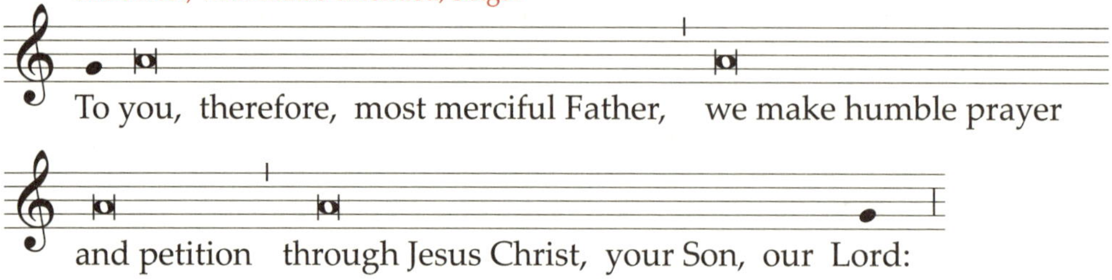

He joins his hands and makes the Sign of the Cross once over the bread and chalice together, singing:

With hands extended, the Priest continues:

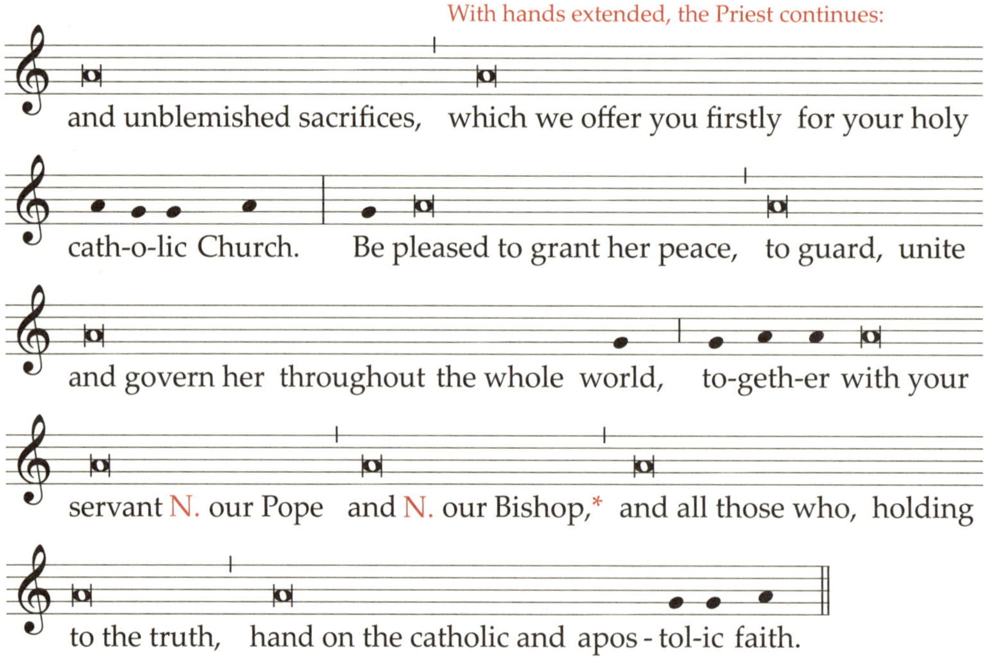

(One of the concelebrants)

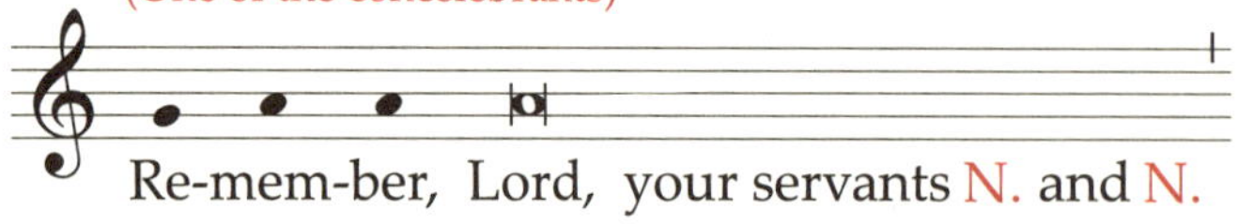

* Mention may be made here of the Coadjutor Bishop, or Auxiliary Bishops, as noted in the *General Instruction of the Roman Missal,* no. 149.

The Priest joins his hands and prays briefly for those for whom he intends to pray.
Then, with hands extended, he continues:

and all gathered here, whose faith and de-vo-tion are known to you.

For them, we offer you this sacrifice of praise or they offer it for

themselves and all who are dear to them: for the redemption of

their souls, in hope of health and well-being, and paying their hom-

-age to you, the eternal God, liv-ing and true.

(Another of the concelebrants) *proper formulas, pp. 190–95*

In communion with those whose memory we venerate, especially

the glorious ever-Virgin Mary, Mother of our God and Lord, Jesus

Christ, † and blessed Joseph, her Spouse, your blessed Apostles

and Martyrs, Peter and Paul, Andrew, (James, John, Thomas,

James, Philip, Bartholomew, Matthew, Simon and Jude; Li-nus,

Cletus, Clement, Sixtus, Cornelius, Cyprian, Lawrence, Chryso-

-gonus, John and Paul, Cosmas and Damian) and all your Saints;

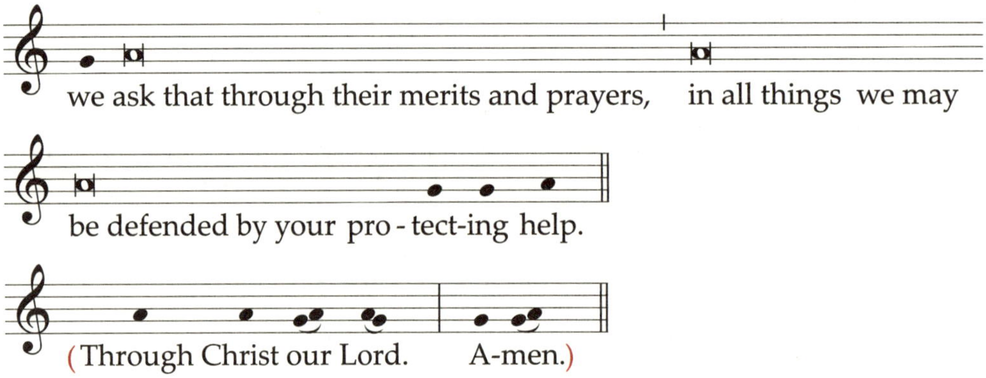

With hands extended, the principal celebrant continues: *proper formulas, pp. 191–94*

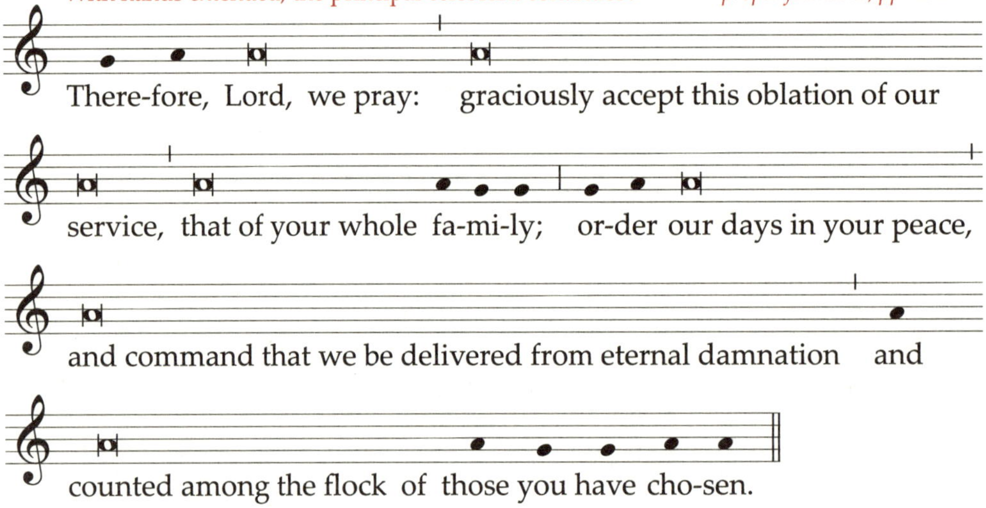

(He joins his hands.)

Holding his hands extended over the offerings, he sings (together with the concelebrants):

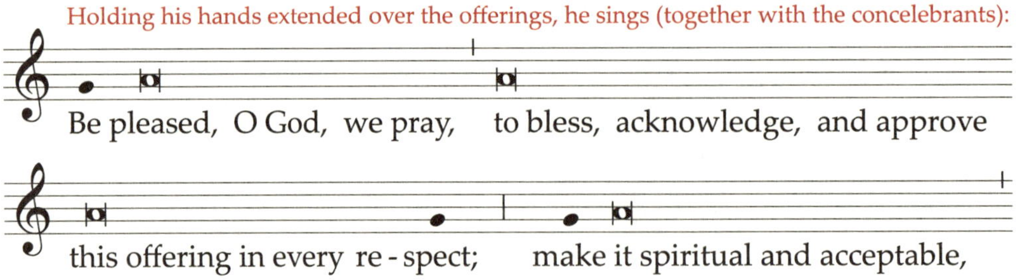

so that it may become for us the Body and Blood of your most be-

-loved Son, our Lord Je-sus Christ.

He joins his hands.

On the day before he was to suf-fer,

The Priest takes the bread, and, holding it slightly raised above the altar, continues:

he took bread in his holy and venerable hands,

He raises his eyes.

and with eyes raised to heaven to you, O God, his almighty Fa-ther,

giv-ing you thanks, he said the blessing, broke the bread and gave it

to his disciples, say-ing:

He bows slightly.

TAKE THIS, ALL OF YOU, AND EAT OF IT, FOR THIS IS MY BOD-Y,

WHICH WILL BE GIV-EN UP FOR YOU.

He shows the consecrated host to the people, places it again on the paten, and genuflects in adoration.

After this, he continues:

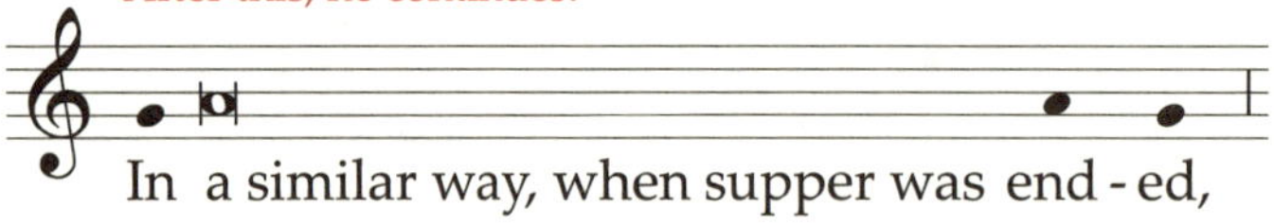

He takes the chalice and, holding it slightly raised above the altar, continues:

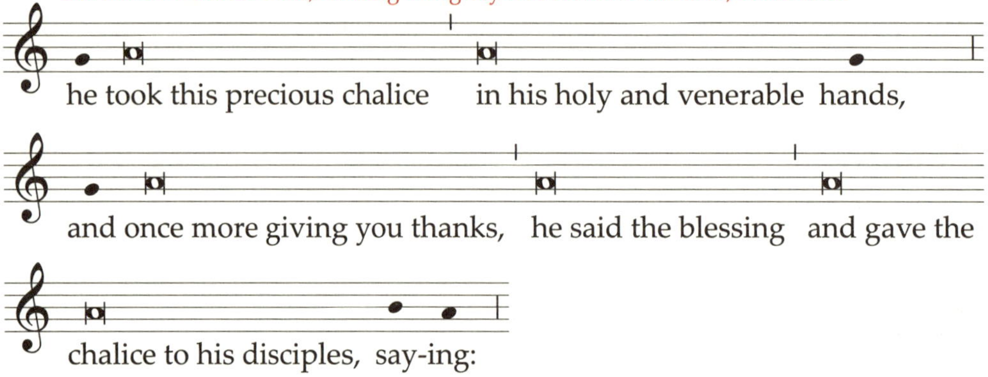

He bows slightly.

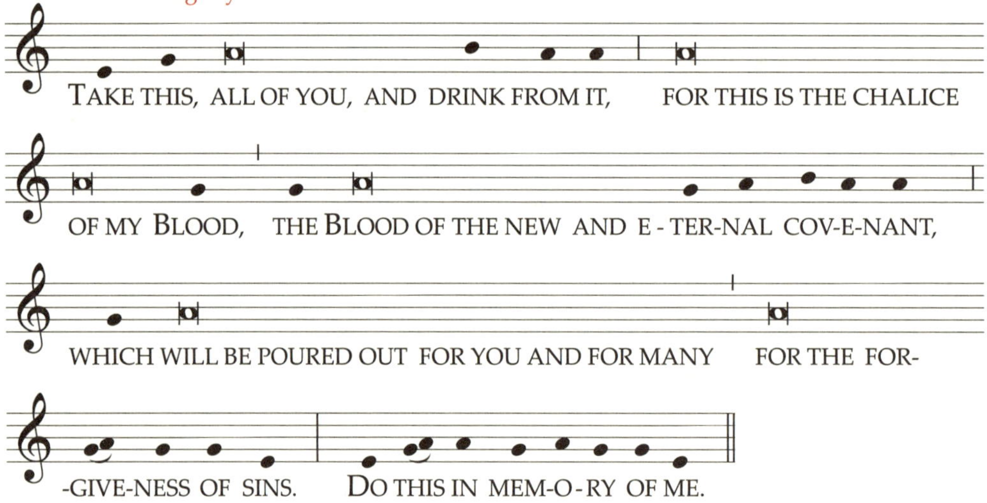

The Priest shows the chalice to the people, places it on the corporal, and genuflects in adoration.

Then he sings:

And the people continue, acclaiming:

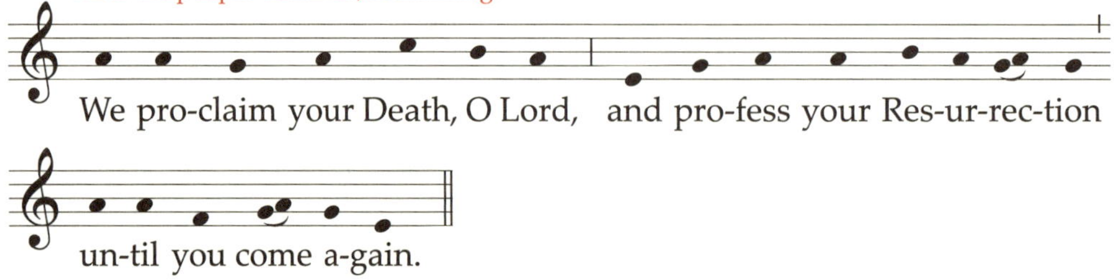

Or:

Or:

Then he, with hands extended, sings (together with the concelebrants):

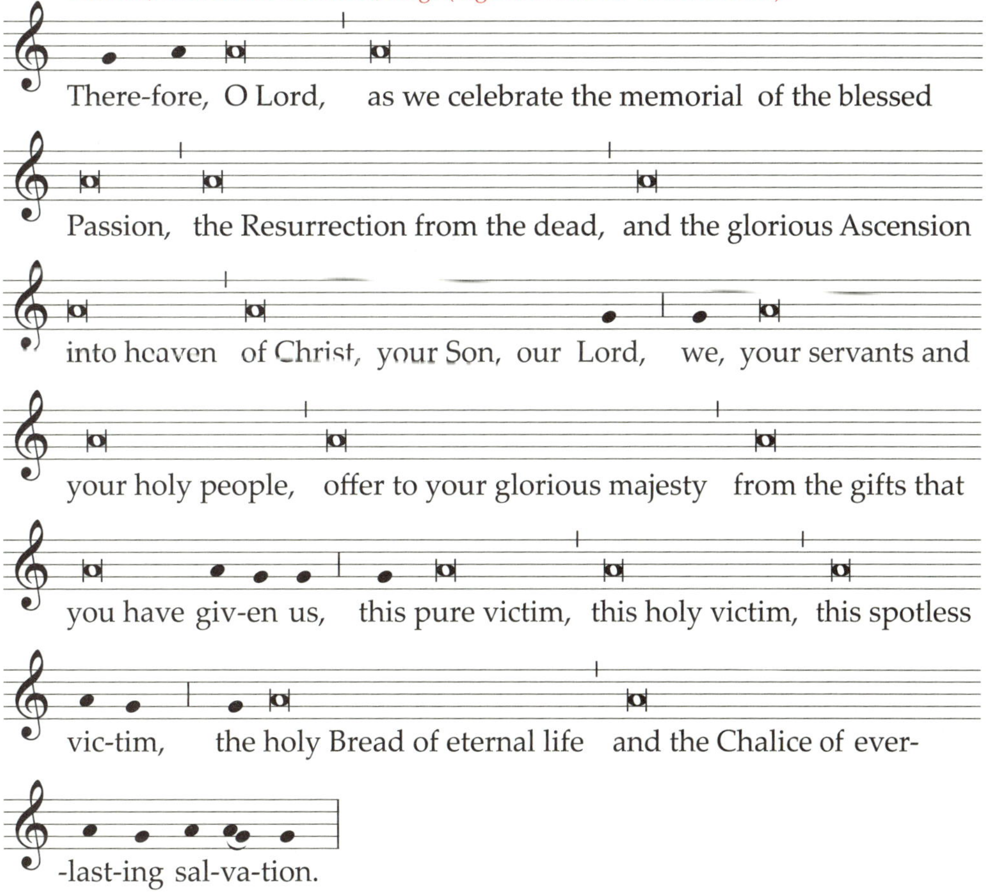

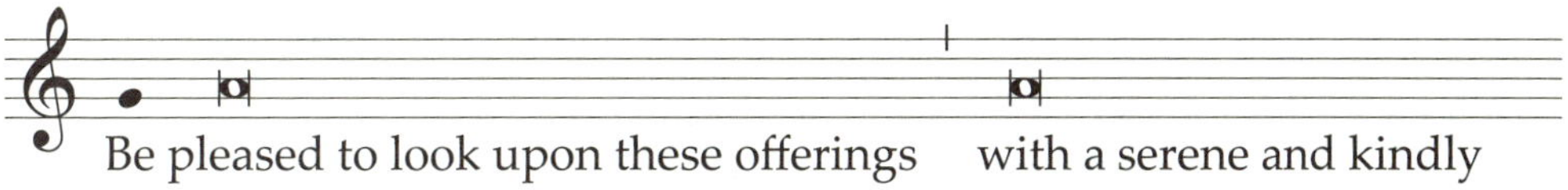

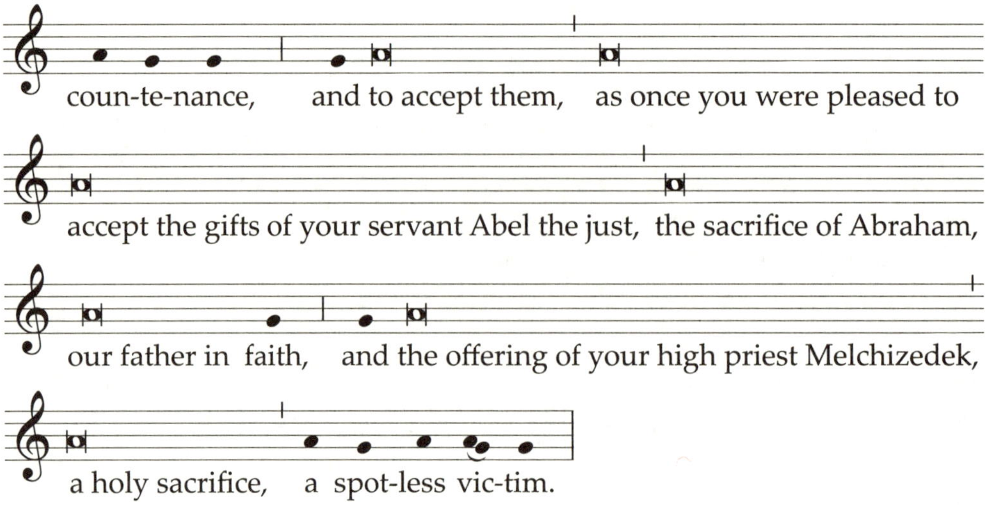

Bowing, with hands joined, he continues:

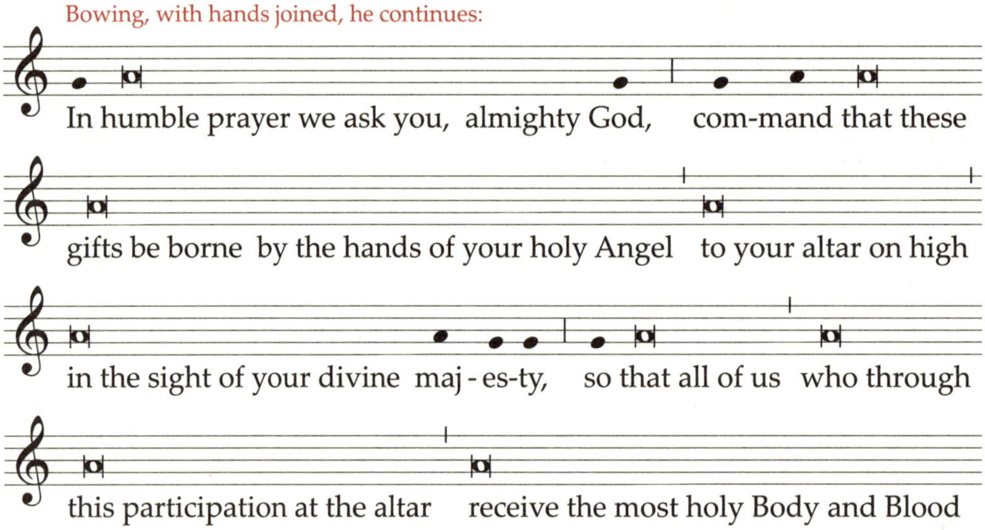

He stands upright again and signs himself with the Sign of the Cross, singing:

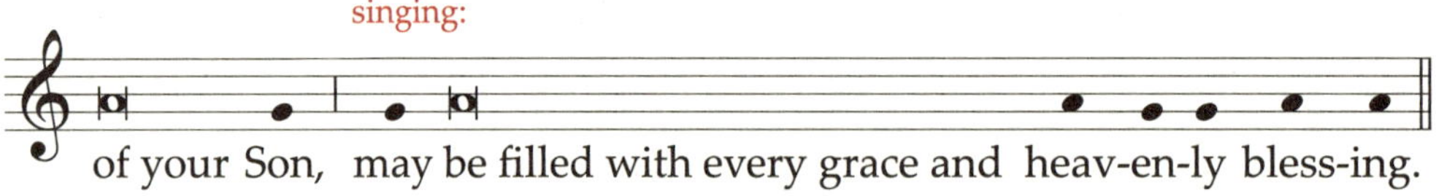

(He joins his hands.)

With hands extended, the Priest sings (one of the concelebrants):

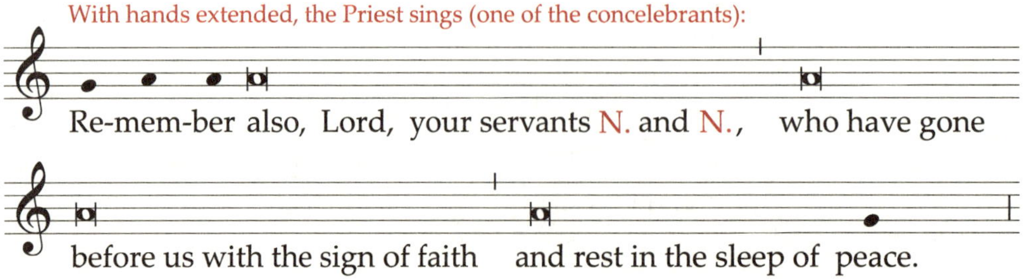

He joins his hands and prays briefly for those who have died and for whom he intends to pray.
Then, with hands extended, he continues:

Grant them, O Lord, we pray, and all who sleep in Christ, a place of refreshment, light and peace. *(He joins his hands.)* (Through Christ our Lord. A-men.)

(Another of the concelebrants)
He strikes his breast with his right hand, singing:

To us, also, your servants, who, though sinners,

And, with hands extended, he continues:

hope in your abun-dant mercies, graciously grant some share and fellowship with your holy Apostles and Mar-tyrs: with John the Baptist, Stephen, Mat-thias, Barnabas, (Ignatius, Alexander, Marcellinus, Peter, Felicity, Perpetua, Agatha, Lucy, Agnes, Cecilia, Anastasia) and all your Saints; ad-mit us, we beseech you, into their company, not weigh-ing our merits, but granting us your par-don,

He joins his hands.

through Christ our Lord.

And the principal celebrant continues, with hands joined:

Through whom you continue to make all these good things, O Lord;

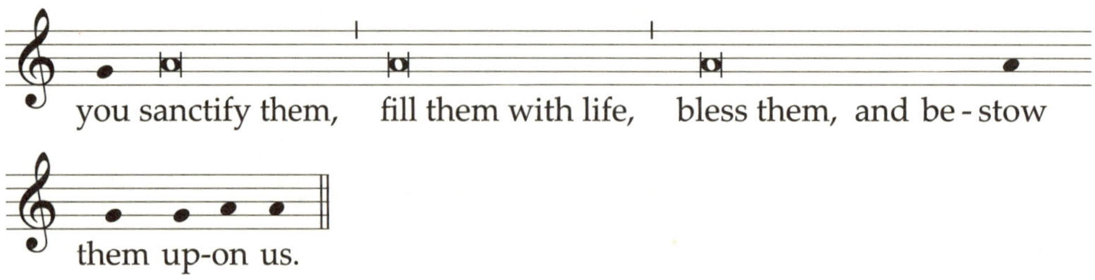

He takes the chalice and the paten with the host and raising both, he sings (together with the concelebrants):

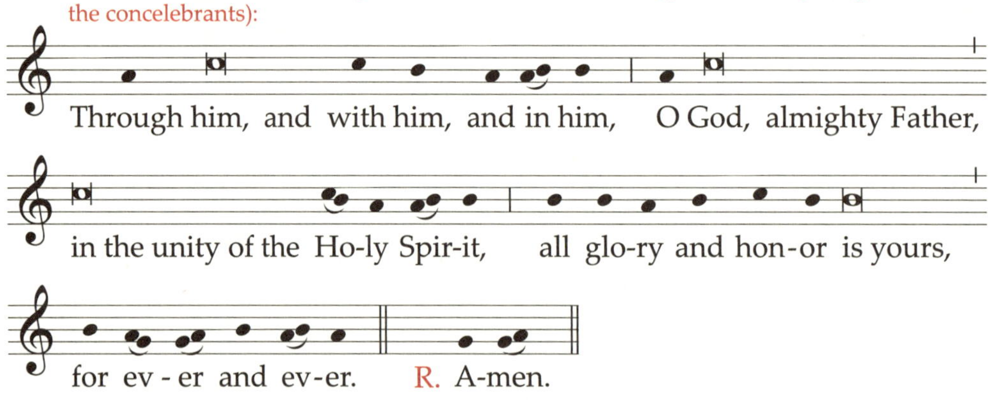

Then follows the Communion Rite, p. 223.

Proper forms of the *Communicantes and Hanc Igitur*

On the Nativity of the Lord and throughout the Octave

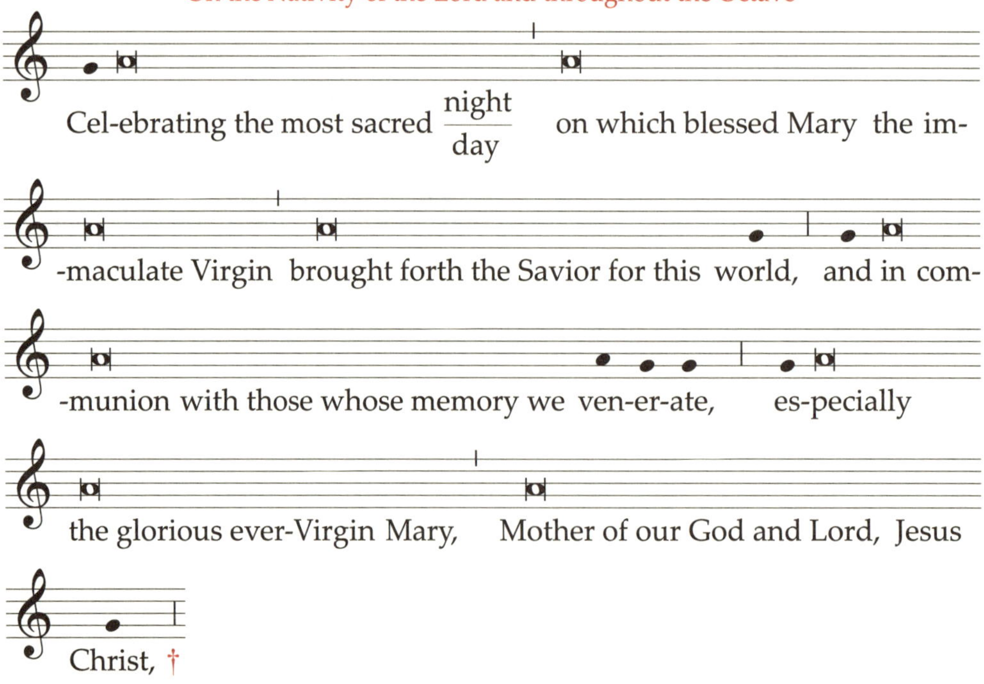

On the Epiphany of the Lord

Cel-ebrating the most sacred day on which your Only Begotten Son,
eternal with you in your glory, appeared in a human body, truly
sharing our flesh, and in communion with those whose memory we
ven-er-ate, es-pecially the glorious ever-Virgin Mary, Mother of
our God and Lord, Jesus Christ, †

Thursday of the Lord's Supper

Cel-ebrating the most sacred day on which our Lord Jesus Christ
was handed over for our sake, and in communion with those whose
memory we ven-er-ate, es-pecially the glorious ever-Virgin Mary,
Mother of our God and Lord, Jesus Christ, †

With hands extended, the Priest continues:

There-fore, Lord, we pray: graciously accept this oblation of our
service, that of your whole fa-mi-ly, which we make to you as we

observe the day on which our Lord Jesus Christ handed on the mysteries of his Body and Blood for his disciples to cel-e-brate; or-der our days in your peace, and command that we be delivered from eternal damnation and counted among the flock of those you have cho-sen.

(He joins his hands.)

(Through Christ our Lord. A-men.)

Holding his hands extended over the offerings, he sings (together with the concelebrants):

Be pleased, O God, we pray, to bless, acknowledge, and approve this offering in every re-spect; make it spiritual and acceptable, so that it may become for us the Body and Blood of your most beloved Son, our Lord Je-sus Christ.

He joins his hands.

On the day before he was to suffer for our salvation and the salvation of all, that is, to-day,

He takes the bread and, holding it slightly raised above the altar, continues:

he took bread in his holy and venerable hands,

He raises his eyes.

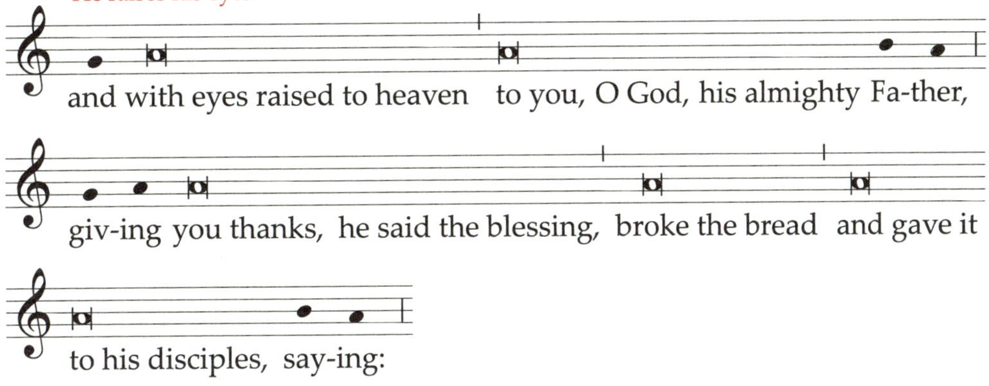

He bows slightly.

He shows the consecrated host to the people, places it again on the paten, and genuflects in adoration.

From the Mass of the Easter Vigil until the Second Sunday of Easter

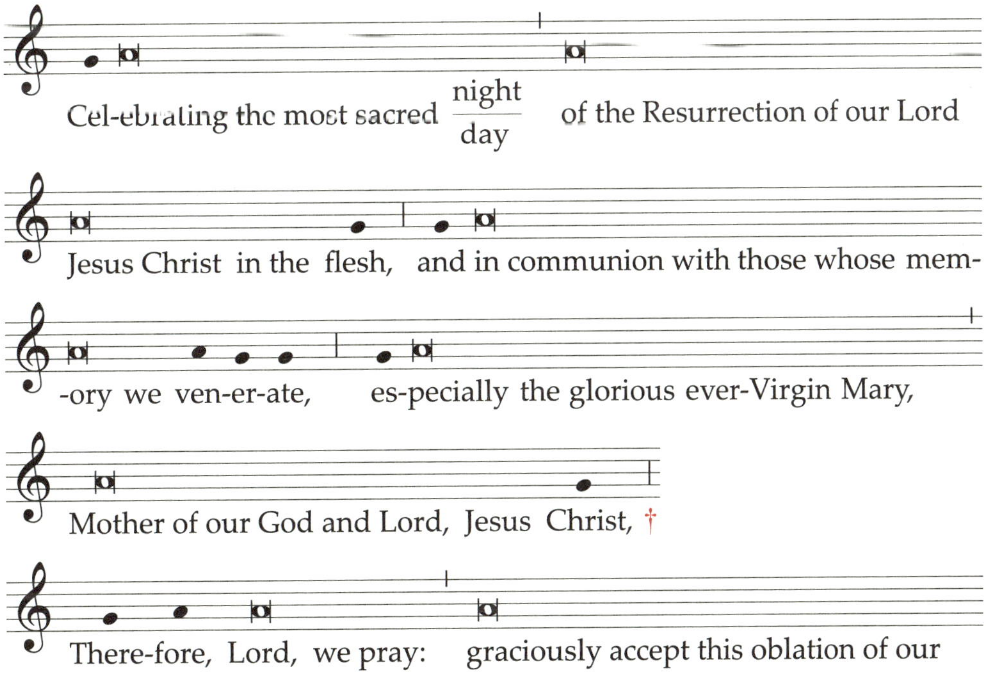

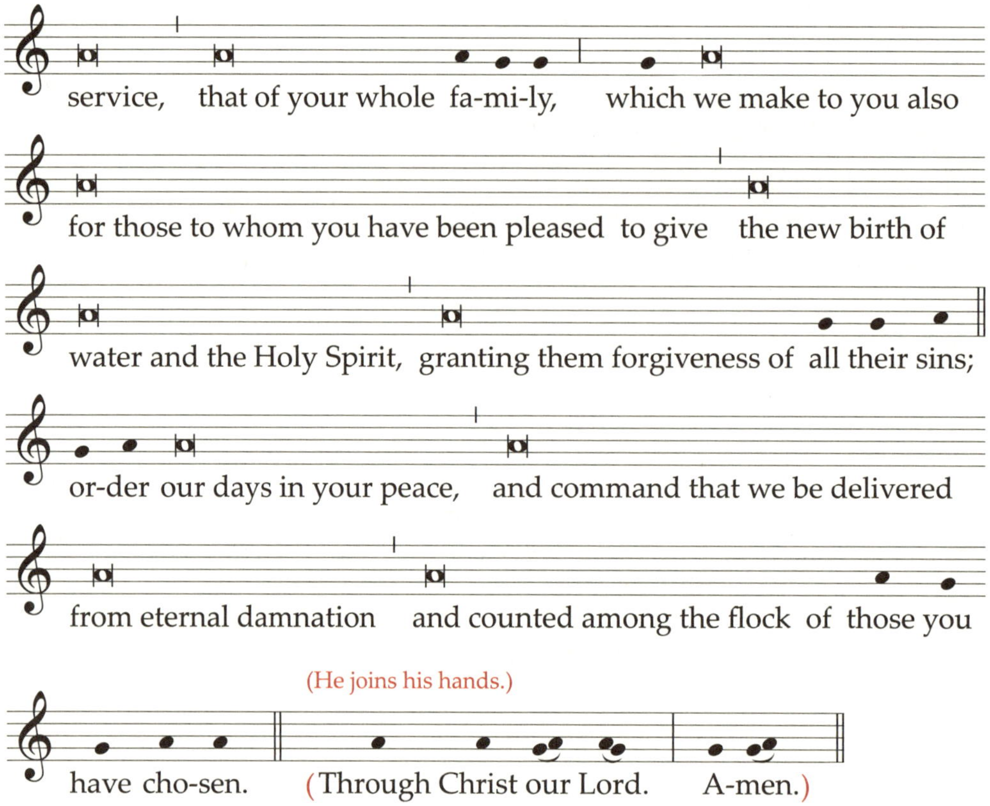

On the Ascension of the Lord

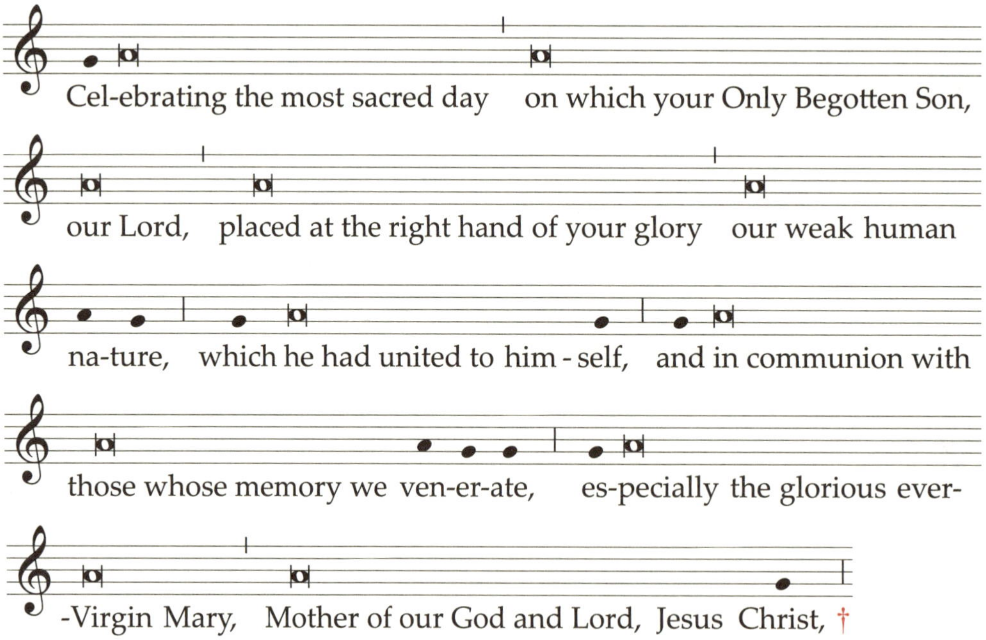

On Pentecost Sunday

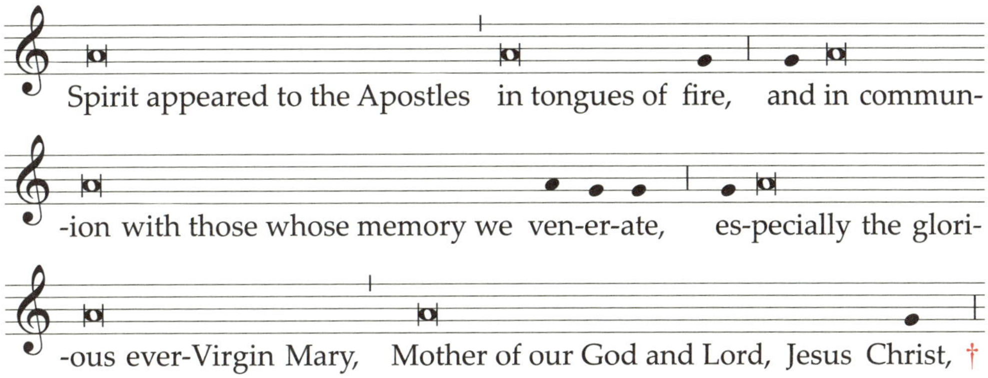

Eucharistic Prayer I (or The Roman Canon)

Solemn Tone

The Priest, with hands extended, sings:

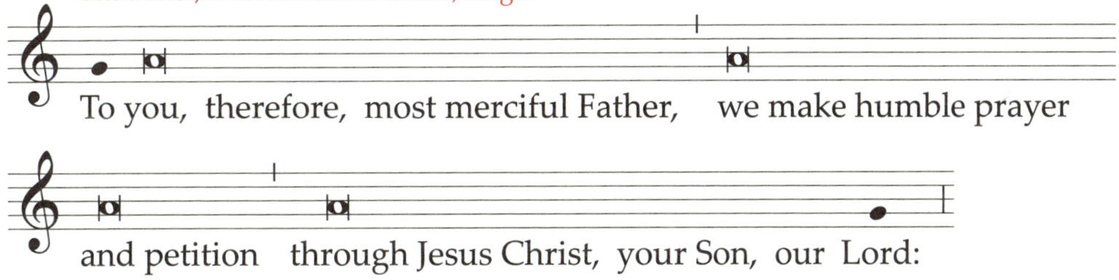

He joins his hands and makes the Sign of the Cross once over the bread and chalice together, singing:

With hands extended, he continues:

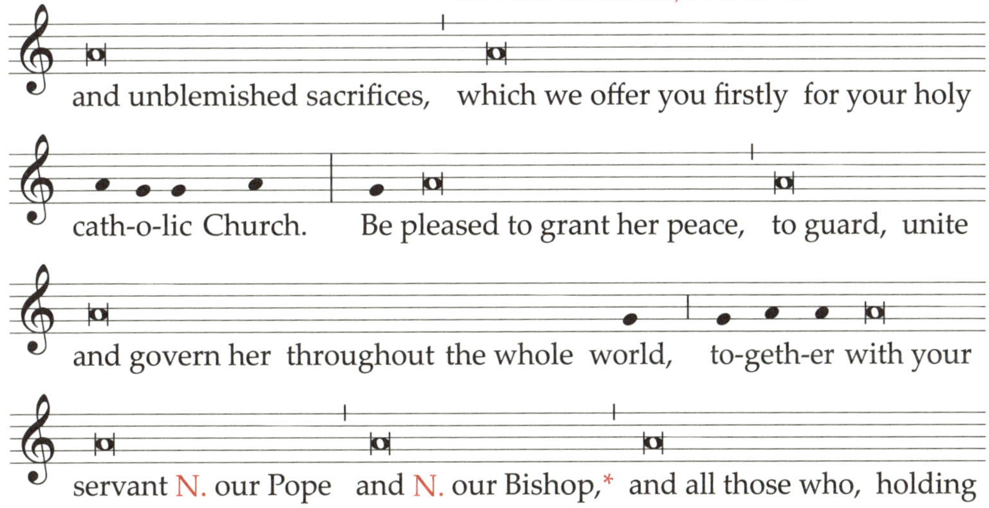

* Mention may be made here of the Coadjutor Bishop, or Auxiliary Bishops, as noted in the *General Instruction of the Roman Missal*, no. 149.

to the truth, hand on the catholic and apos - tol-ic faith.

(One of the concelebrants)

Re-mem-ber, Lord, your servants N. and N.

The Priest joins his hands and prays briefly for those for whom he intends to pray. Then, with hands extended, he continues:

and all gathered here, whose faith and de - vo-tion are known to you.

For them, we offer you this sacrifice of praise or they offer it for

themselves and all who are dear to them: for the redemption of

their souls, in hope of health and well-being, and paying their hom-

-age to you, the eternal God, liv-ing and true.

(Another of the concelebrants) *proper formulas, pp. 190–95*

In communion with those whose memory we venerate, especially

the glorious ever-Virgin Mary, Mother of our God and Lord, Jesus

Christ, † and blessed Joseph, her Spouse, your blessed Apostles

and Martyrs, Peter and Paul, Andrew, (James, John, Thomas,

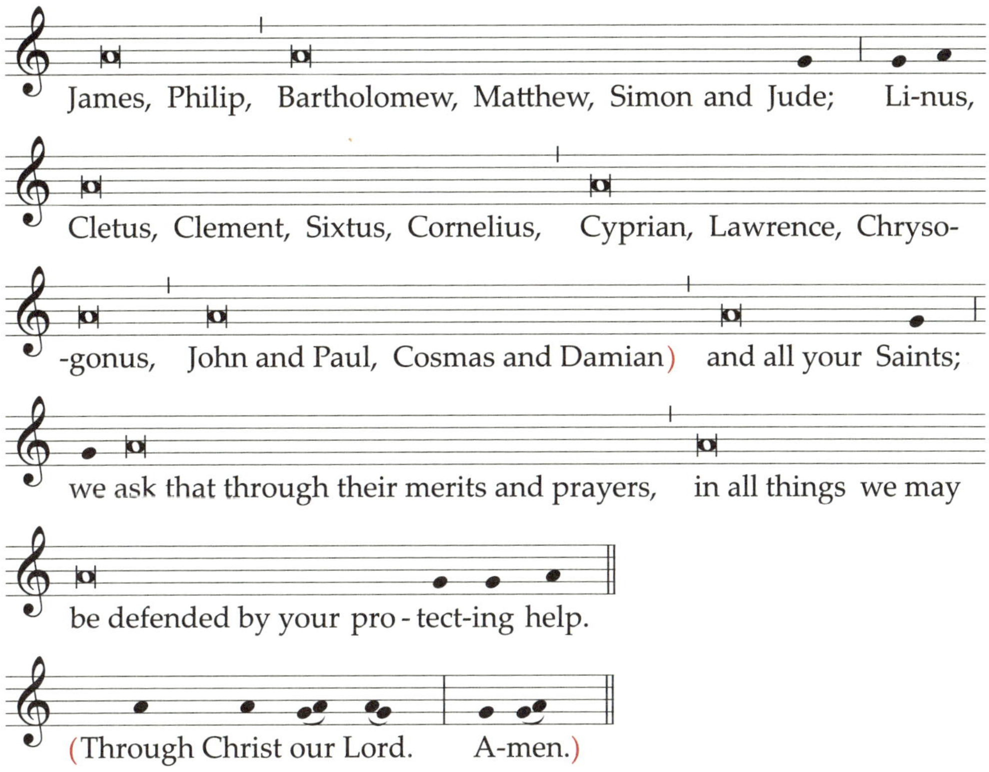

With hands extended, the principal celebrant continues: *proper formulas, pp. 191–94*

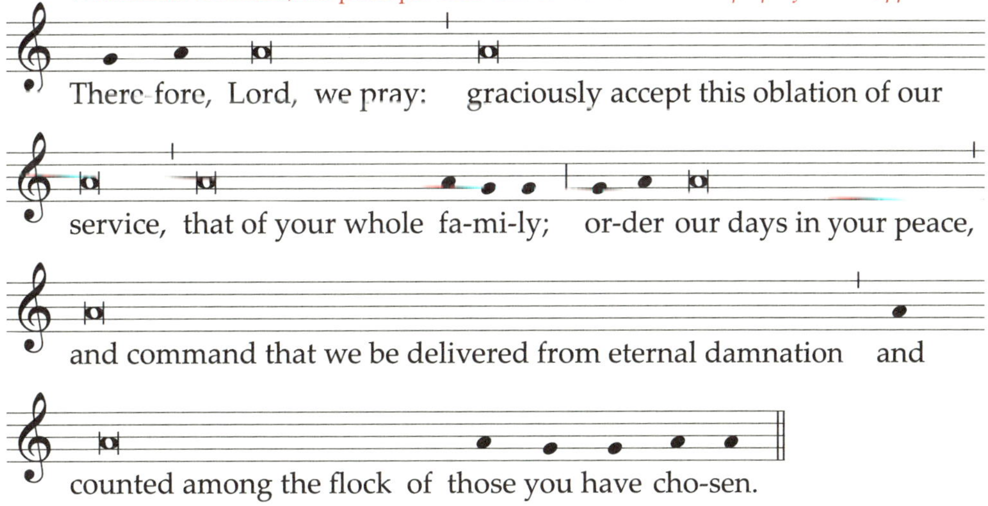

(He joins his hands.)

Holding his hands extended over the offerings, he sings (together with the concelebrants):

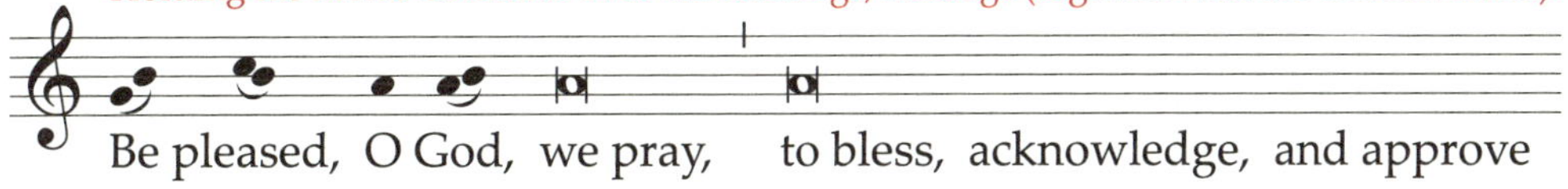

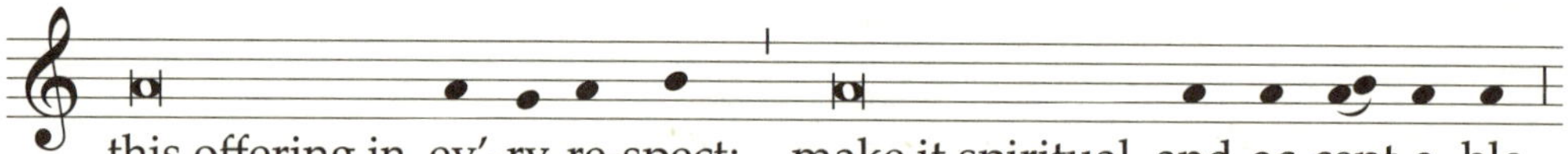

this offering in ev'-ry re-spect; make it spiritual and ac-cept-a-ble,

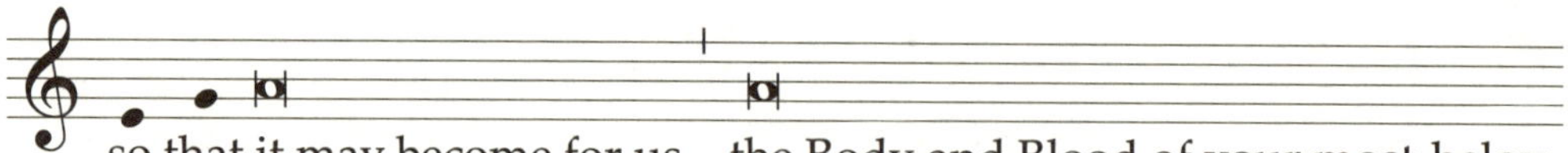

so that it may become for us the Body and Blood of your most belov-

-ed Son, our Lord Je-sus Christ.

He joins his hands.

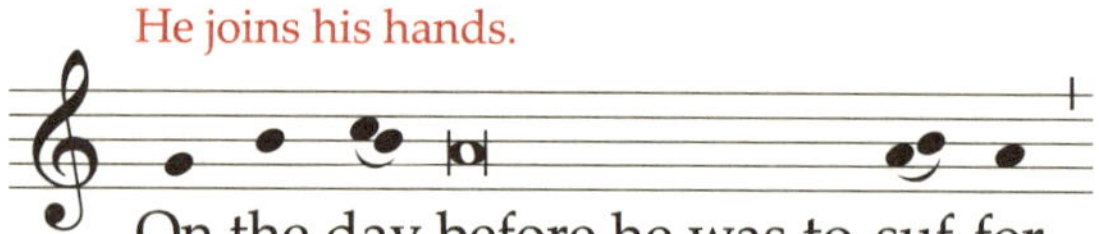

On the day before he was to suf-fer,

He takes the bread and, holding it slightly raised above the altar, continues:

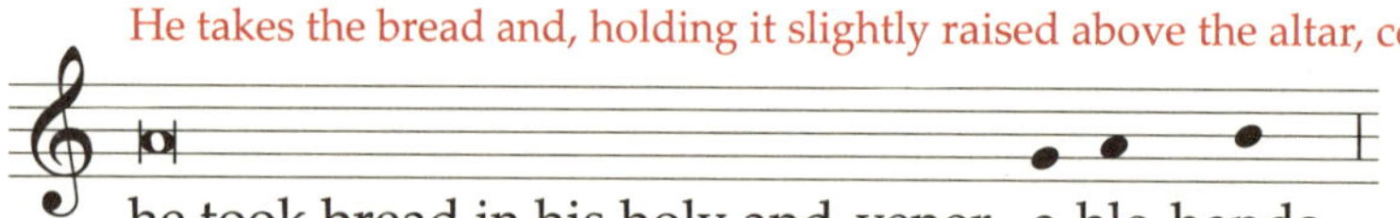

he took bread in his holy and vener - a-ble hands,

He raises his eyes.

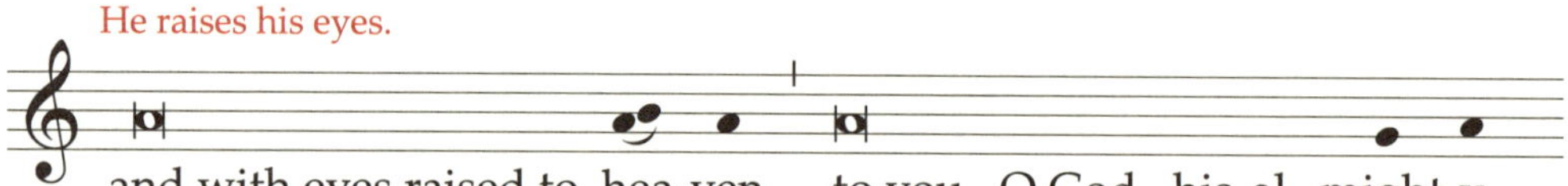

and with eyes raised to hea-ven to you, O God, his al - might-y

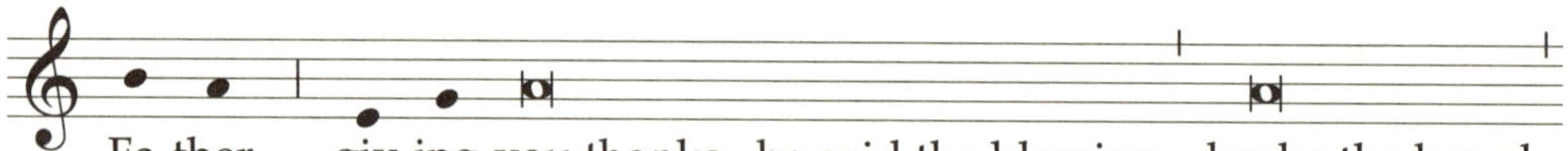

Fa-ther, giv-ing you thanks, he said the blessing, broke the bread

and gave it to his disciples, say-ing:

He bows slightly.

TAKE THIS, ALL OF YOU, AND EAT OF IT, FOR THIS IS MY BOD-Y,

WHICH WILL BE GIV-EN UP FOR YOU.

He shows the consecrated host to the people, places it again on the paten, and genuflects in adoration.

After this, he continues:

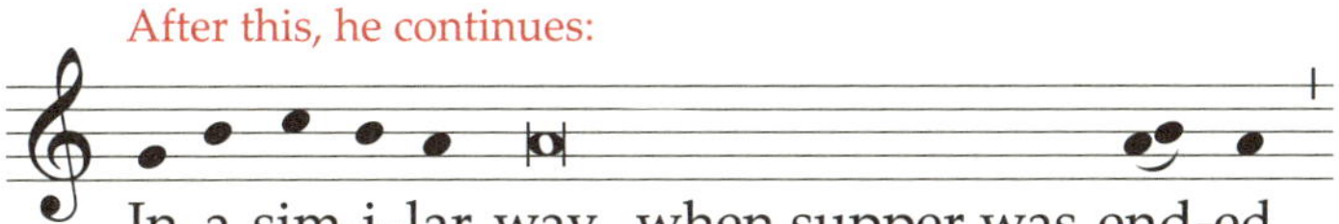

In a sim-i-lar way, when supper was end-ed,

He takes the chalice and, holding it slightly raised above the altar, continues:

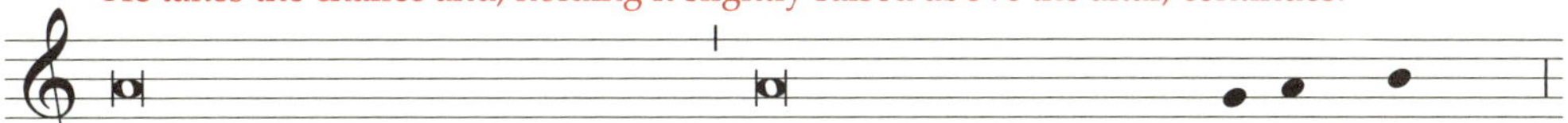

he took this precious chalice in his holy and vener-a-ble hands,

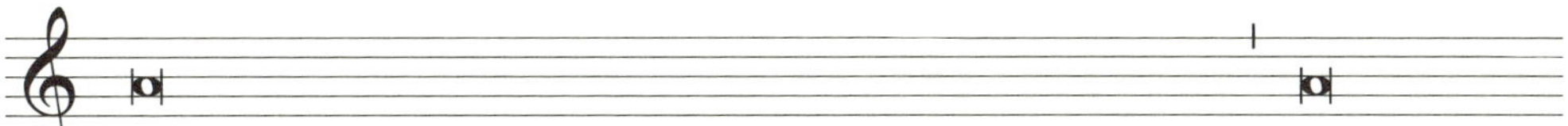

and once more giving you thanks, he said the blessing and gave the

chalice to his disciples, say-ing:

He bows slightly.

TAKE THIS, ALL OF YOU, AND DRINK FROM IT, FOR THIS IS THE CHALICE

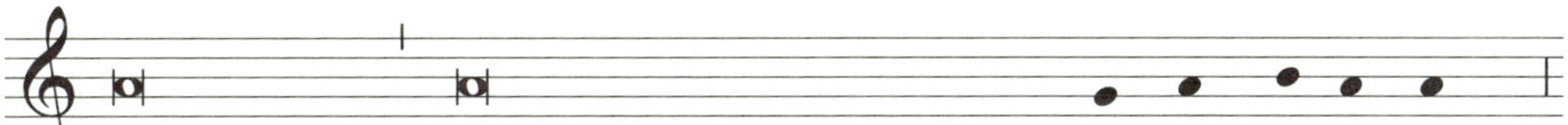

OF MY BLOOD, THE BLOOD OF THE NEW AND E-TER-NAL COV-E-NANT,

WHICH WILL BE POURED OUT FOR YOU AND FOR MAN-Y FOR THE

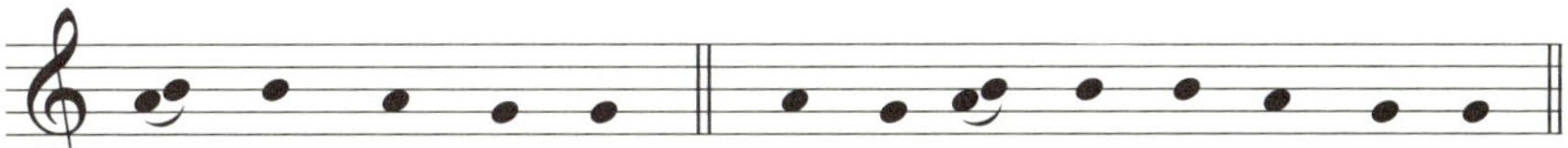

FOR-GIVE-NESS OF SINS. DO THIS IN MEM-O-RY OF ME.

The Priest shows the chalice to the people, places it on the corporal, and genuflects in adoration.

Then he sings:

The mys-ter-y of faith.

Or:

The mys-ter-y of faith.

And the people continue, acclaiming:

We pro-claim your Death, O Lord, and pro-fess your Res-ur-rec-tion

un-til you come a-gain.

Or:

Or:

Then he, with hands extended, sings (together with the concelebrants):

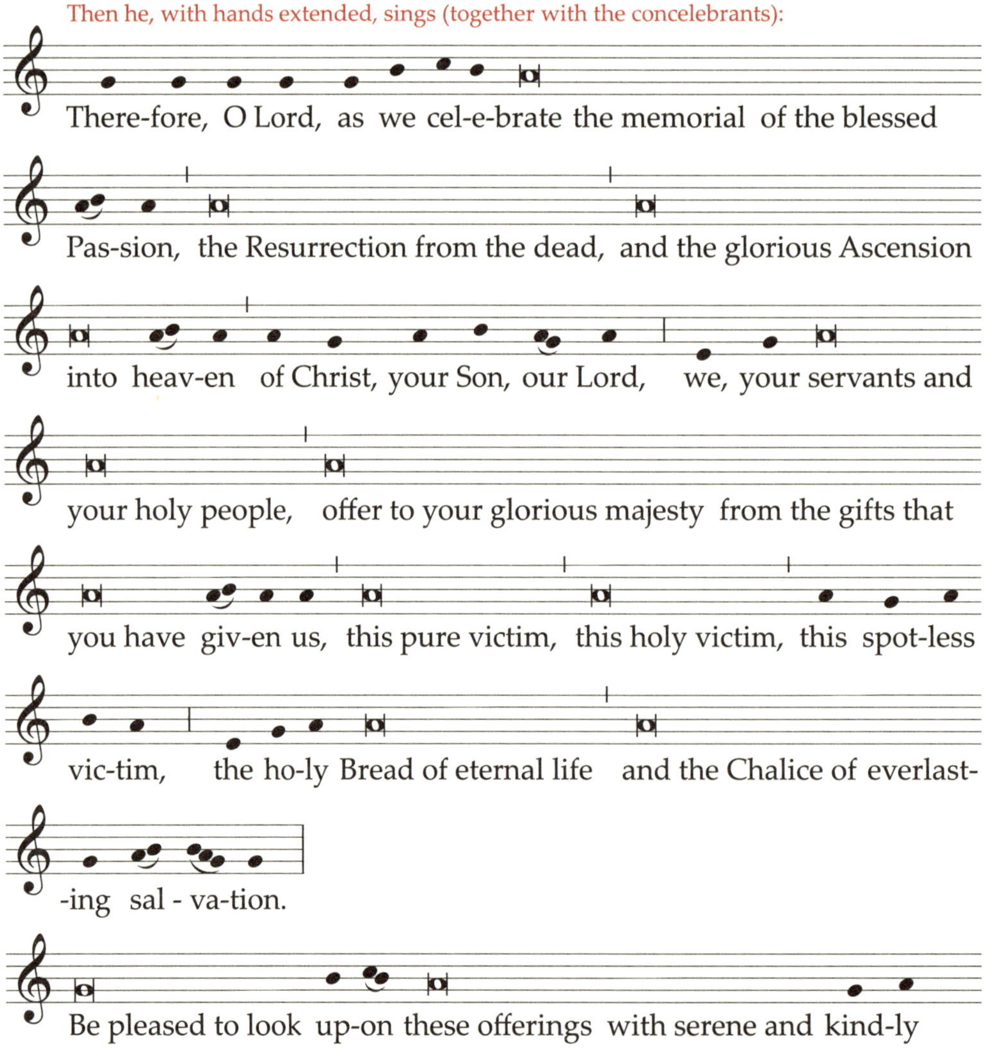

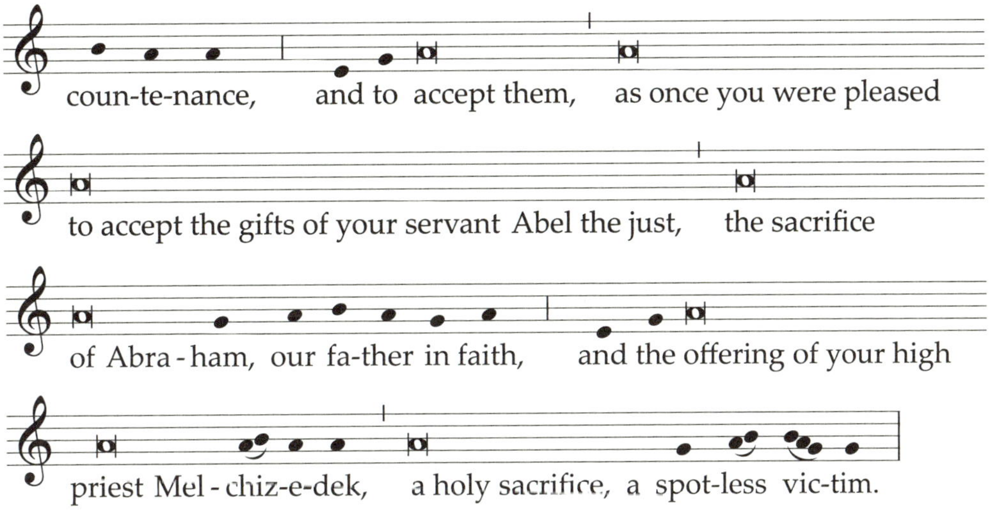

Bowing, with hands joined, he continues:

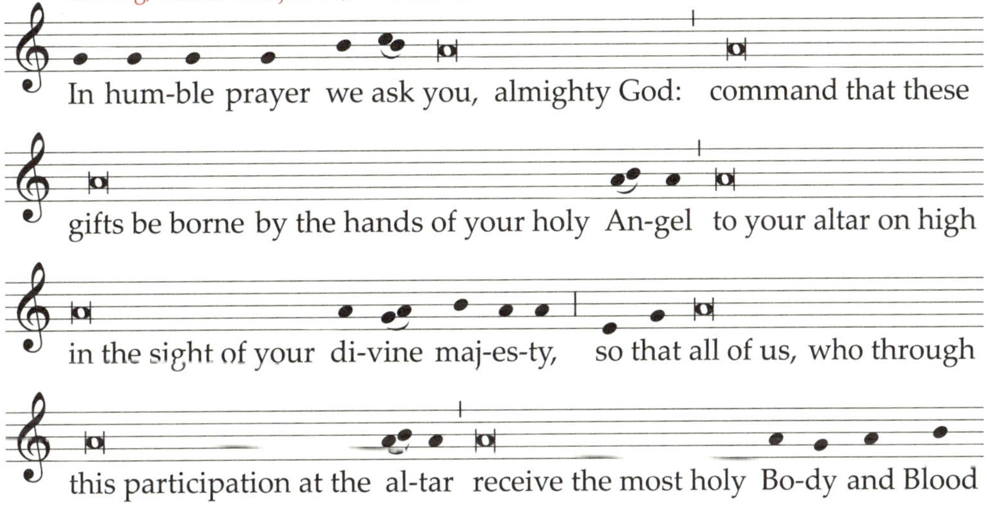

He stands upright again and signs himself with the Sign of the Cross, singing:

(He joins his hands.)

With hands extended, the Priest sings (one of the concelebrants):

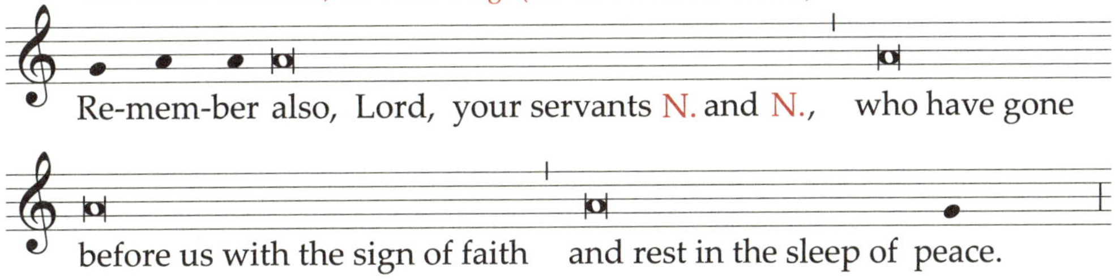

He joins his hands and prays briefly for those who have died and for whom he intends to pray.
Then, with hands extended, he continues:

Grant them, O Lord, we pray, and all who sleep in Christ, a place of refreshment, light and peace.

(He joins his hands.)

(Through Christ our Lord. A-men.)

(Another of the concelebrants)
He strikes his breast with his right hand, singing:

To us, also, your servants, who, though sinners,

And, with hands extended, he continues:

hope in your abundant mercies, graciously grant some share and fellowship with your holy Apostles and Mar-tyrs: with John the Baptist, Stephen, Matthias, Barnabas, (Ignatius, Alexander, Marcellinus, Peter, Felicity, Perpetua, Agatha, Lucy, Agnes, Cecilia, Anastasia) and all your Saints; ad-mit us, we beseech you, into their company, not weighing our merits, but granting us your par-don,

He joins his hands.

through Christ our Lord.

And the principal celebrant continues, with hands joined:

Through whom you continue to make all these good things, O Lord;

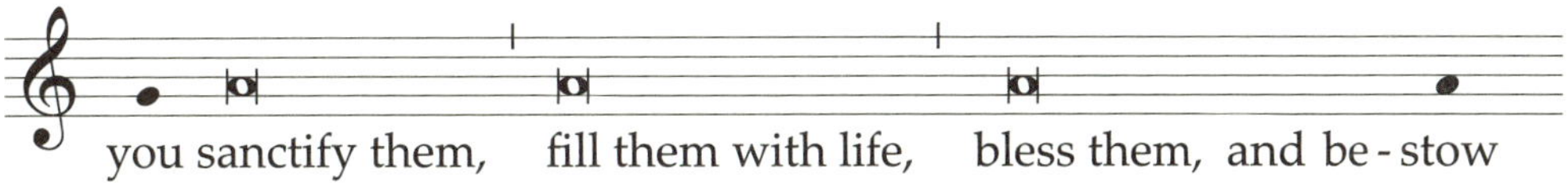

He takes the chalice and the paten with the host and raising both, he sings (together with the concelebrants):

Then follows the Communion Rite, p. 223.

Eucharistic Prayer II

Although it is provided with its own Preface, this Eucharistic Prayer may also be used with other Prefaces, especially those that present an overall view of the mystery of salvation, such as the Common Prefaces.

At the end of the Preface he joins his hands and concludes the Preface with the people, singing aloud:

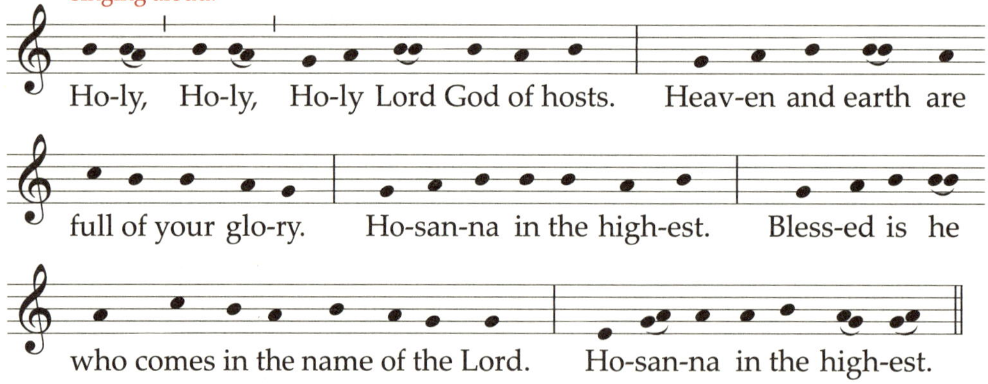

The principal celebrant, with hands extended, sings:

He joins his hands and, holding them extended over the offerings, sings (together with the concelebrants):

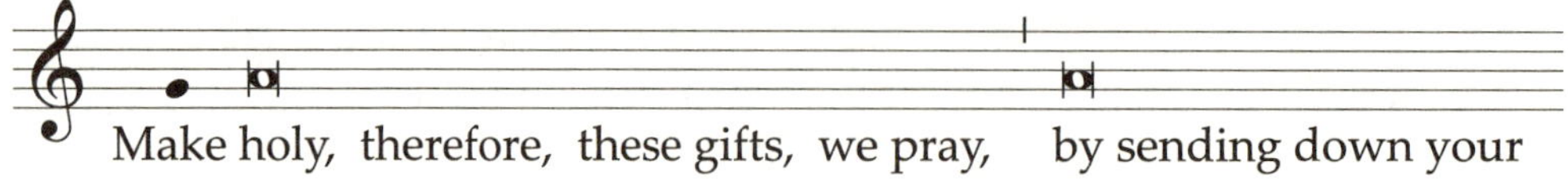

He joins his hands and makes the Sign of the Cross once over the bread and the chalice together, singing:

He joins his hands.

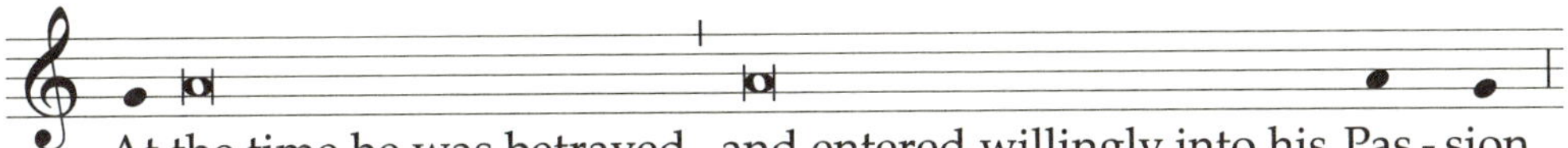

He takes the bread and, holding it slightly raised above the altar, continues:

He bows slightly.

He shows the consecrated host to the people, places it again on the paten, and genuflects in adoration.

After this, he continues:

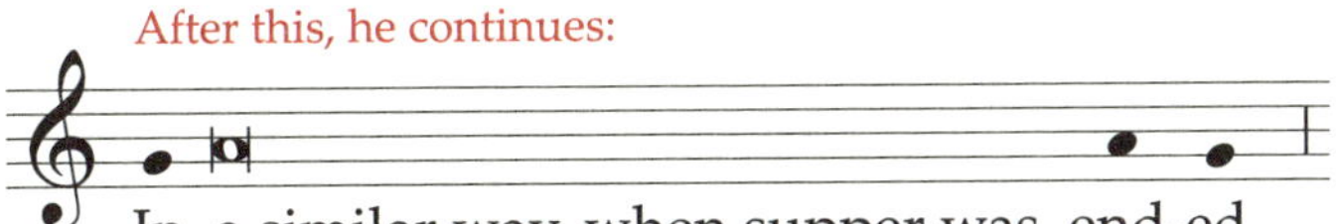

He takes the chalice and, holding it slightly raised above the altar, continues:

He bows slightly.

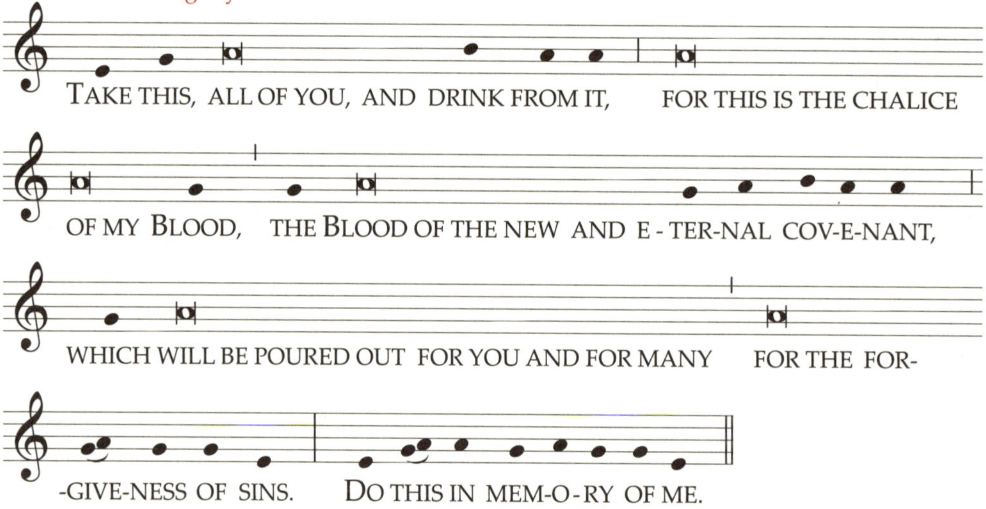

He shows the chalice to the people, places it on the corporal, and genuflects in adoration.

Then he sings:

And the people continue, acclaiming:

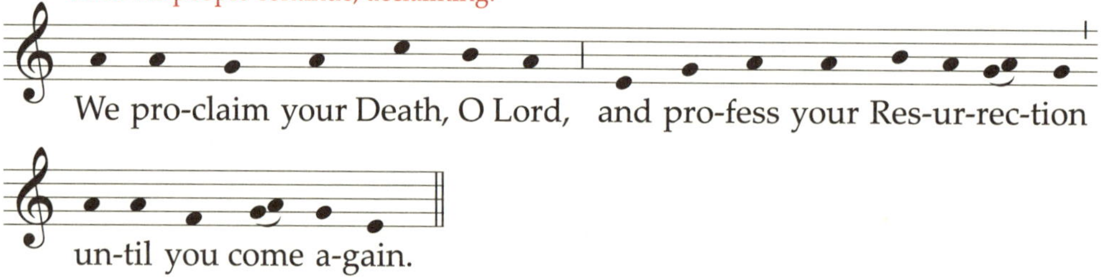

Or:

Or:

Then he, with hands extended, sings (together with the concelebrants):

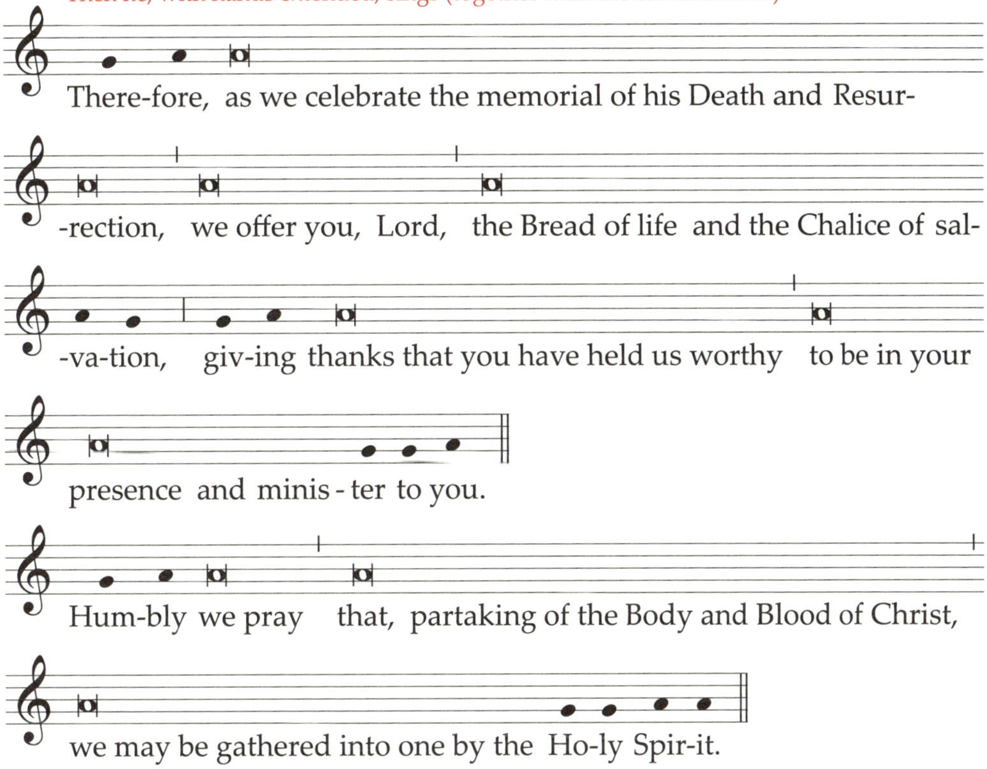

(One of the concelebrants)

* Mention may be made here of the Coadjutor Bishop, or Auxiliary Bishops, as noted in the *General Instruction of the Roman Missal*, no. 149.

(Another of the concelebrants)

In Masses for the Dead, the proper from of the remembrance of the dead (Remember your servant N. is sung (p. 209); and, after it has been sung, the prayer Have mercy on us all immediately follows.

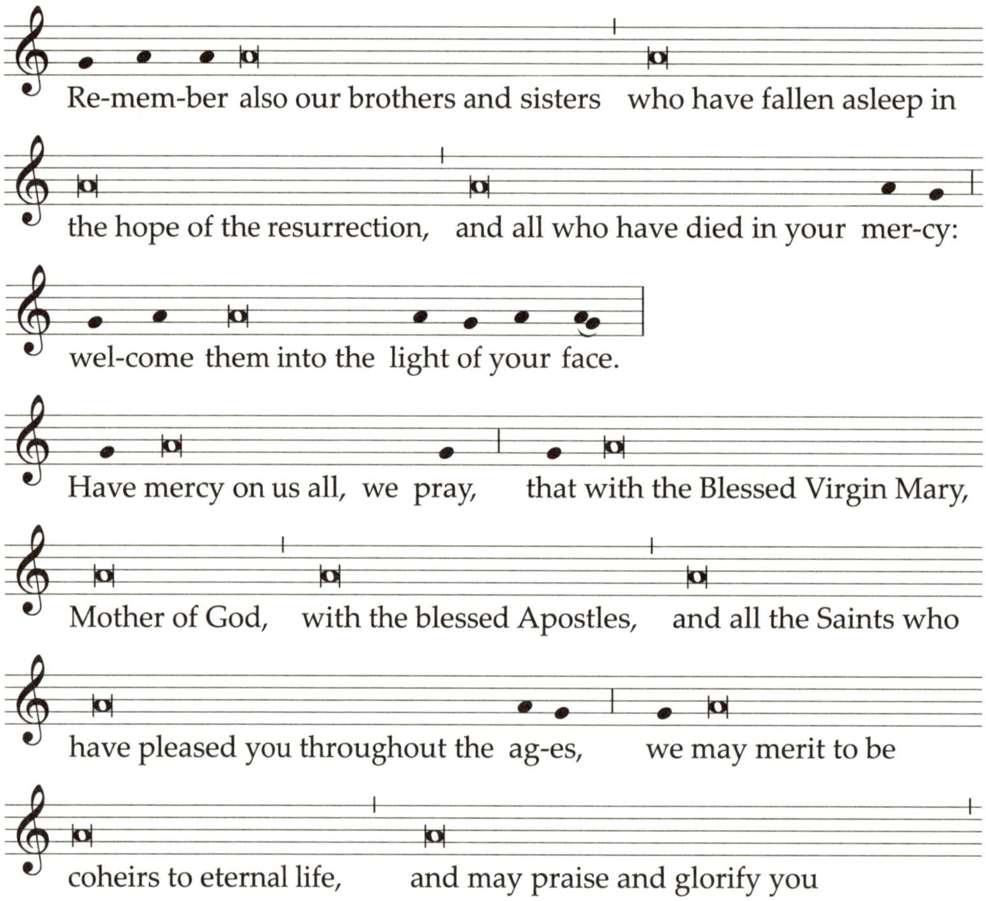

He joins his hands.

He takes the chalice and paten with the host and raising both, he sings (together with the concelebrants):

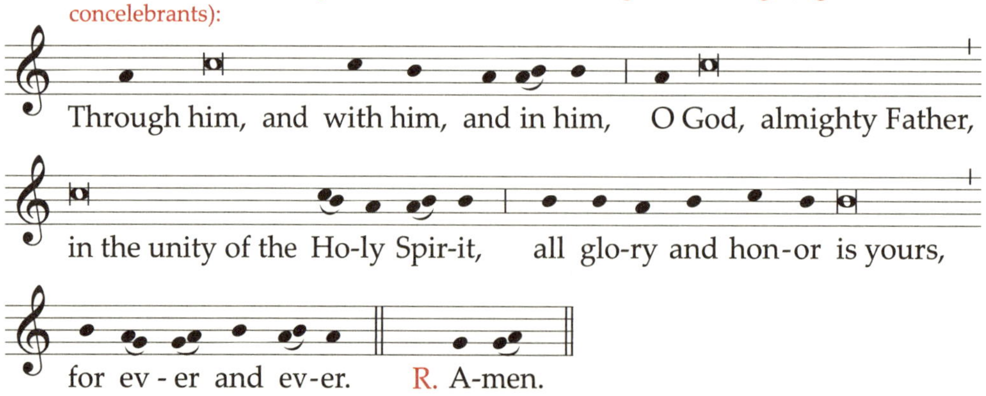

Then follows the Communion Rite, p. 223.

In Masses for the Dead, the following may be sung:

Re-mem-ber your servant N., whom you have called (today) from this world to your - self. Grant that he/she who was united with your Son in a death like his, may also be one with him in his Res-ur-rec-tion.

Eucharistic Prayer III

The principal celebrant, with hands extended, sings:

You are indeed Holy, O Lord, and all you have created rightly gives you praise, for through your Son our Lord Jesus Christ, by the power and working of the Holy Spirit, you give life to all things and make them ho-ly, and you never cease to gather a people to yourself, so that from the rising of the sun to its setting a pure sacrifice may be offered to your name.

He joins his hands and, holding them extended over the offerings, sings (together with the concelebrants):

There-fore, O Lord, we humbly implore you: by the same Spirit

He joins his hands and makes the Sign of the Cross once over the bread and chalice together, singing:

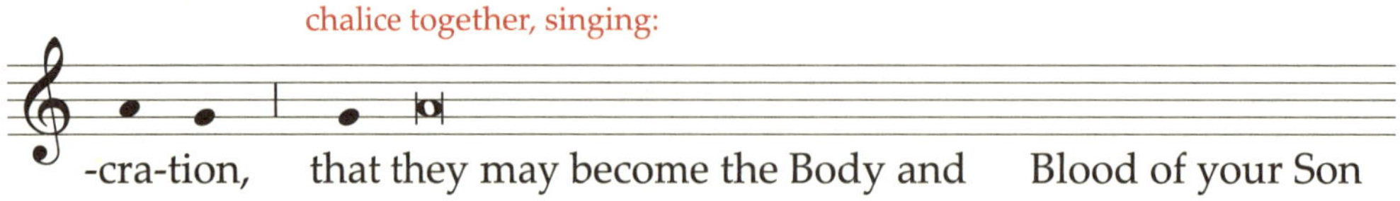

He joins his hands.

He takes the bread and, holding it slightly raised above the altar, continues:

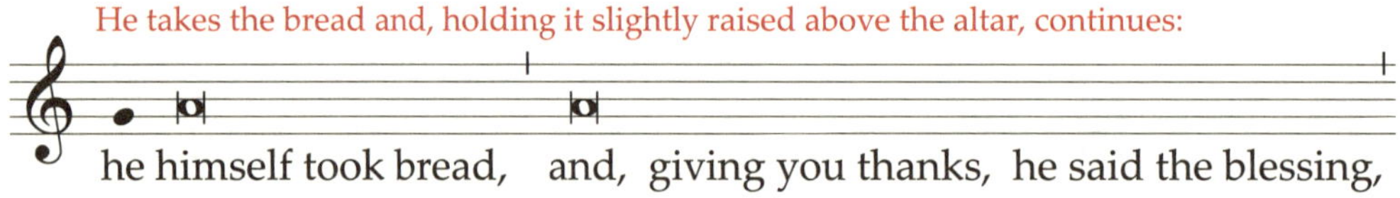

He bows slightly.

He shows the consecrated host to the people, places it again on the paten, and genuflects in adoration.

After this, he continues:

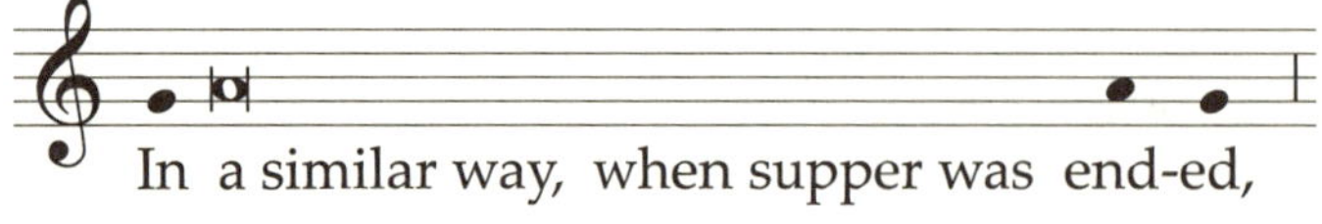

He takes the chalice and, holding it slightly raised above the altar, continues:

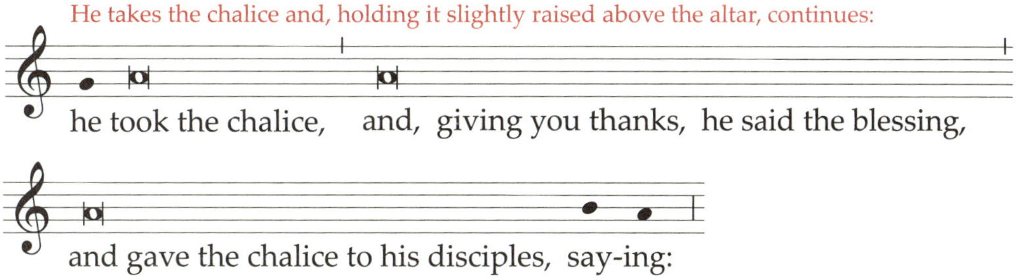

He bows slightly.

He shows the chalice to the people, places it on the corporal, and genuflects in adoration.

Then he sings:

And the people continue, acclaiming:

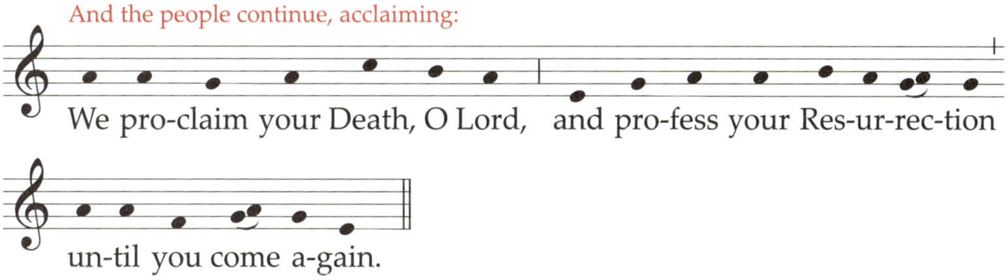

Or:

Or:

Then he, with hands extended, sings (together with the concelebrants):

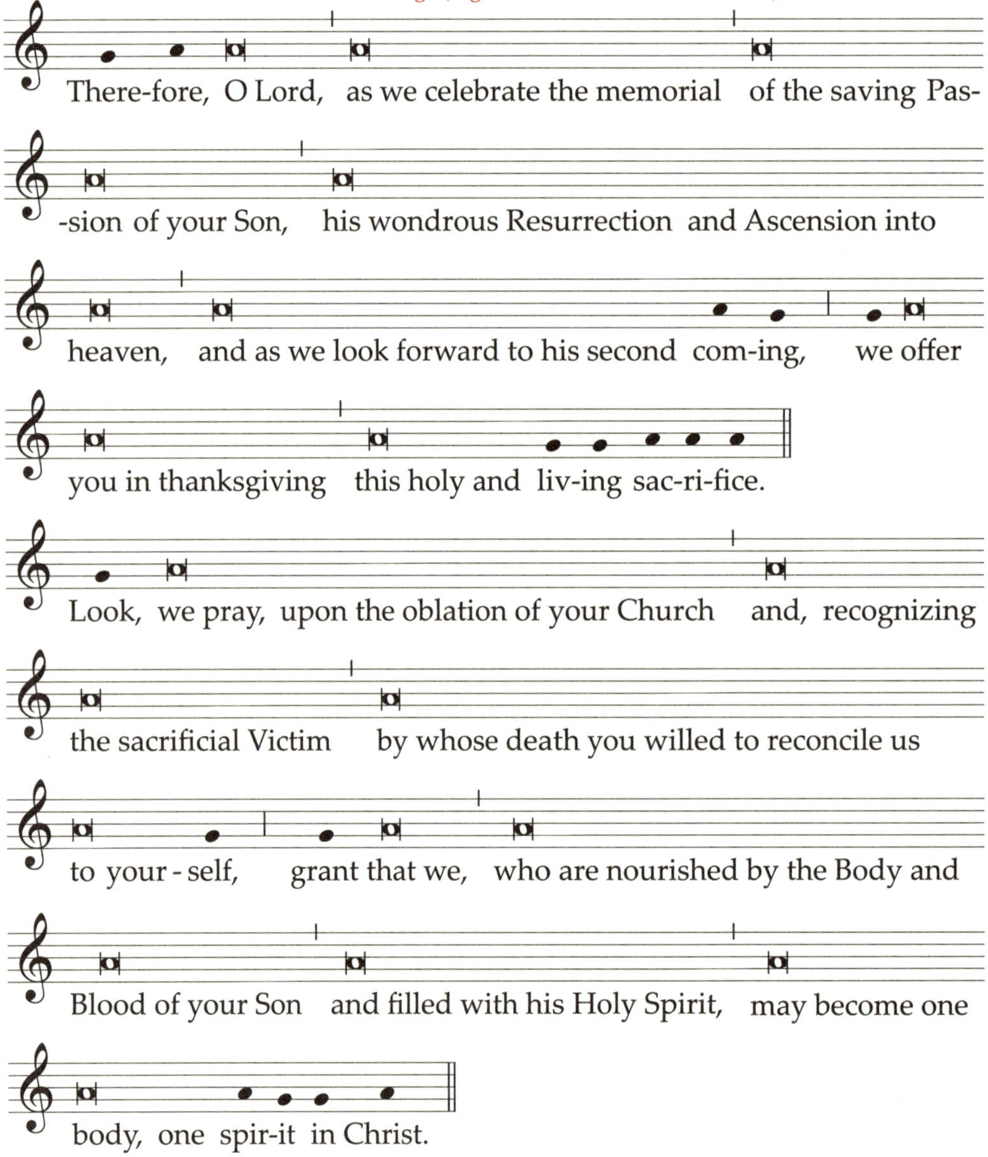

(One of the concelebrants)

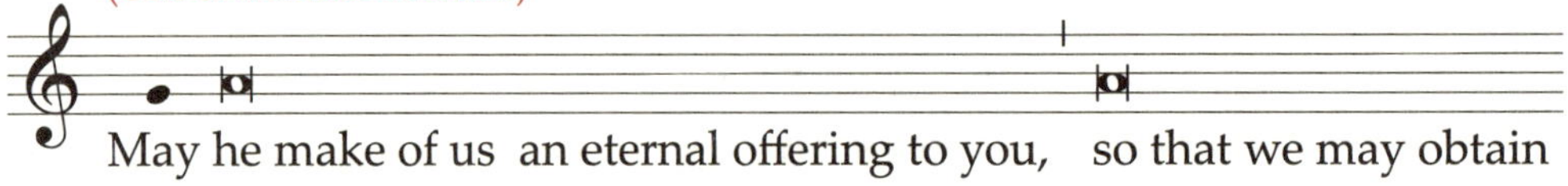

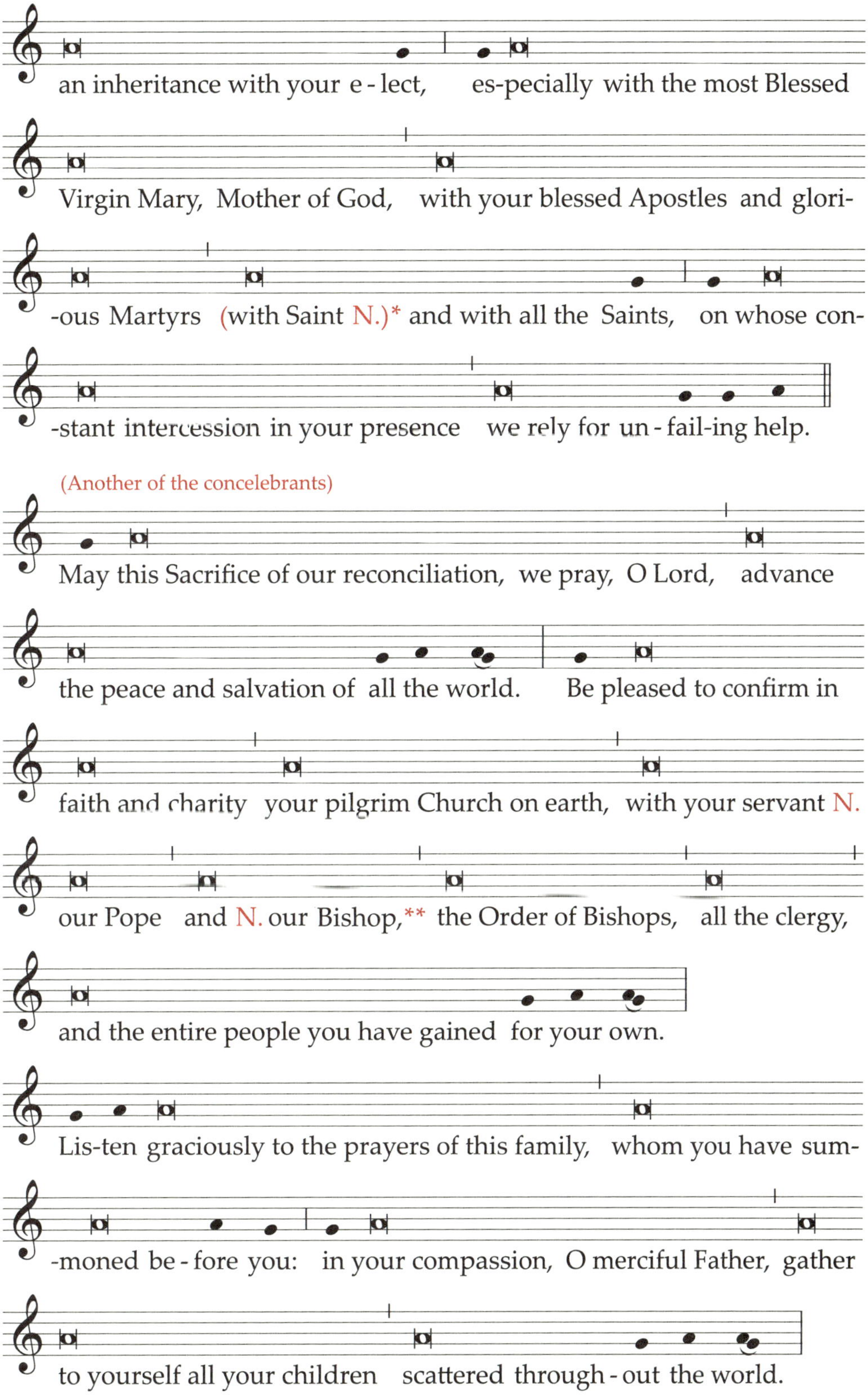

* the Saint of the day or Patron Saint

** Mention may be made here of the Coadjutor Bishop, or Auxiliary Bishops, as noted in the *General Instruction of the Roman Missal*, no. 149.

In Masses for the Dead, the proper form of the remembrance of the dead (Remember your servant N.) is said (below); and, after it has been said, the doxology (Through him) immediately follows.

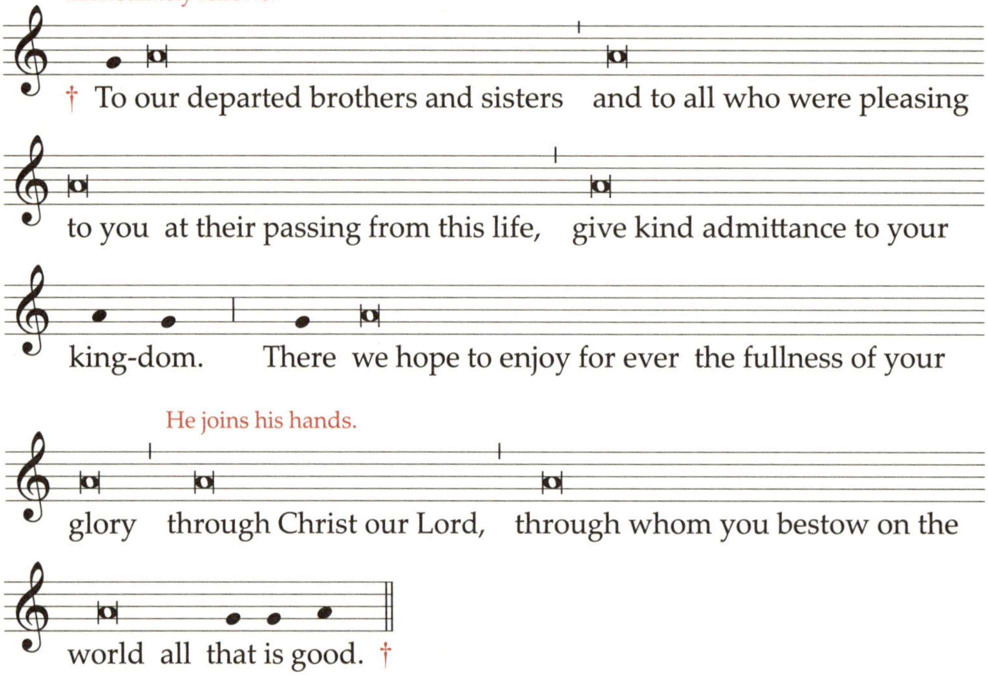

He takes the chalice and the paten with the host and raising both, he sings (together with the concelebrants):

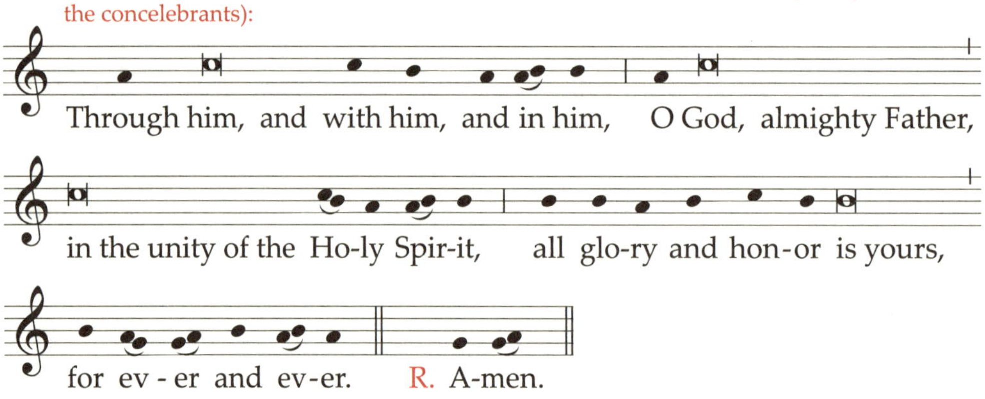

Then follows the Communion Rite, p. 223.

In Masses for the Dead, the following may be sung:

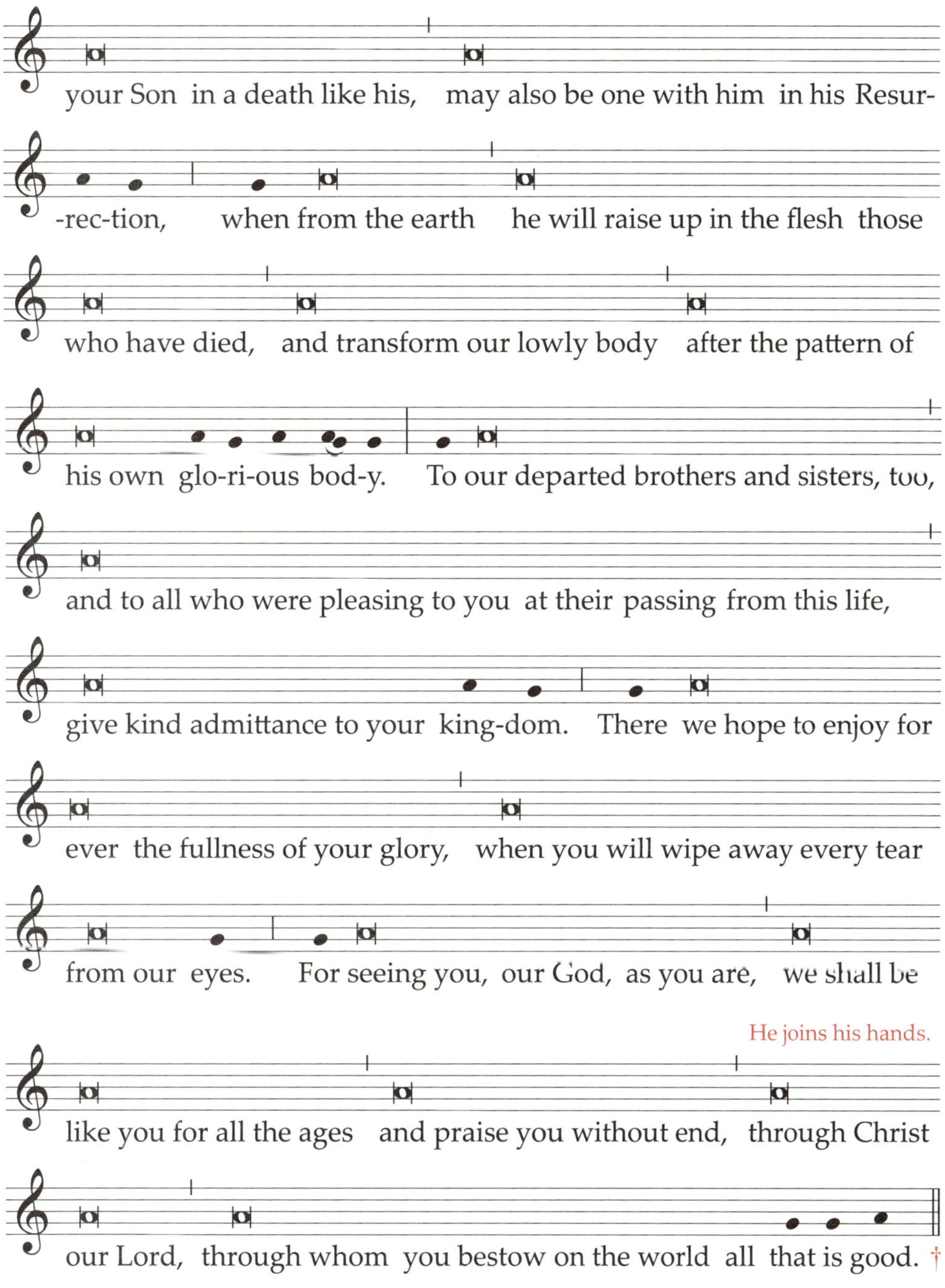
your Son in a death like his, may also be one with him in his Resur-
-rec-tion, when from the earth he will raise up in the flesh those
who have died, and transform our lowly body after the pattern of
his own glo-ri-ous bod-y. To our departed brothers and sisters, too,
and to all who were pleasing to you at their passing from this life,
give kind admittance to your king-dom. There we hope to enjoy for
ever the fullness of your glory, when you will wipe away every tear
from our eyes. For seeing you, our God, as you are, we shall be
He joins his hands.
like you for all the ages and praise you without end, through Christ
our Lord, through whom you bestow on the world all that is good. †

Eucharistic Prayer IV

It is not permitted to change the Preface of this Eucharistic Prayer because of the structure of the Prayer itself, which presents a summary of the history of salvation.

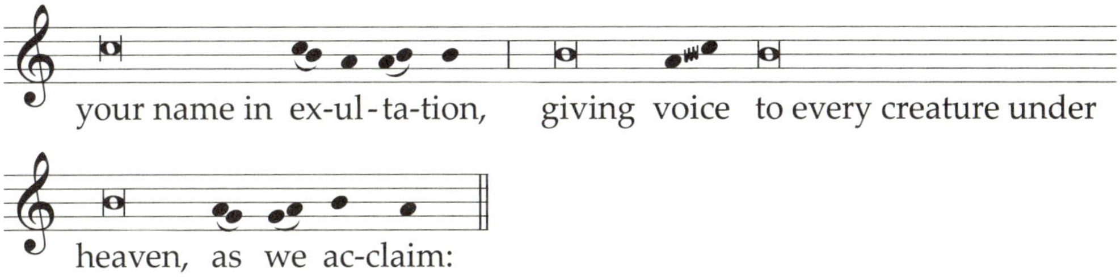

At the end of the Preface he joins his hands and concludes the Preface with the people, singing aloud:

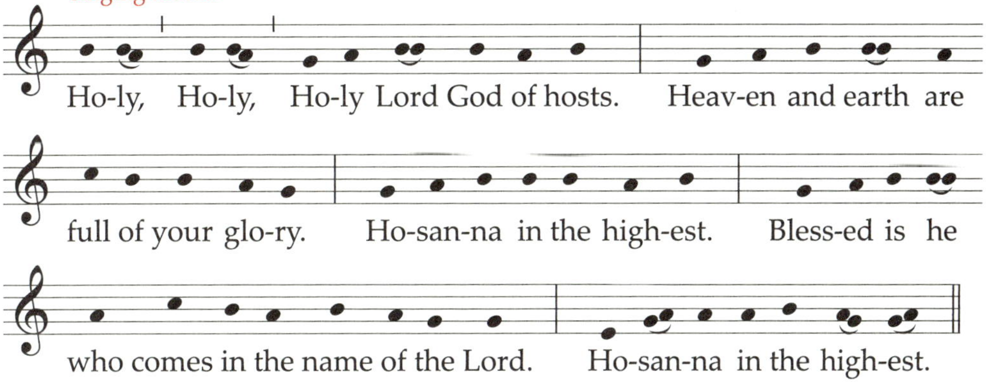

The principal celebrant, with hands extended, sings:

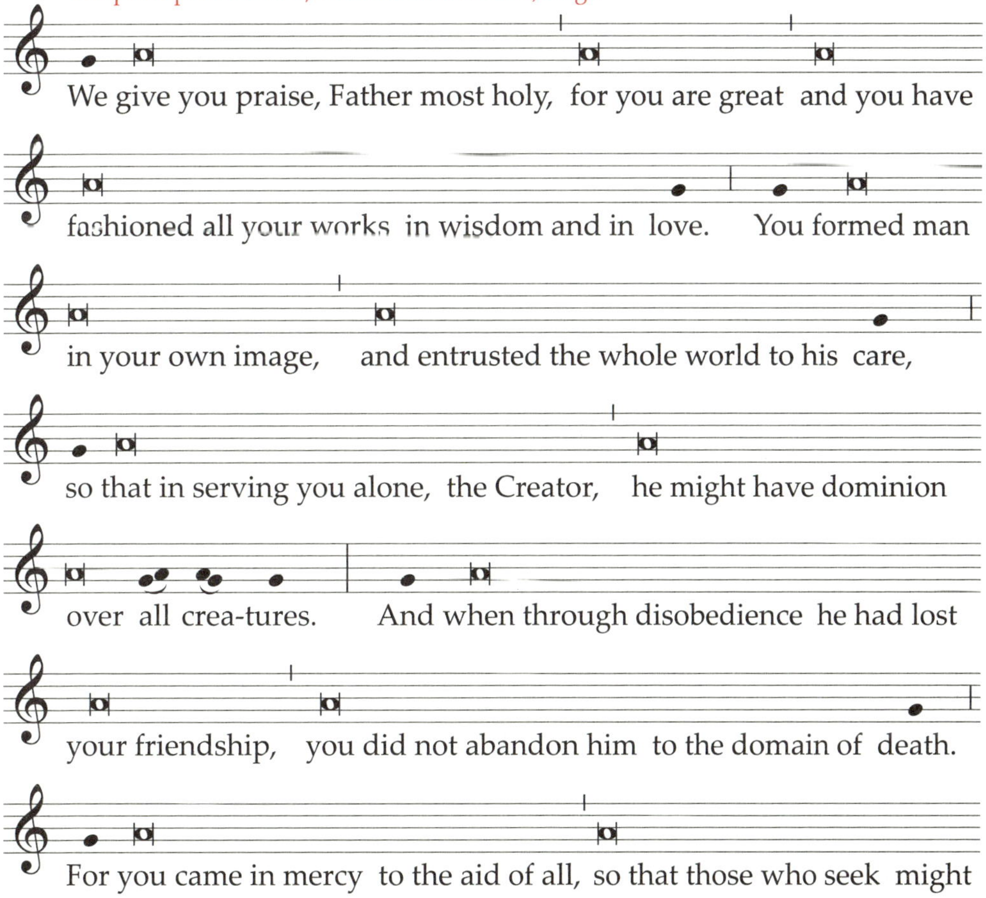

find you. Time and again you offered them covenants and through
the prophets taught them to look forward to sal-va-tion. And
you so loved the world, Father most holy, that in the fullness of time
you sent your Only Begotten Son to be our Sav-ior. Made incarnate
by the Holy Spirit and born of the Virgin Mary, he shared our hu-
-man nature in all things but sin. To the poor he proclaimed the
good news of salvation, to prisoners, freedom, and to the sorrow-
-ful of heart, joy. To accomplish your plan, he gave himself up to
death, and, rising from the dead, he destroyed death and re-
-stored life. And that we might live no longer for ourselves but for
him who died and rose a - gain for us, he sent the Holy Spirit from
you, Father, as the first fruits for those who be - lieve, so that, bring-
-ing to perfection his work in the world, he might sanctify creation

to the full.

He joins his hands and, holding them extended over the offerings, sings (together with the concelebrants):

There-fore, O Lord, we pray: may this same Holy Spirit graciously

He joins his hands and makes the Sign of the Cross once over the bread and chalice together, singing:

sanctify these of-fer-ings, that they may become the Body and

He joins his hands.

Blood of our Lord Jesus Christ for the celebration of this great mys-

-tery, which he himself left us as an e - ter-nal cov-e-nant.

For when the hour had come for him to be glorified by you, Father

most holy, having loved his own who were in the world, he loved

them to the end: and while they were at supper,

He takes the bread and, holding it slightly raised above the altar, continues:

he took bread, blessed and broke it, and gave it to his disciples,

say-ing:

He bows slightly.

TAKE THIS, ALL OF YOU, AND EAT OF IT, FOR THIS IS MY BOD-Y,

He shows the consecrated host to the people, places it again on the paten, and genuflects in adoration.

After this, he continues: He takes the chalice and, holding it slightly raised above the altar, continues:

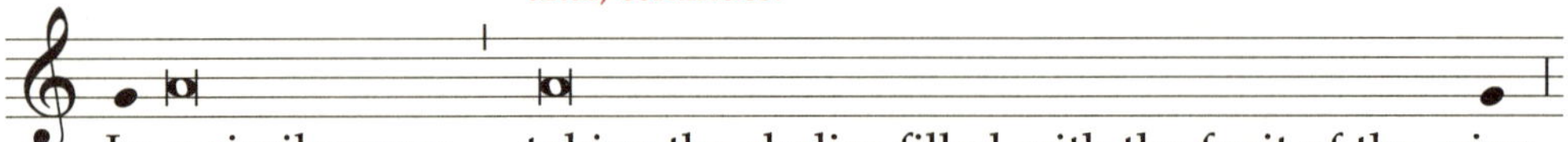

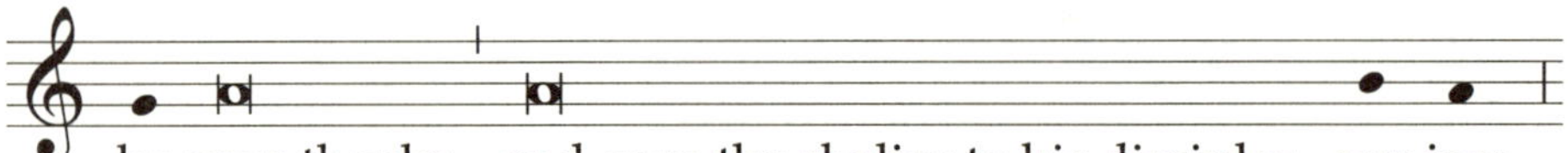

He bows slightly.

He shows the chalice to the people, places it on the corporal, and genuflects in adoration.

Then he sings:

And the people continue, acclaiming:

Or:

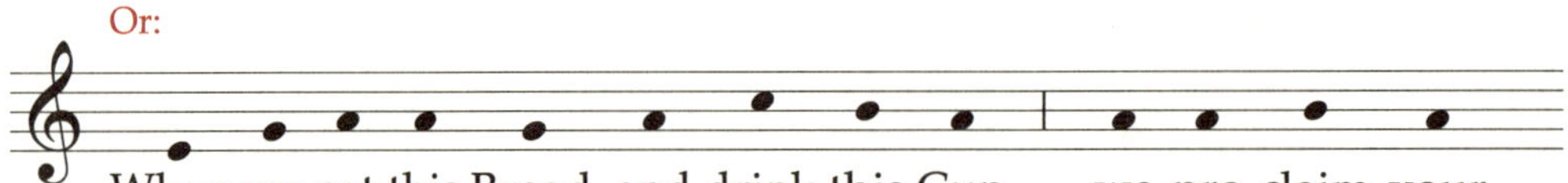

Or:

Then he, with hands extended, sings (together with the concelebrants):

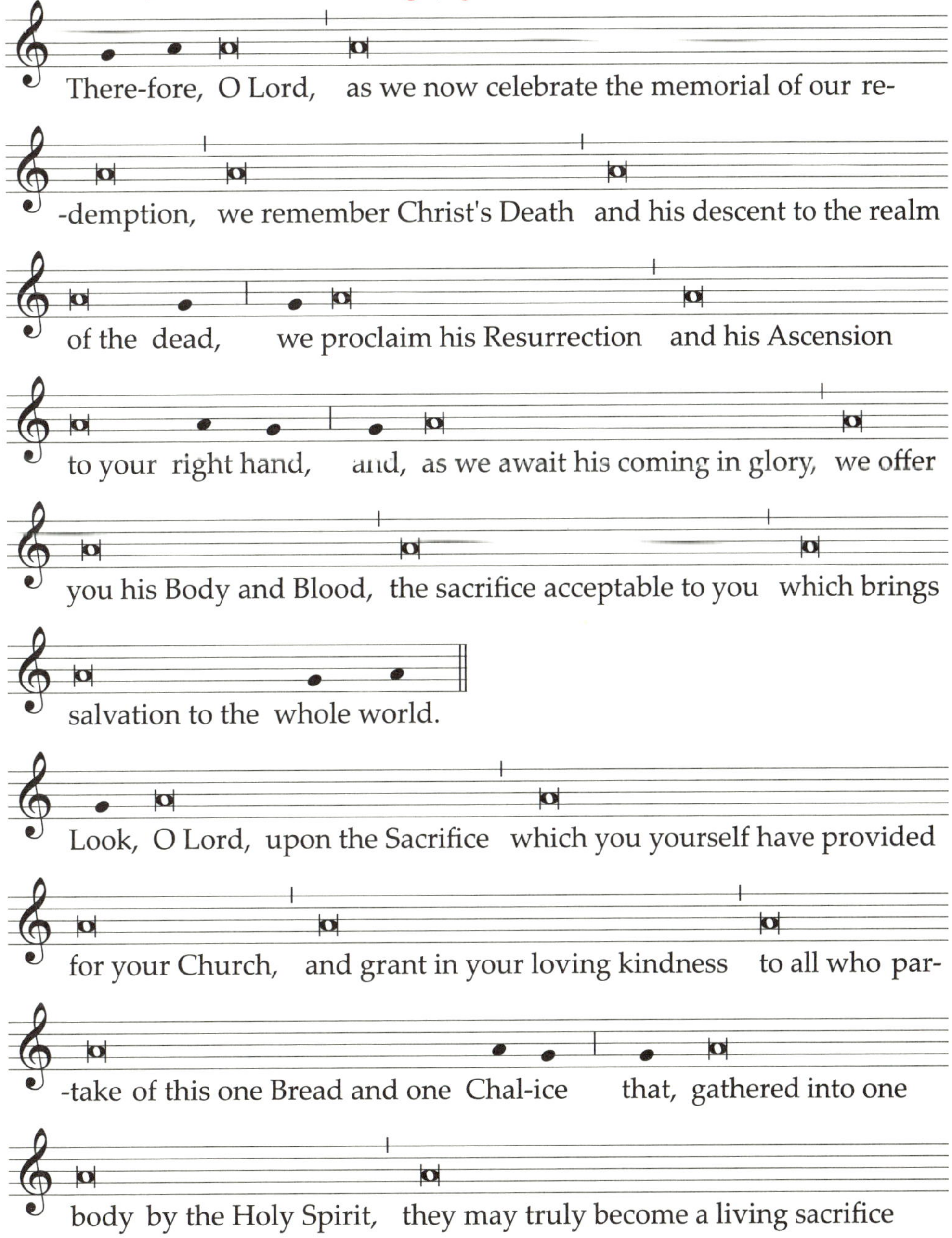

* Mention may be made here of the Coadjutor Bishop, or Auxiliary Bishops, as noted in the *General Instruction of the Roman Missal,* no. 149.

He joins his hands.

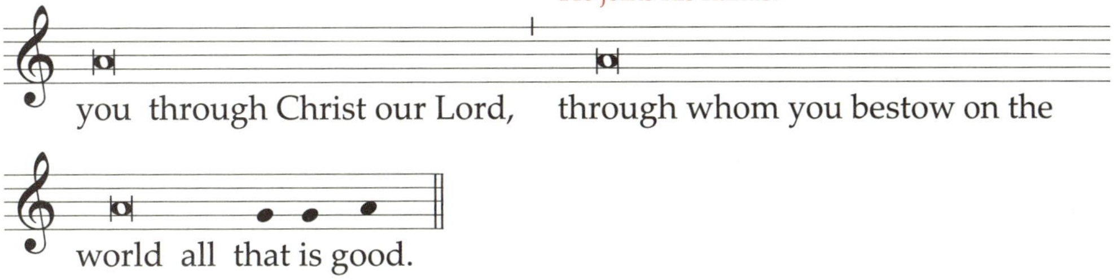

He takes the chalice and the paten with the host and raising both, he sings (together with the concelebrants):

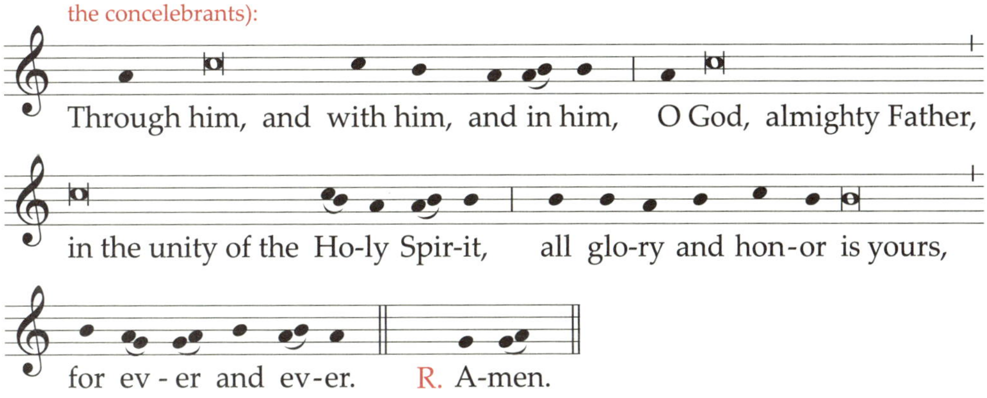

Then follows the Communion Rite.

THE COMMUNION RITE

The Lord's Prayer

USA Version

124.

Priest:

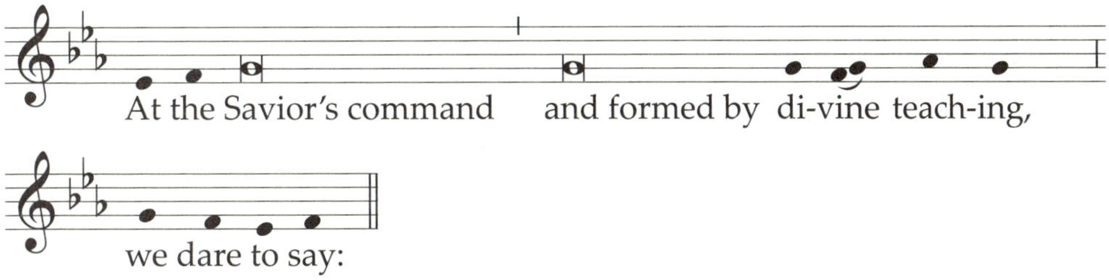

All:

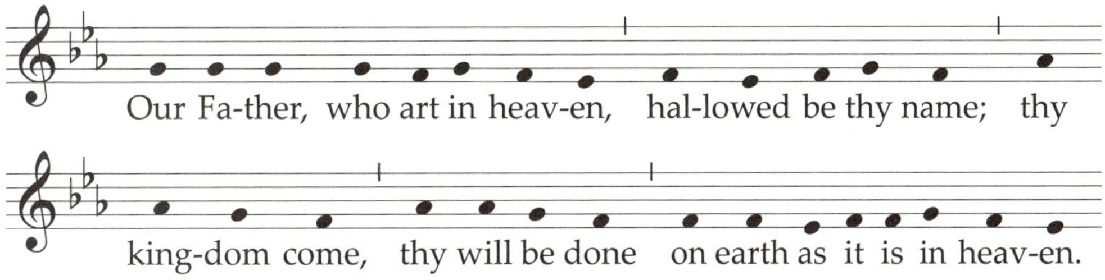

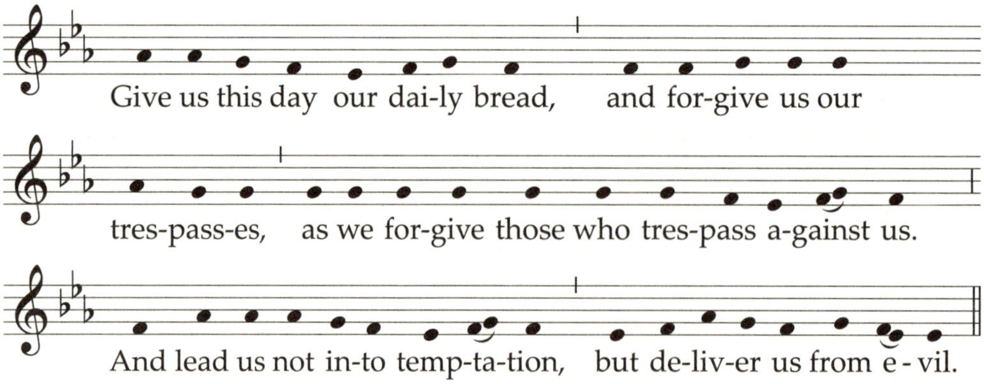

ICEL Version

Priest:

All:

Or:

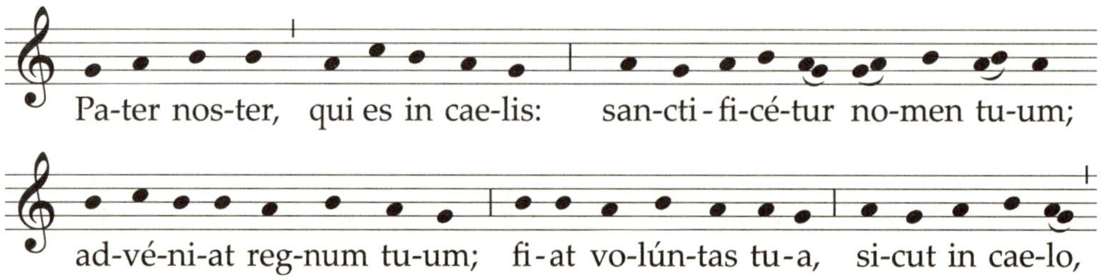

USA Version

125.

Priest:

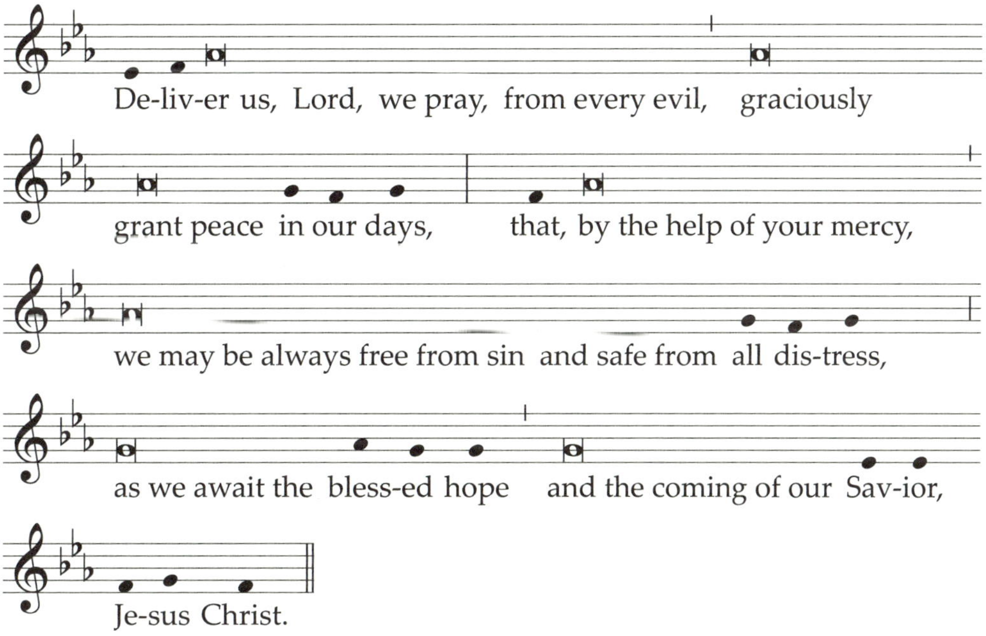

People:

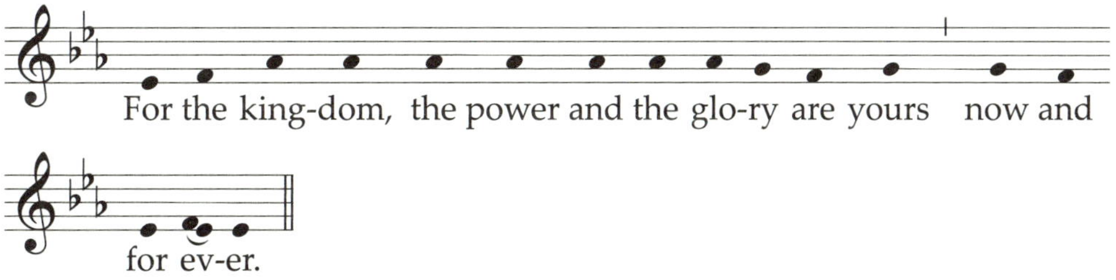

ICEL Version

Or:
Priest:

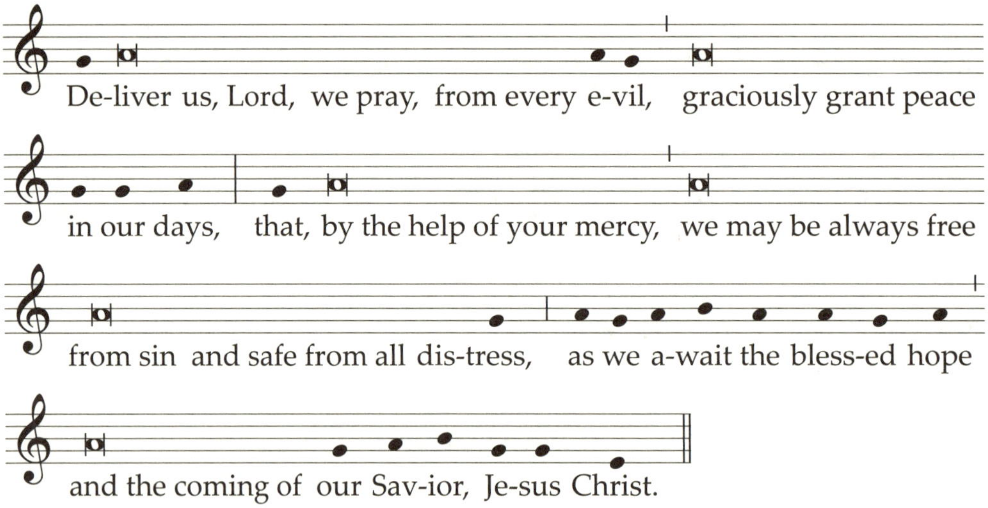

People:

Sign of Peace

125.

Priest:

The people reply:

127.

Priest:

The people reply:

128.

Deacon, or the Priest:

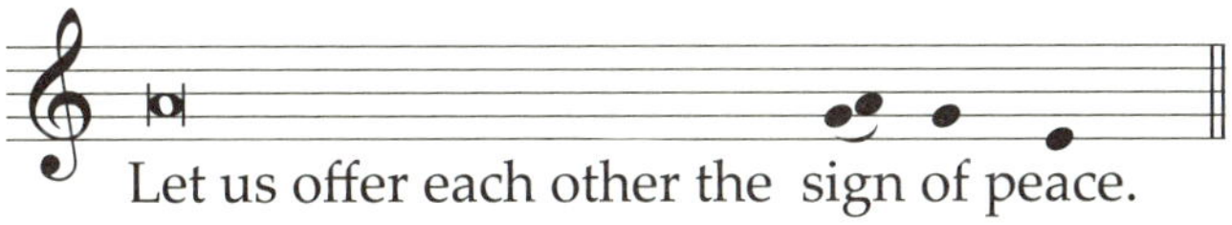

Lamb of God

130.

Or:

Invitation to Communion

132.

Priest:

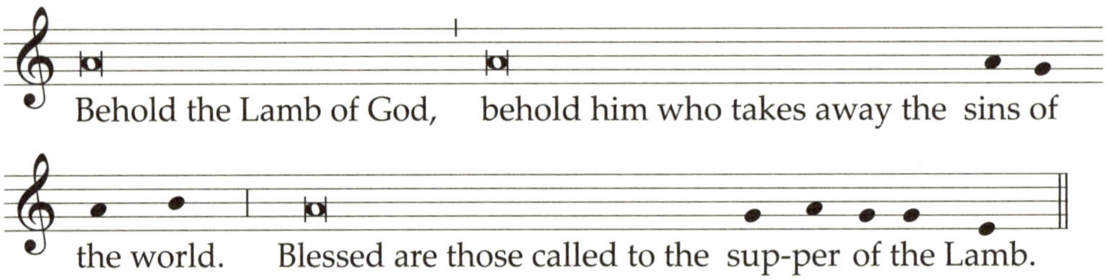

Priest and people:

THE CONCLUDING RITES

Final Blessing

141.

Priest:

The people reply:

Priest:

The people reply:

143. In a Pontifical Mass:

Celebrant:

All reply:

Celebrant:

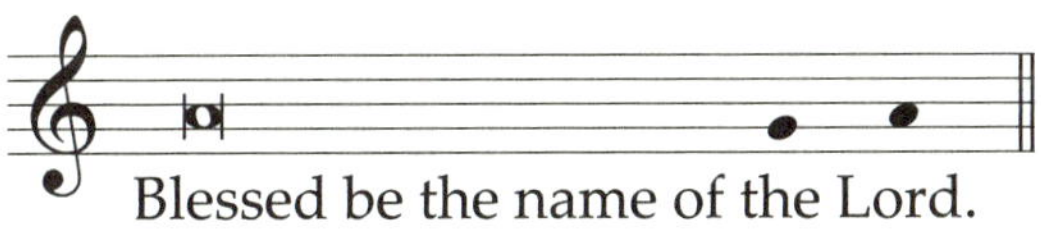

All reply:

Celebrant:

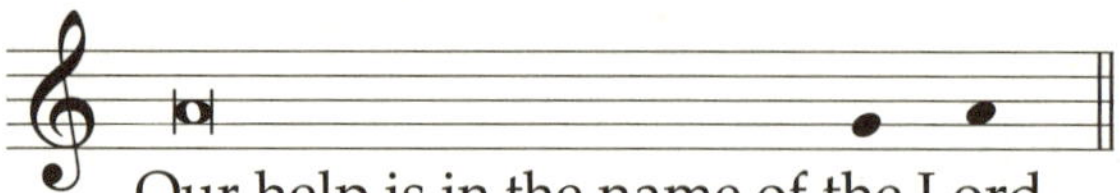

Our help is in the name of the Lord.

All reply:

Who made heav-en and earth.

Celebrant:

May almighty God bless you,

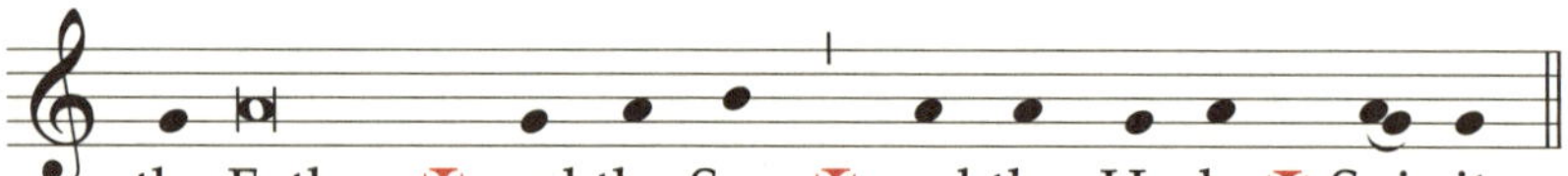

the Father, ✠ and the Son, ✠ and the Ho-ly ✠ Spir-it.

All reply:

A-men.

Dismissal

144.

V. Go forth, the Mass is end-ed. R. Thanks be to God.

Or:

V. Go and an-nounce the Gos-pel of the Lord. R. Thanks be to God.

Or:

V. Go in peace, glorifying the Lord by your life. R. Thanks be to God.

Or:

V. Go in peace. R. Thanks be to God.

APPENDIX TO THE ORDER OF MASS

Eucharistic Prayer for Reconciliation I

Preface

be un-done. E-ven now you set before your people a time of grace
and recon - ci - li - a - tion, and, as they turn back to you in spirit,
you grant them hope in Christ Je-sus and a desire to be of ser-vice
to all, while they entrust them - selves more ful-ly to the Ho-ly
Spir-it. And so, filled with wonder, we extol the power of your
love, and, proclaiming our joy at the salvation that comes from
you, we join in the heavenly hymn of count-less hosts, as without
end we ac-claim:

Eucharistic Prayer for Reconciliation II

Preface

Eucharistic Prayer for Use in Masses for Various Needs

I

The Church on the Path to Unity

Preface

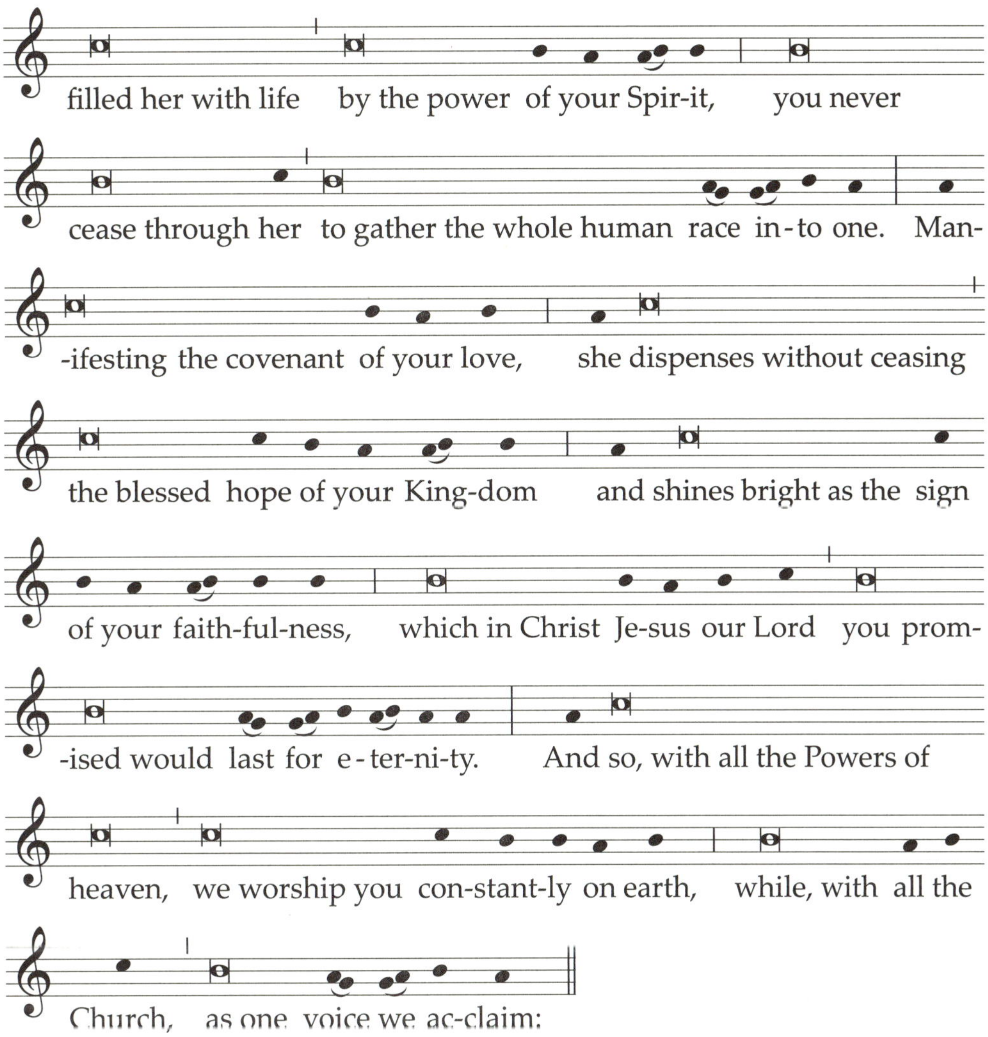

II

God Guides His Church along the Way of Salvation

Preface

It is truly right and just, our duty and our sal-va-tion, al-ways and
everywhere to give you thanks, Lord, holy Father, creator of the
world and source of all life. For you never forsake the works of
your wis-dom, but by your prov-i-dence are even now at work in
our midst. With mighty hand and out-stretched arm you led your
peo-ple Is-ra-el through the de-sert. Now, as your Church makes
her pilgrim journey in the world, you always accompany her by the
power of the Ho-ly Spir-it and lead her along the paths of time
to the eternal joy of your King-dom, through Christ our Lord.
And so, with the An-gels and Saints, we, too, sing the hymn of your
glo-ry, as without end we ac-claim:

III

Jesus, the Way to the Father

Preface

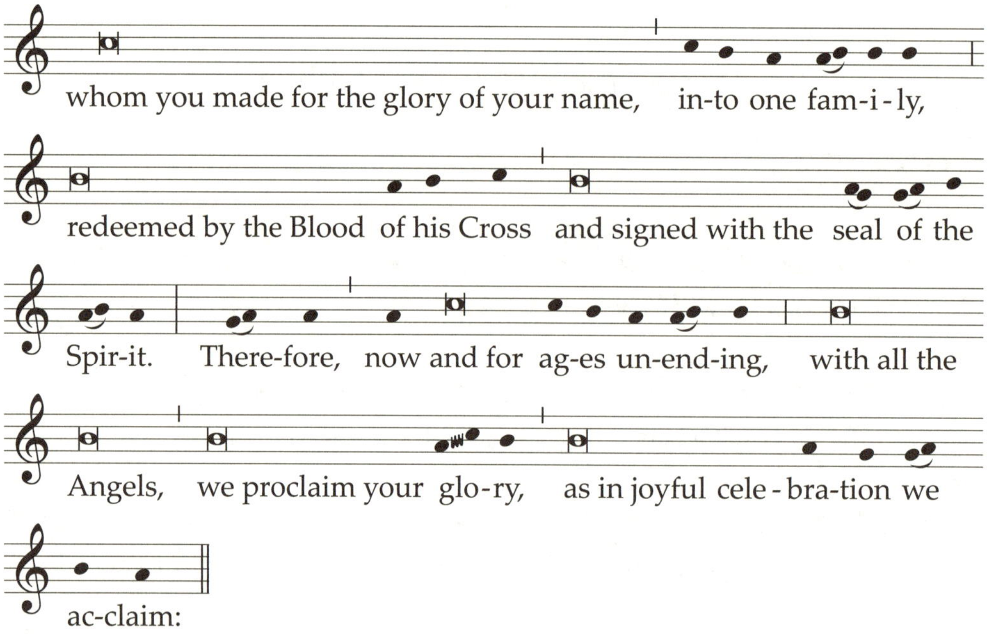

IV

Jesus, Who Went About Doing Good

Preface

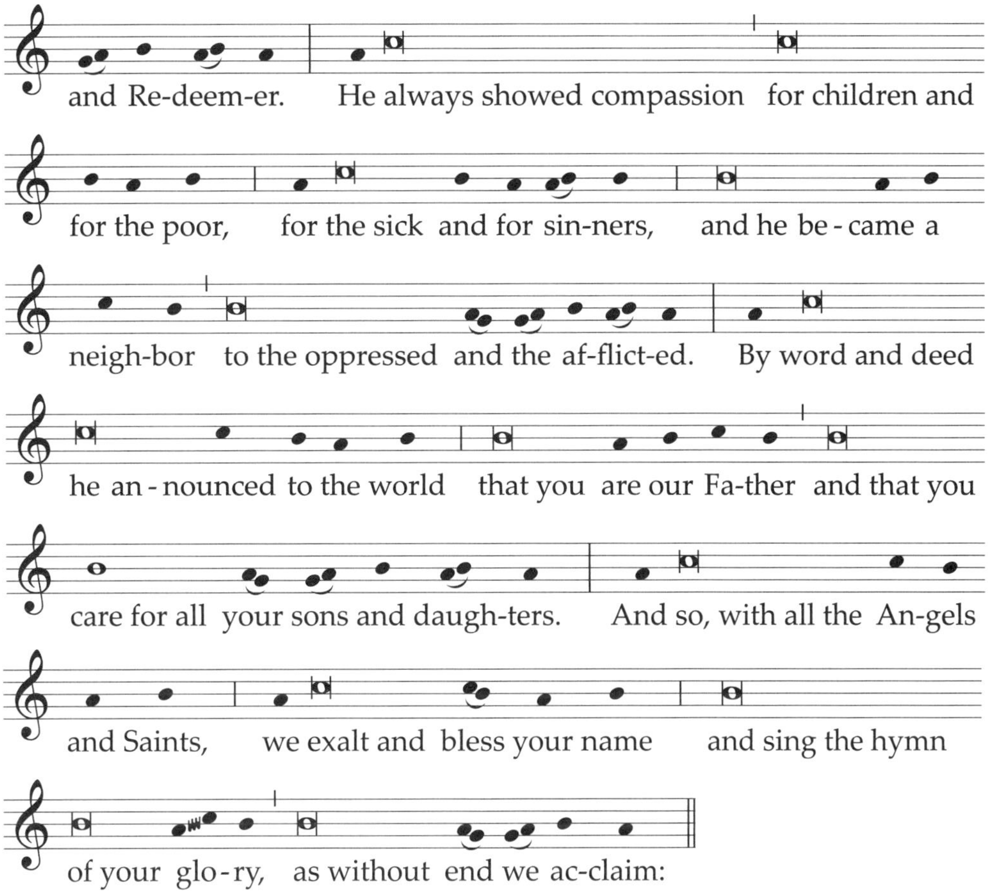
and Re-deem-er. He always showed compassion for children and
for the poor, for the sick and for sin-ners, and he be-came a
neigh-bor to the oppressed and the af-flict-ed. By word and deed
he an-nounced to the world that you are our Fa-ther and that you
care for all your sons and daugh-ters. And so, with all the An-gels
and Saints, we exalt and bless your name and sing the hymn
of your glo-ry, as without end we ac-claim:

PROPER OF SAINTS

FEBRUARY

February 2
The Presentation of the Lord

First Form: The Procession

3.

Or:

6.

Deacon, or if there is no Deacon, the Priest:

Or:

In this latter case, all respond:

7. Antiphon

Lk 2: 29-32

Or:

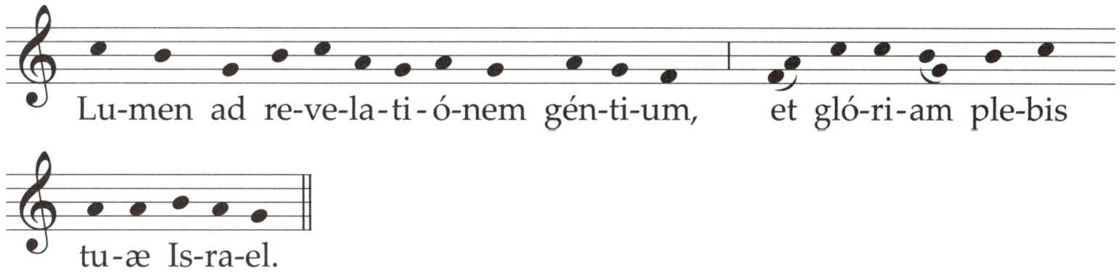

Verse 1:

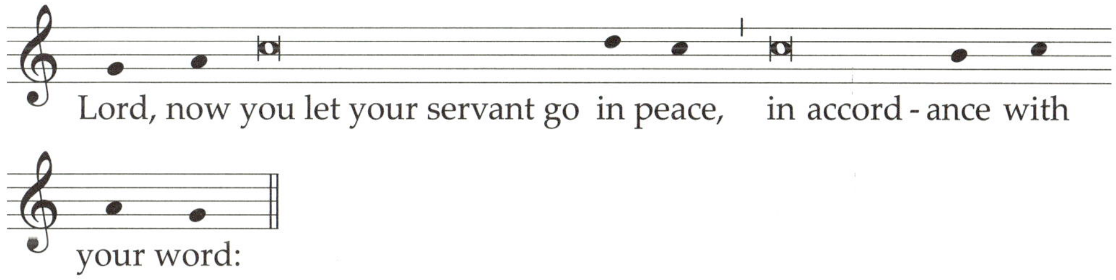

Repeat Antiphon

Verse 2:

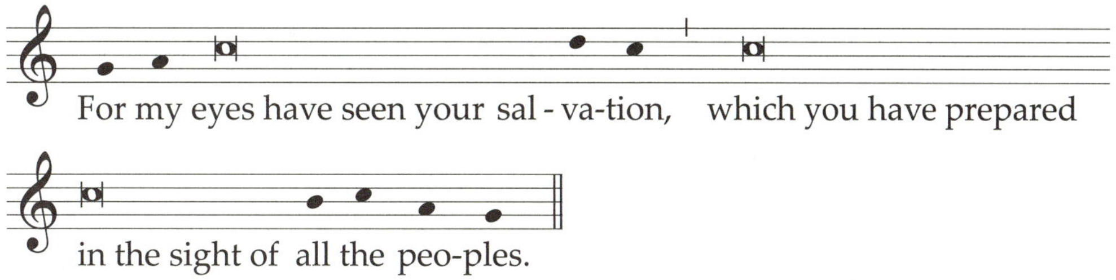

Repeat Antiphon.

Preface: The mystery of the Presentation of the Lord.

MARCH

March 19
Saint Joseph, Spouse of the Blessed Virgin Mary

Preface: The mission of Saint Joseph.

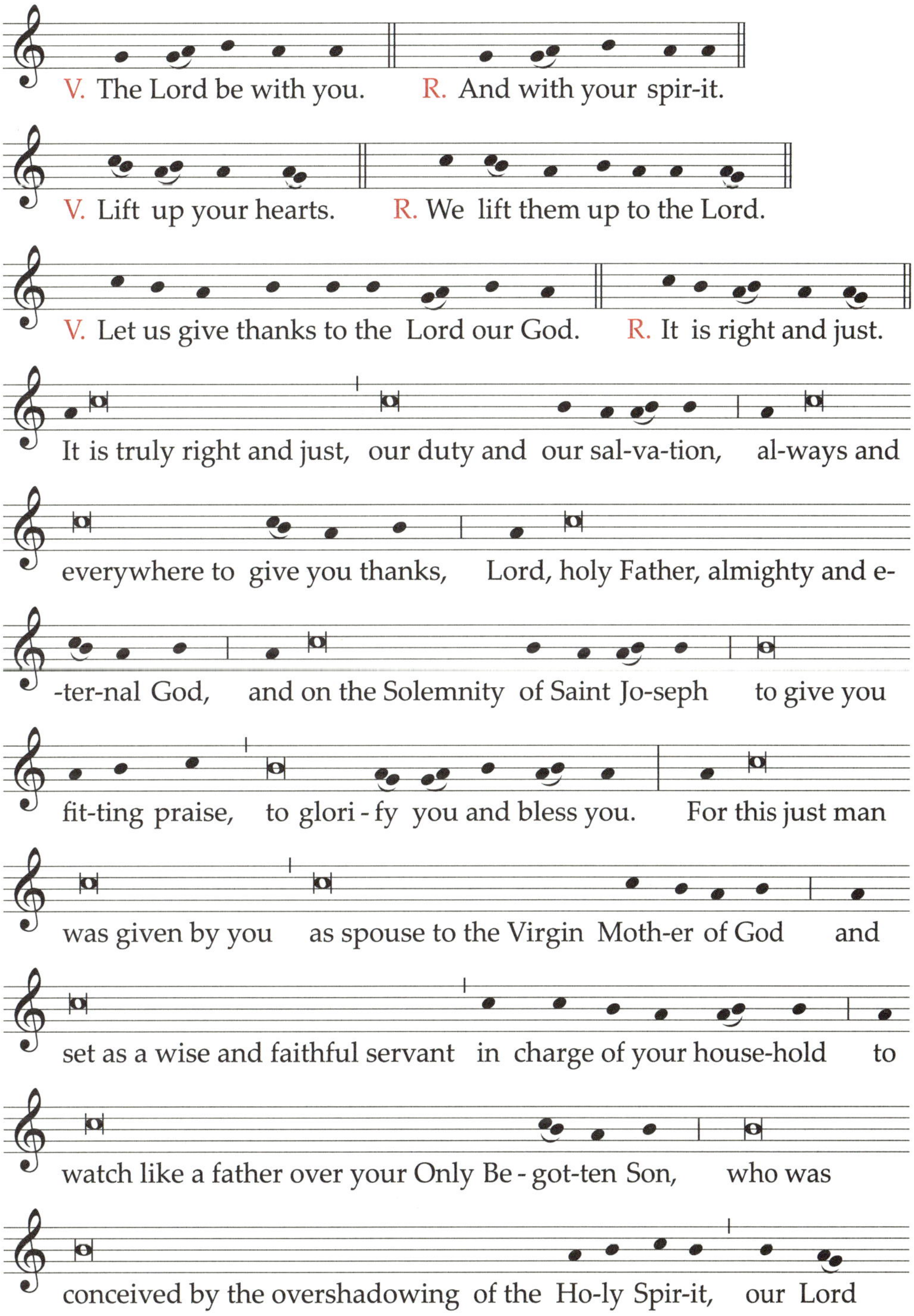

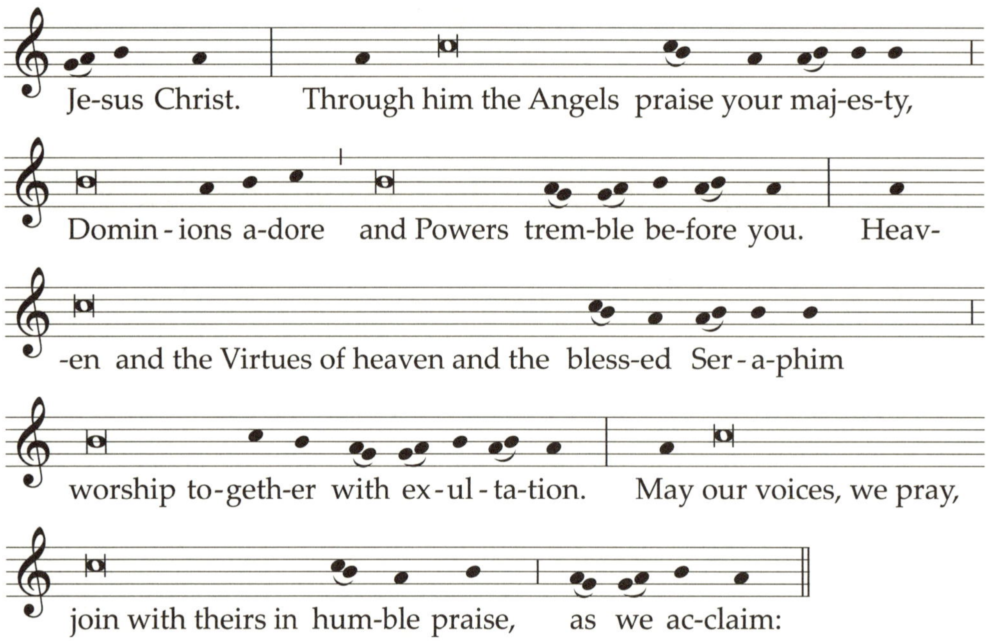

March 25
The Annunciation of the Lord

Preface: The mystery of the Incarnation.

-ter-nal God, through Christ our Lord. For the Virgin Mary heard
with faith that the Christ was to be born among men and for
men's sake by the over - shad-ow-ing pow-er of the Ho-ly Spir-it.
Lov-ingly she bore him in her im - mac-u-late womb, that the prom-
-ises to the children of Israel might come a-bout and the hope of
na-tions be accomplished be-yond all tell-ing. Through him the
host of Angels a - dores your maj-es-ty and re-joic-es in your
pres-ence for ev-er. May our voices, we pray, join with theirs in one
chorus of ex - ult-ant praise, as we ac-claim:

MAY

May 1
Saint Joseph the Worker

Preface: The mission of Saint Joseph.

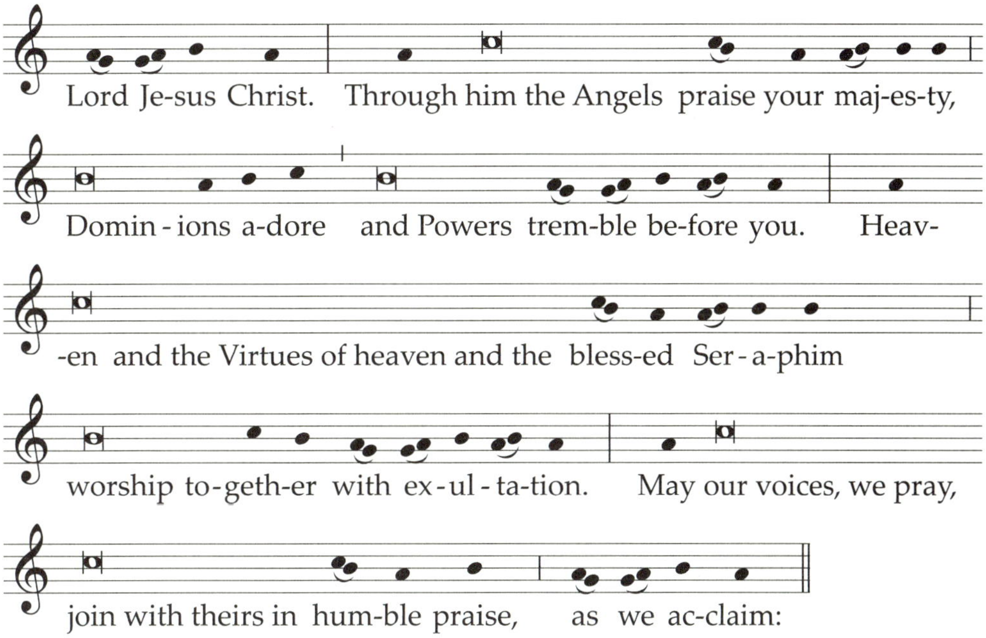

JUNE

June 24
The Nativity of Saint John the Baptist

Preface: The mission of the Precursor.

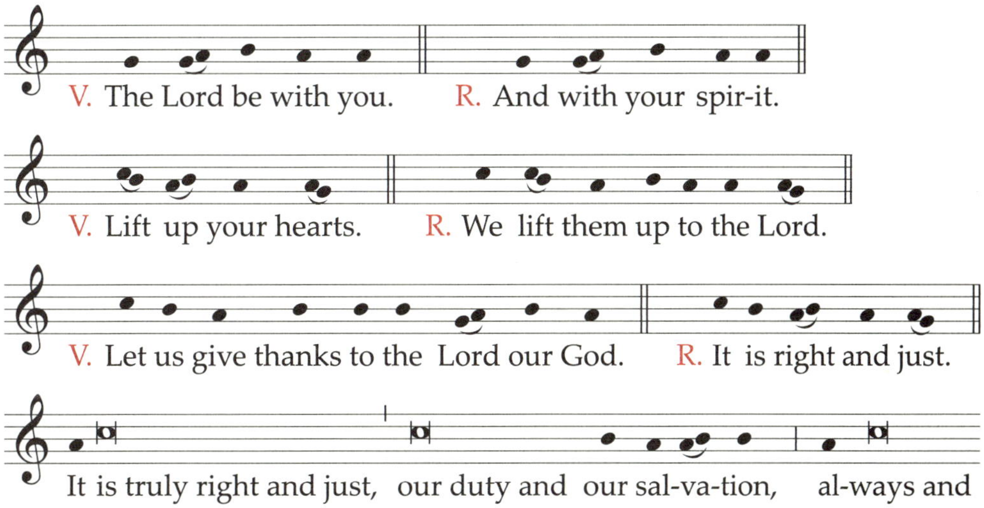

everywhere to give you thanks, Lord, holy Father, almighty and e-
-ter-nal God, through Christ our Lord. In his Precursor, Saint
John the Baptist, we praise your great glo-ry, for you consecrated
him for a sin-gu-lar hon-or among those born of wom-en. His
birth brought great re-joic-ing; even in the womb he leapt for joy
at the coming of hu-man sal-va-tion. He alone of all the proph-ets
pointed out the Lamb of re-demp-tion. And to make holy the flow-
-ing waters, he baptized the very au-thor of Bap-tism and was priv-
-ileged to bear him supreme wit-ness by the shed-ding of his blood.
And so, with the Pow-ers of heav-en, we worship you con-stant-ly
on earth, and before your maj-es-ty without end we ac-claim:

June 29
Saints Peter and Paul, Apostles

Preface: The twofold mission of Peter and Paul in the Church.

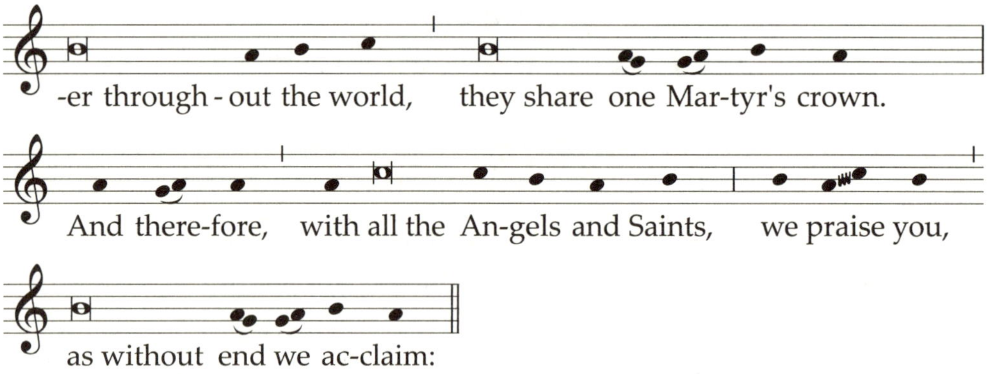

JULY

July 4
Independence Day (USA)

Preface: Independence Day I.

Or:

Preface: Independence Day II.

AUGUST

August 6
The Transfiguration of the Lord

Preface: The mystery of the Transfiguration.

It is truly right and just, our duty and our sal-va-tion, al-ways and
everywhere to give you thanks, Lord, holy Father, almighty and e-
-ter-nal God, through Christ our Lord. For he revealed his glory
in the presence of cho-sen wit-ness-es and filled with the greatest
splendor that bod-i-ly form which he shares with all hu-man-i-ty,
that the scandal of the Cross might be removed from the hearts of
his dis-ci-ples and that he might show how in the Body of the
whole Church is to be ful-filled what so wonderfully shone forth
first in its Head. And so, with the Pow-ers of heav-en, we
worship you con-stant-ly on earth, and before your maj-es-ty
without end we ac-claim:

August 15
The Assumption of the Blessed Virgin Mary

Preface: The Glory of Mary assumed into heaven.

of all life. And so, in company with the choirs of An-gels, we

praise you, and with joy we pro-claim:

SEPTEMBER

September 14
The Exaltation of the Holy Cross

Preface: The victory of the glorious Cross.

V. The Lord be with you. R. And with your spir-it.

V. Lift up your hearts. R. We lift them up to the Lord.

V. Let us give thanks to the Lord our God. R. It is right and just.

It is truly right and just, our duty and our sal-va-tion, al-ways and

everywhere to give you thanks, Lord, holy Father, almighty and e-

-ter-nal God. For you placed the salvation of the human race

on the wood of the Cross, so that, where death a-rose, life might

a-gain spring forth and the evil one, who conquered on a tree,

September 29
Saints Michael, Gabriel, and Raphael, Archangels

Preface: God glorified through the Angels.

NOVEMBER

November 1
All Saints

Preface: The glory of Jerusalem, our mother.

V. Let us give thanks to the Lord our God. R. It is right and just.
It is truly right and just, our duty and our sal-va-tion, al-ways and
everywhere to give you thanks, Lord, holy Father, almighty and e-
-ter-nal God. For today by your gift we celebrate the festival of your
city, the heavenly Jerusa-lem, our moth-er, where the great array
of our broth-ers and sis-ters already gives you e-ter-nal praise.
Towards her, we eagerly hasten as pilgrims ad-vanc-ing by faith,
re-joicing in the glory bestowed upon those exalted members of the
Church through whom you give us, in our frailty, both strength and
good ex-am-ple. And so, we glorify you with the multitude of
Saints and An-gels, as with one voice of praise we ac-claim:

November 9
The Dedication of the Lateran Basilica

Preface: The mystery of the Church, the Bride of Christ and the Temple of the Spirit.

Thanksgiving Day (USA)

Preface: Thanksgiving Day.

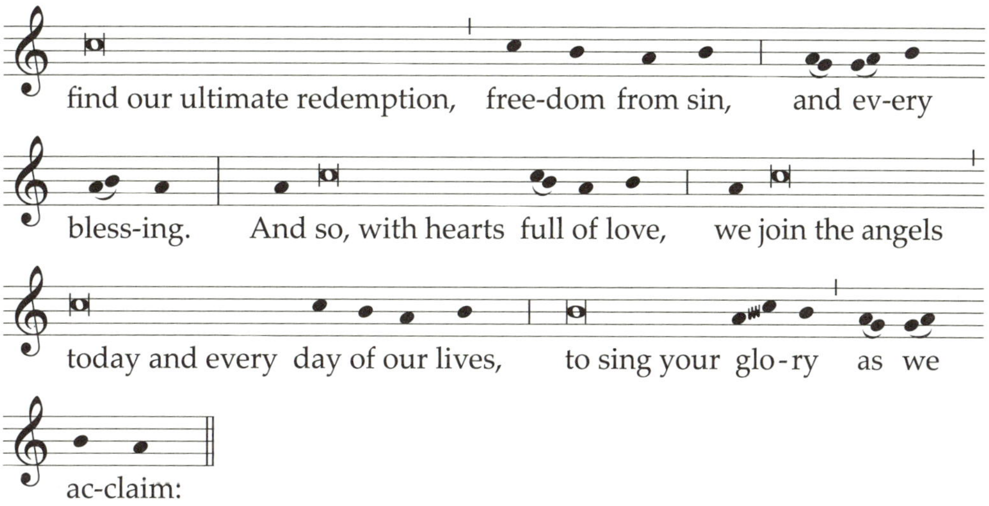

DECEMBER

December 8
The Immaculate Conception of the Blessed Virgin Mary

Preface: The mystery of Mary and the Church.

from all stain of o-rig-i-nal sin, so that in her, endowed with the rich
fullness of your grace, you might prepare a worthy Mother for your
Son and signify the beginning of the Church, his beautiful
Bride with-out spot or wrin-kle. She, the most pure Virgin, was
to bring forth a Son, the in-no-cent Lamb who would wipe a-way
our of-fens-es; you placed her above all others to be for your peo-
-ple an ad-vo-cate of grace and a mod-el of ho-li-ness. And so, in
company with the choirs of An-gels, we praise you, and with joy
we pro-claim:

COMMONS

COMMON OF THE DEDICATION OF A CHURCH

On the Anniversary of the Dedication

I. In the Church that was Dedicated

Preface: The mystery of the Temple of God, which is the Church.

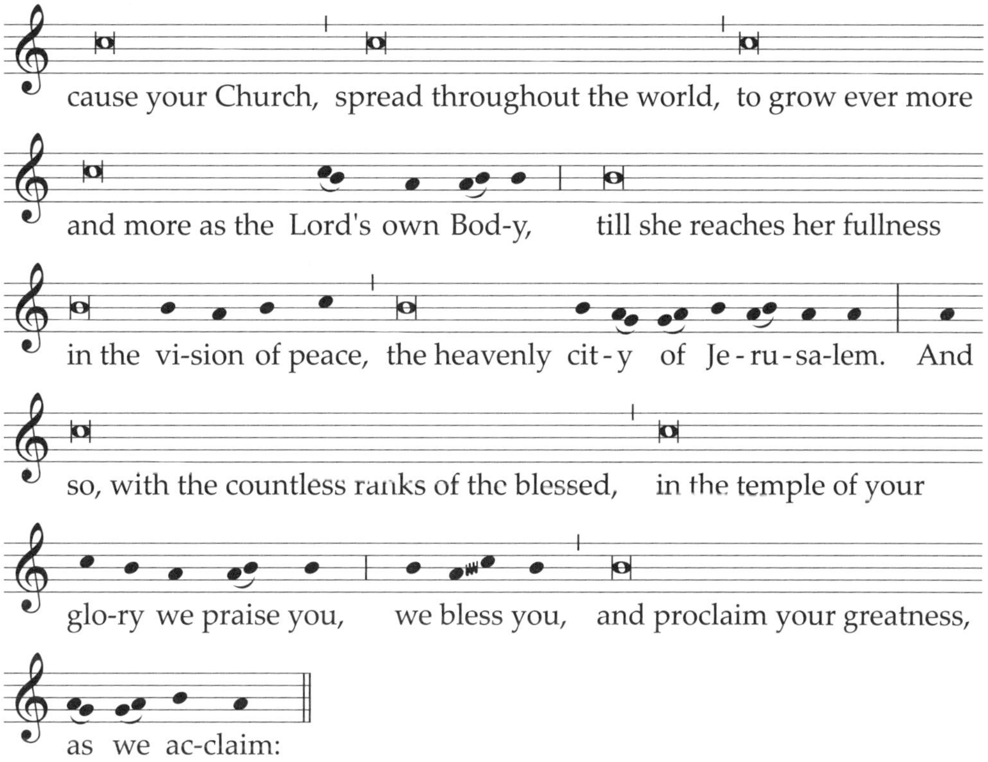
cause your Church, spread throughout the world, to grow ever more
and more as the Lord's own Bod-y, till she reaches her fullness
in the vi-sion of peace, the heavenly cit-y of Je-ru-sa-lem. And
so, with the countless ranks of the blessed, in the temple of your
glo-ry we praise you, we bless you, and proclaim your greatness,
as we ac-claim:

RITUAL MASSES

IV. FOR THE CONFERRAL OF HOLY ORDERS

(For Bishops and Priests, see the Chrism Mass Preface, pp. 76–77)

3. For the Ordination of Deacons

Preface: Christ, source of all ministry in the Church.

V. FOR THE CELEBRATION OF MARRIAGE

A

Preface: The dignity of the marriage covenant.

V. Lift up your hearts. R. We lift them up to the Lord.
V. Let us give thanks to the Lord our God. R. It is right and just.
It is truly right and just, our duty and our sal-va-tion, al-ways and
everywhere to give you thanks, Lord, holy Father, almighty and e-
-ter-nal God. For you have forged the covenant of marriage
as a sweet yoke of har-mo-ny and an unbreakable bond of peace,
so that the chaste and fruitful love of ho-ly Mat-rimony may serve to
increase the children you a-dopt as your own. By your providence
and grace, O Lord, you accomplish the wonder of this two-fold
de-sign: that, while the birth of children brings beauty to the world,
their rebirth in Bap-tism gives increase to the Church, through Christ
our Lord. Through him, with the Angels and all the Saints, we sing
the hymn of your praise, as without end we ac-claim:

B

Preface: The great Sacrament of Matrimony.

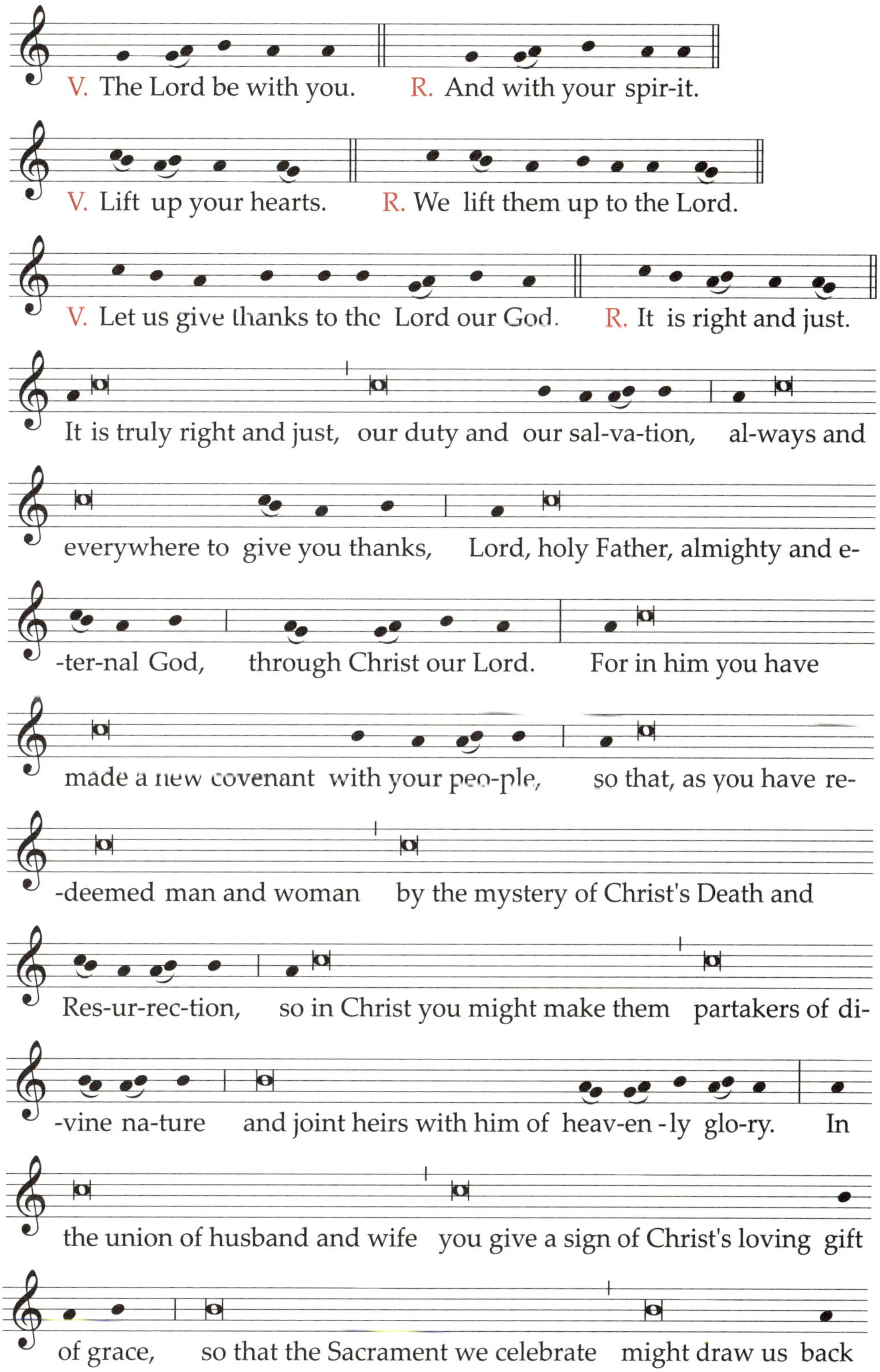

C

Preface: Matrimony as a sign of divine love.

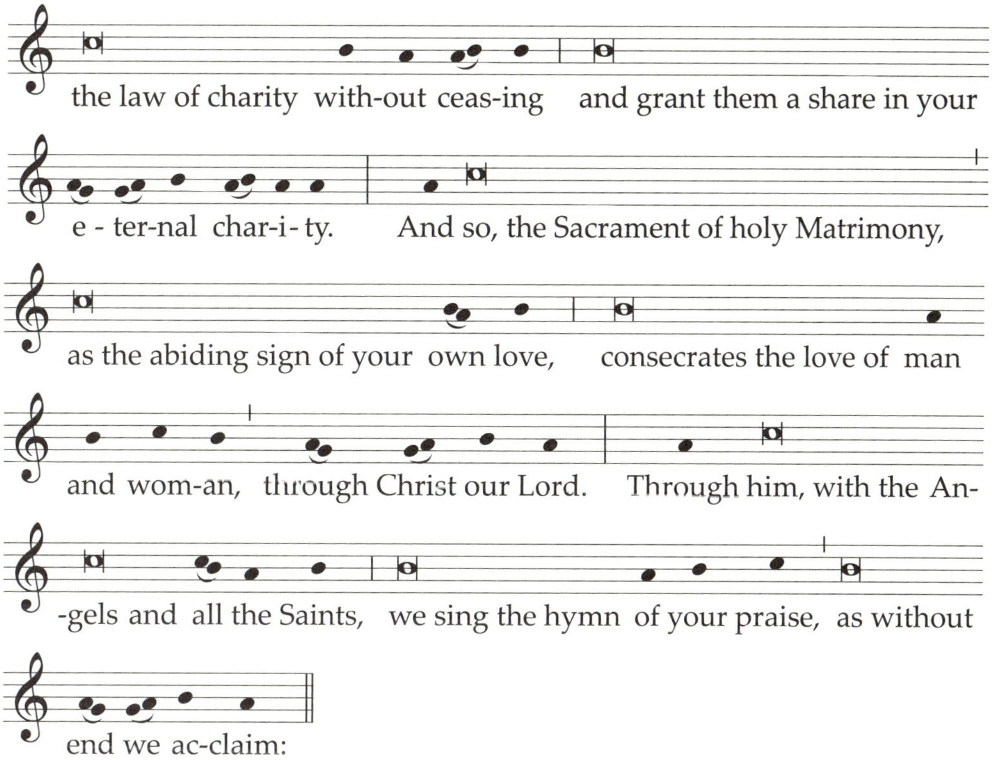

VIII. FOR RELIGIOUS PROFESSION

2. FOR PERPETUAL PROFESSION

Preface: Religious life as service of God through the imitation of Christ.

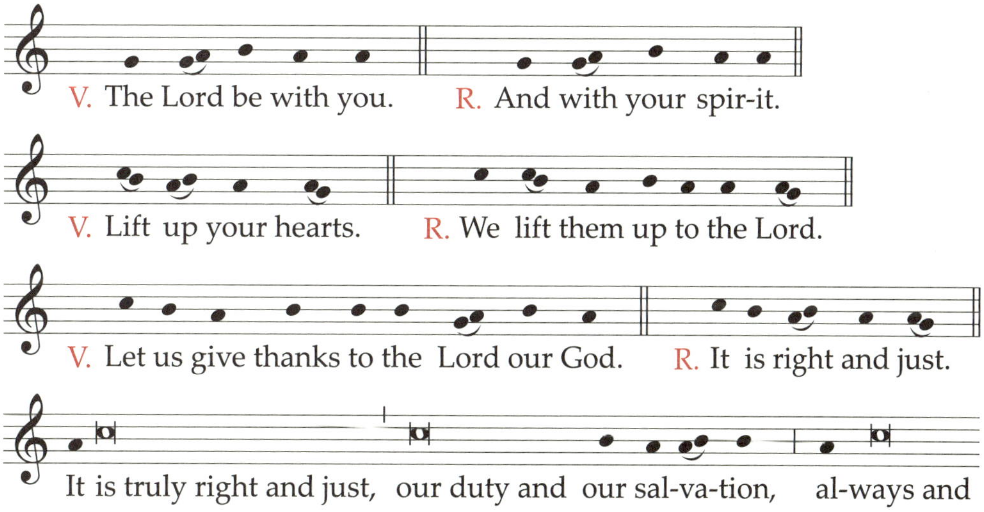

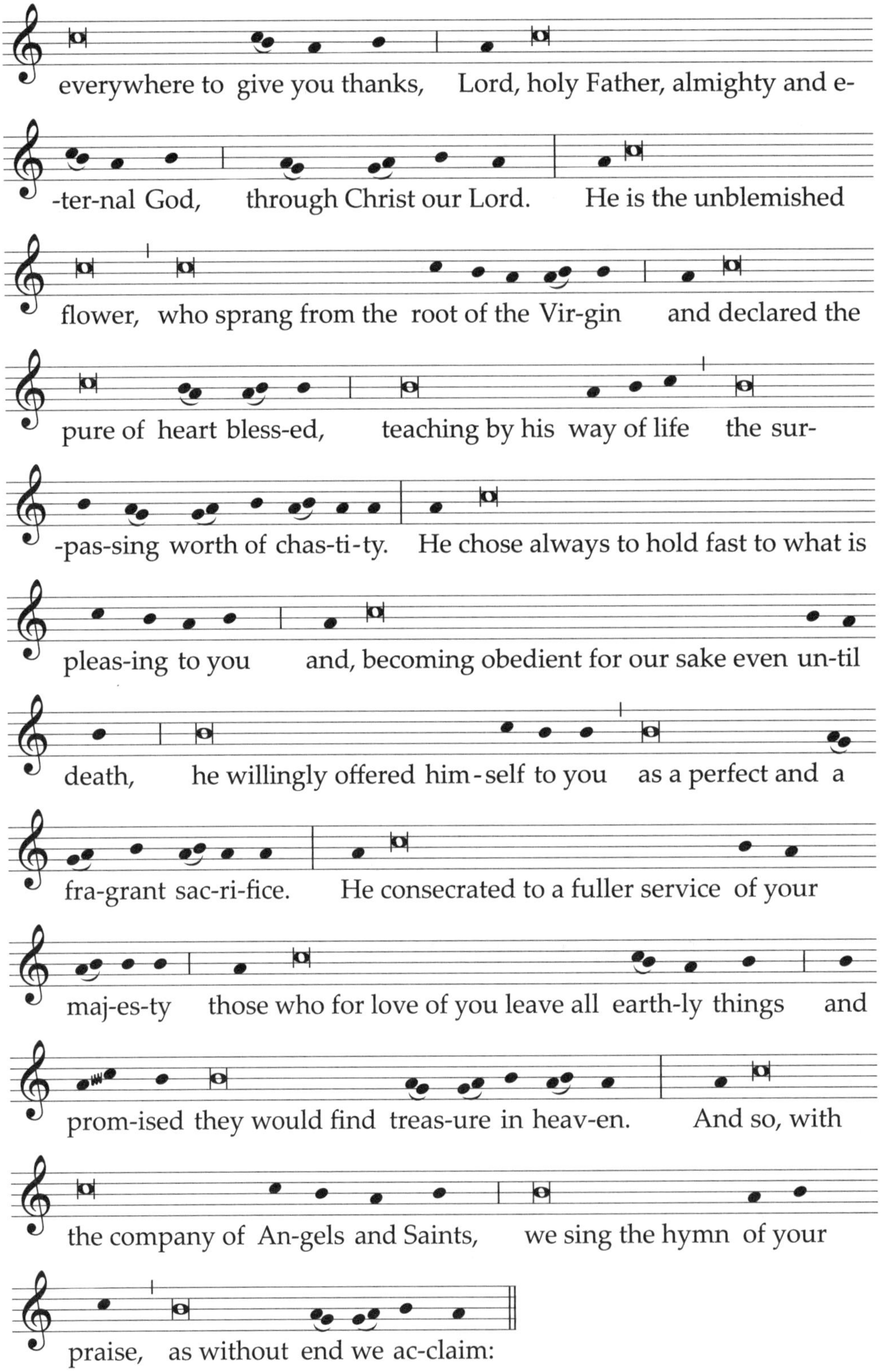
everywhere to give you thanks, Lord, holy Father, almighty and e-
-ter-nal God, through Christ our Lord. He is the unblemished
flower, who sprang from the root of the Vir-gin and declared the
pure of heart bless-ed, teaching by his way of life the sur-
-pas-sing worth of chas-ti-ty. He chose always to hold fast to what is
pleas-ing to you and, becoming obedient for our sake even un-til
death, he willingly offered him-self to you as a perfect and a
fra-grant sac-ri-fice. He consecrated to a fuller service of your
maj-es-ty those who for love of you leave all earth-ly things and
prom-ised they would find treas-ure in heav-en. And so, with
the company of An-gels and Saints, we sing the hymn of your
praise, as without end we ac-claim:

X. FOR THE DEDICATION OF A CHURCH AND AN ALTAR

1. For the Dedication of a Church

Preface: The mystery of God's Temple.

2. For the Dedication of an Altar

Preface: Christ himself is the altar.

It is truly right and just, our duty and our sal-va-tion, al-ways and
everywhere to give you thanks, Lord, holy Father, almighty and e-
-ter-nal God, through Christ our Lord. Hav-ing become both the
true Priest and the true ob-la-tion, he has taught us to celebrate for
ever the memorial of the Sac-ri-fice that he himself of-fered to you
on the al-tar of the Cross. There-fore, Lord, your people have
raised this al-tar, which we dedicate to you with joy-ful praise.
Tru-ly this is an ex-alt-ed place, where the Sacrifice of Christ is ever
of-fered in mys-ter-y, where perfect praise is ren-dered to you
and redemption flows forth for us. Here is prepared the table of
the Lord, where your children, fed by the Bod-y of Christ, are gath-
-ered into the one, the ho-ly Church. Here the faithful drink of
your Spirit from the streams that flow from Christ, the spir-it-ual

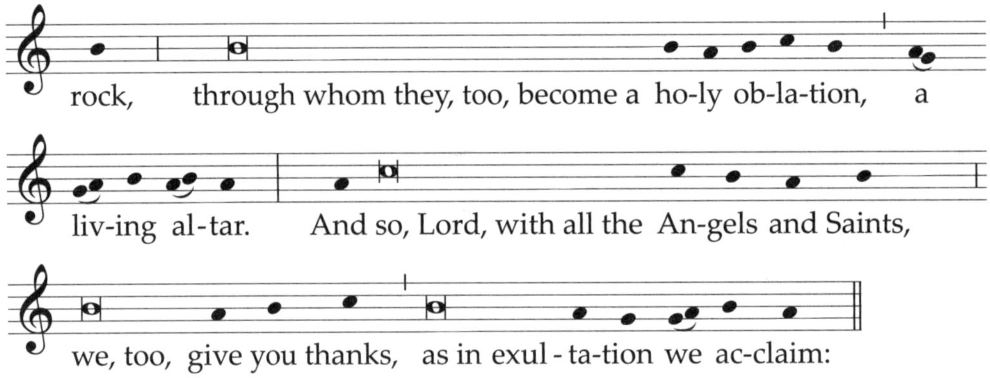
rock, through whom they, too, become a ho-ly ob-la-tion, a
liv-ing al-tar. And so, Lord, with all the An-gels and Saints,
we, too, give you thanks, as in exul - ta-tion we ac-claim:

MASSES AND PRAYERS FOR VARIOUS NEEDS AND OCCASIONS

I. FOR HOLY CHURCH

17. For The Unity of Christians

Preface: The unity of the Body of Christ, which is the Church.

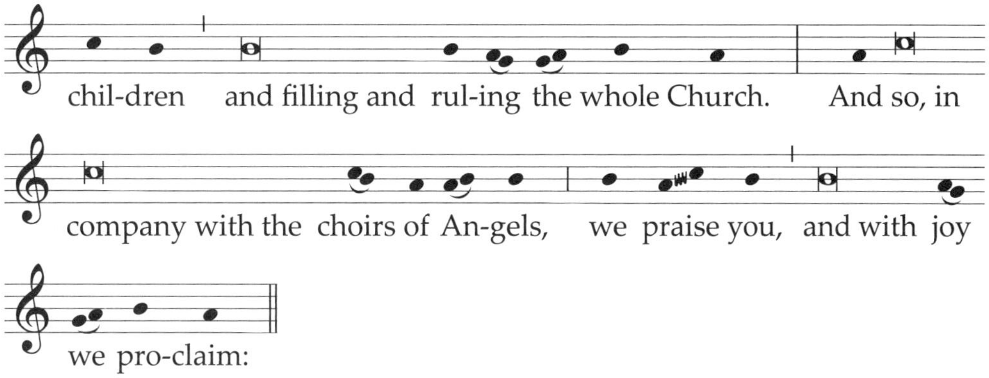
chil-dren and filling and rul-ing the whole Church. And so, in
company with the choirs of An-gels, we praise you, and with joy
we pro-claim:

VOTIVE MASSES

9. The Holy Spirit

A

Preface I of the Holy Spirit: The sending of the Spirit by the Lord upon the Church.

B

Preface II of the Holy Spirit: The action of the Spirit in the Church.

10. The Blessed Virgin Mary

B

Our Lady, Mother of the Church

Preface: Mary, Model and Mother of the Church.

13. Saint Joseph

Preface: The mission of Saint Joseph.

It is truly right and just, our duty and our sal-va-tion, al-ways and
everywhere to give you thanks, Lord, holy Father, almighty and e-
-ter-nal God, and in honor - ing Saint Jo-seph to give you fit-ting
praise, to glori - fy you and bless you. For this just man was given
by you as spouse to the Virgin Moth-er of God and set as a wise
and faithful servant in charge of your house-hold to watch like a
father over your Only Be - got-ten Son, who was conceived by the
overshadowing of the Ho-ly Spir-it, our Lord Je-sus Christ.
Through him the Angels praise your maj-es-ty, Domin - ions a-dore
and Powers trem-ble be-fore you. Heav-en and the Virtues of
heaven and the bless-ed Ser - a-phim worship to-geth-er with
ex - ul - ta-tion. May our voices, we pray, join with theirs in hum-ble
praise, as we ac-claim:

APPENDICES

APPENDIX I
VARIOUS CHANTS FOR THE ORDER OF MASS

The Introductory Rites
(Simple Tone)

Greeting

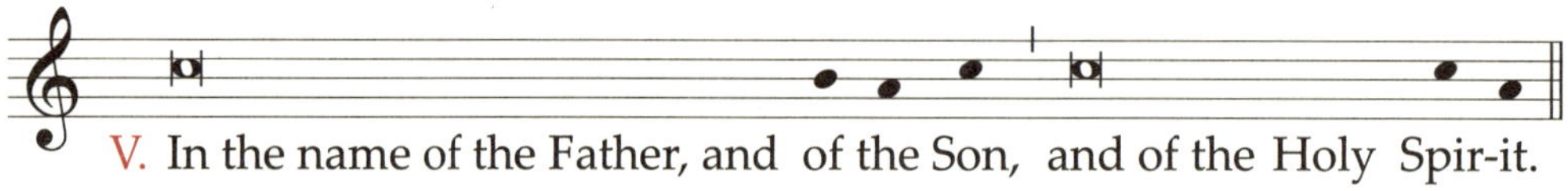

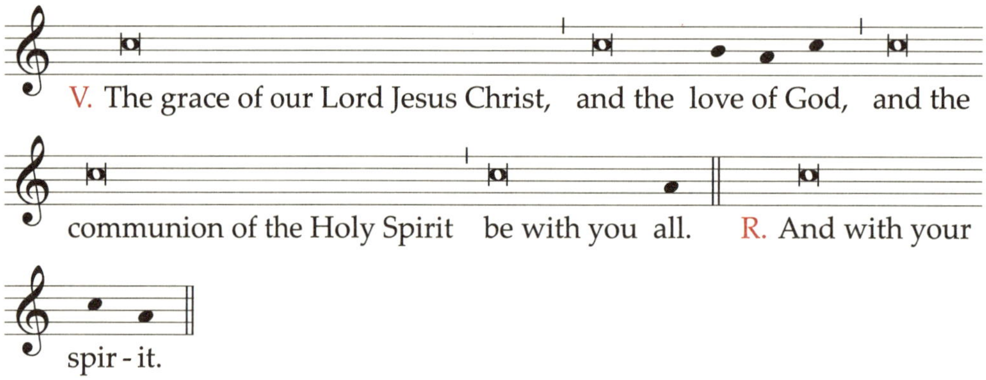

Or:

Or:

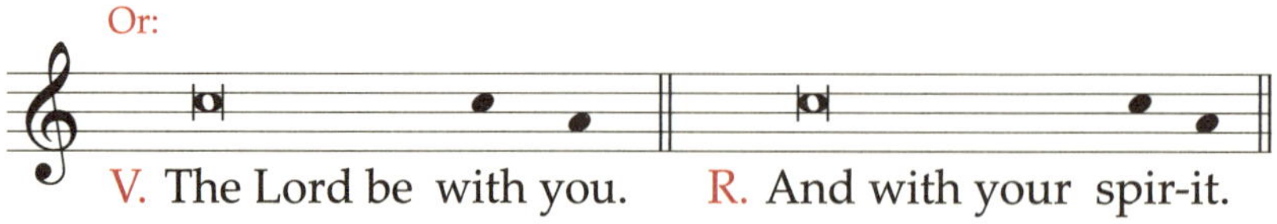

Greeting at a Pontifical Mass:

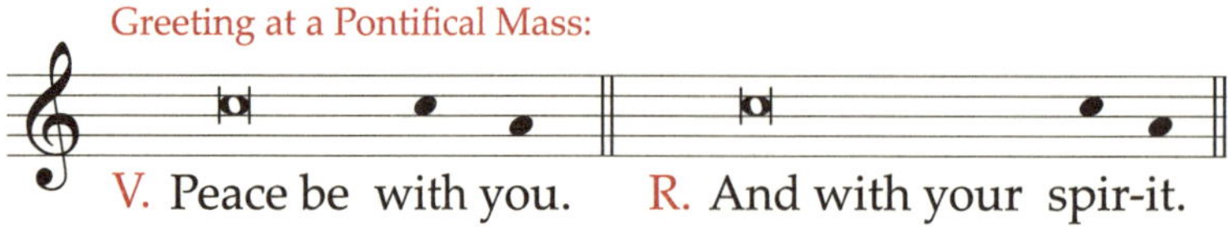

Penitential Act

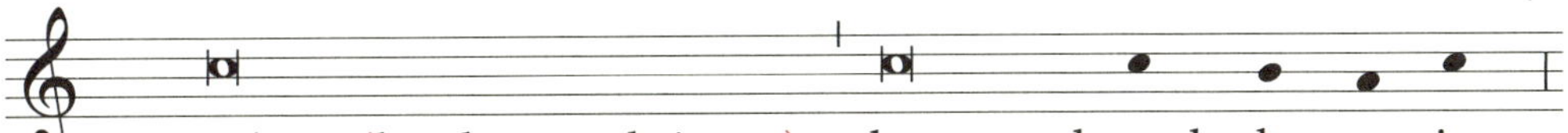

V. Brethren (brothers and sisters), let us ac - knowl-edge our sins,

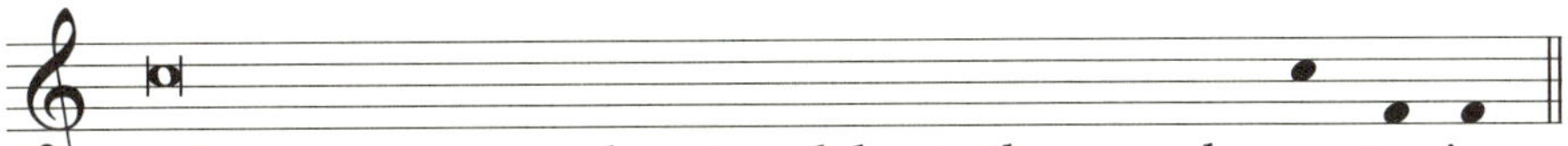

and so prepare ourselves to celebrate the sacred mys-ter-ies.

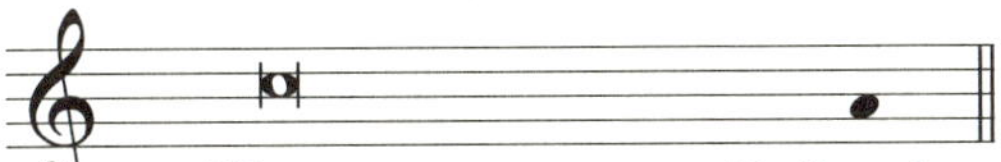

V. Have mercy on us, O Lord.

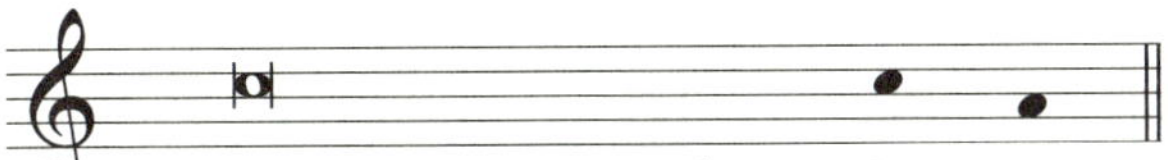

R. For we have sinned a - gainst you.

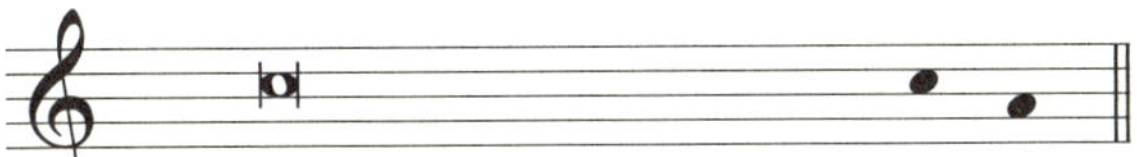

V. Show us, O Lord, your mer-cy.

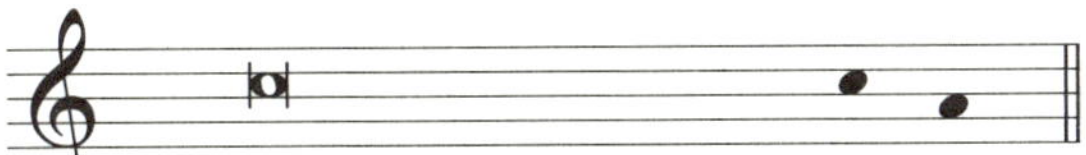

R. And grant us your sal - va-tion.

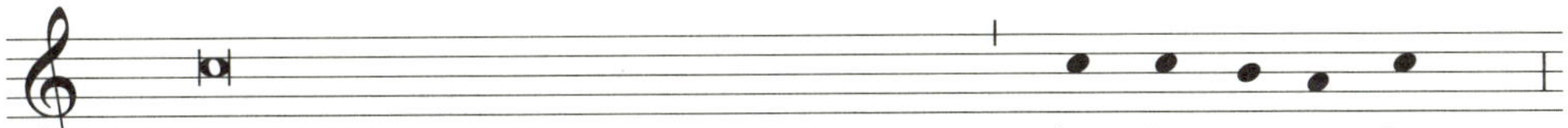

V. May almighty God have mercy on us, for-give us our sins,

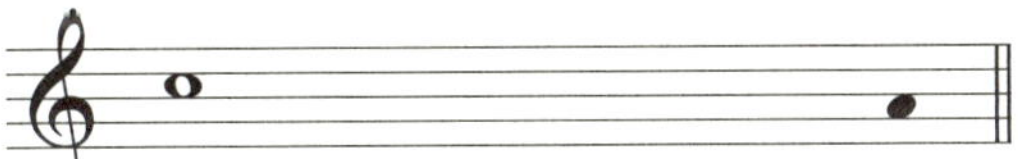

and bring us to everlasting life.

R. A-men.

Or:

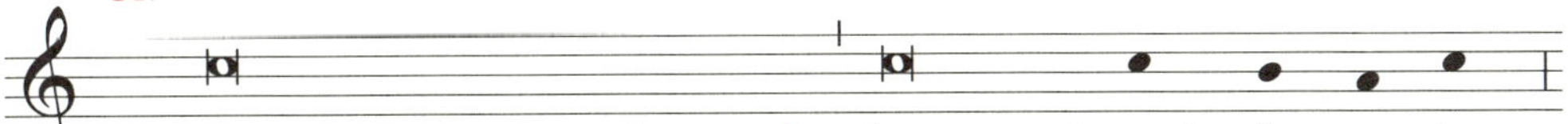

V. Brethren (brothers and sisters), let us ac - knowl-edge our sins,

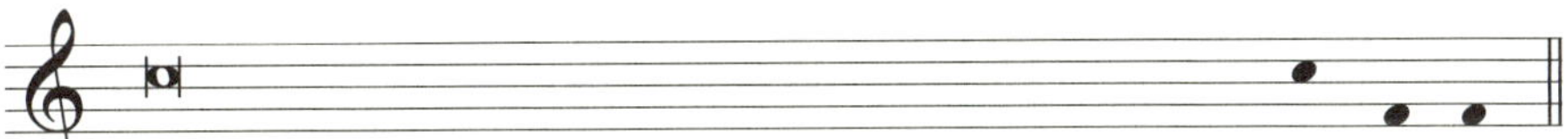

and so prepare ourselves to celebrate the sacred mys-ter-ies.

V. You were sent to heal the con - trite of heart: Lord, have mer-cy.

R. Lord, have mer-cy.

V. You came to call sin-ners: Christ, have mer-cy.

R. Christ, have mer-cy.

V. You are seated at the right hand of the Father to in-ter-cede for us:

Lord, have mer-cy.

R. Lord, have mer-cy.

V. May almighty God have mercy on us, for-give us our sins,

and bring us to everlasting life.

R. A-men.

The Concluding Rites

Blessing

V. The Lord be with you. R. And with your spir-it.

V. May al-might-y God bless you, the Father, and the Son, ✠

and the Holy Spir-it. R. A-men.

Pontifical Blessing

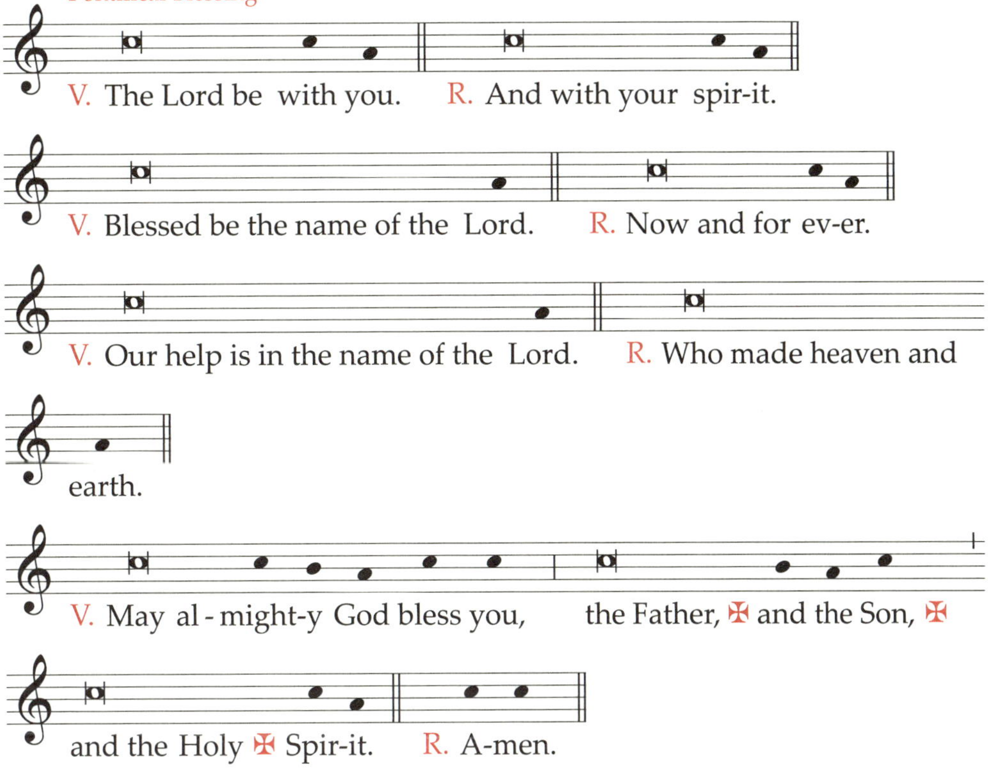

Dismissal

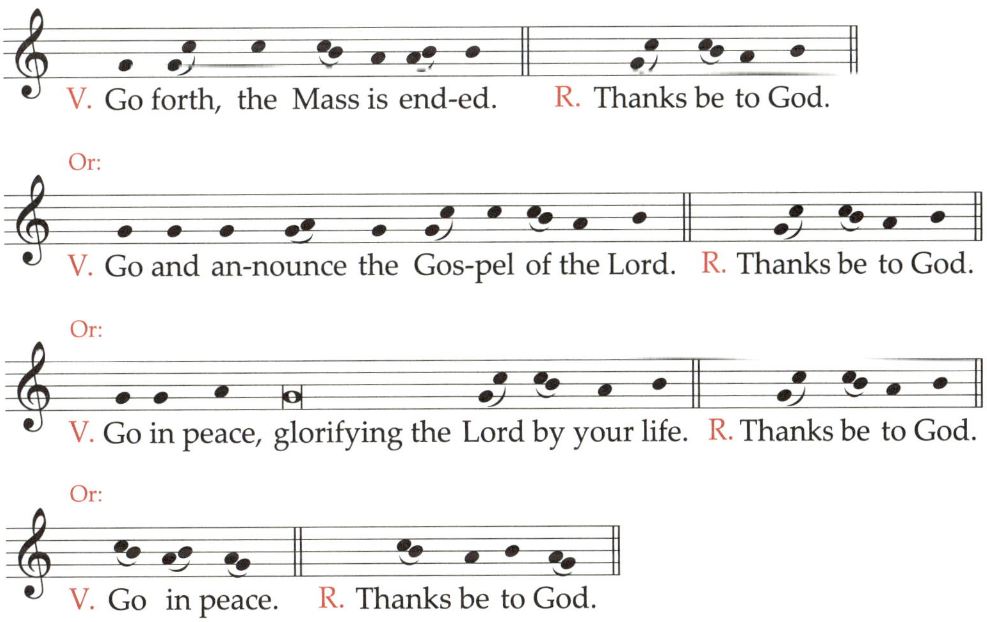

Tones for the Presidential Prayers

Solemn Tone

All the presidential prayers in the Missal (Collects, Prayers over the Offerings, Prayers after Communion) may be pointed for use with the solemn tone according to the following formula. The reciting tone is preceded by one "G" (before ascending to "A"), including after the Flex. At every cadence, whether a Flex or a Full Stop, the grave (\) indicates where to descend to "G," and the acute (/) indicates where to ascend back to "A." The grave at the Flex may or may not fall on the text accent, depending on the textual accent pattern. The grave at the Full Stop is always applied to the second to last syllable before the final accent, without respect to the accentuation of that syllable. When the Eucharistic Prayer is sung according to the tone in the Missal, the Prayer over the Offerings must be sung according to the solemn tone.

INVITATION

RECITING TONE FLEX FULL STOP

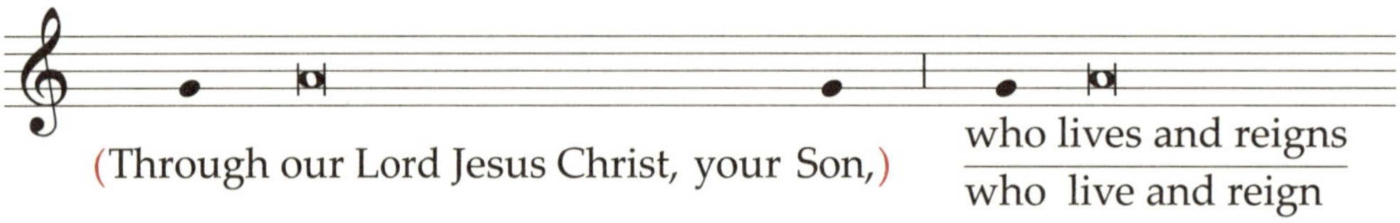

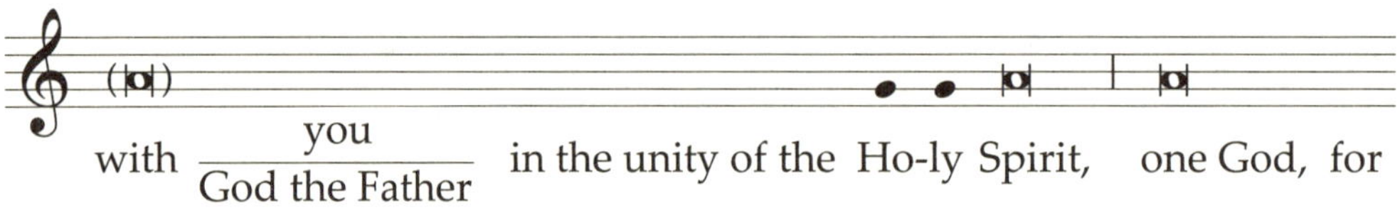

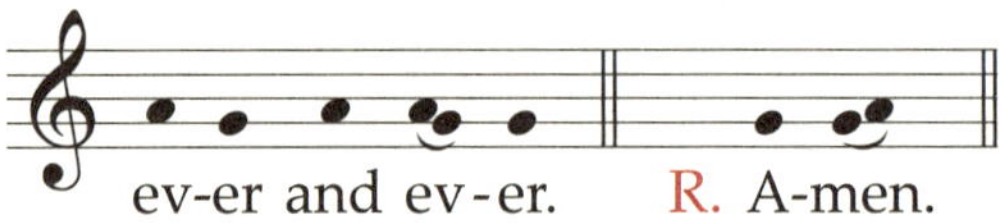

After the other Prayers

Or:

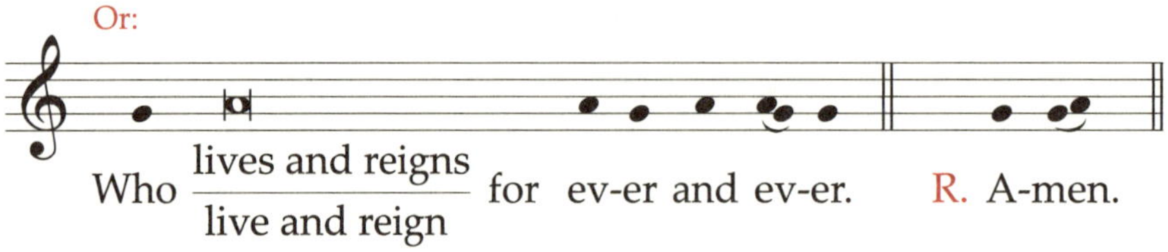

Collect (First Sunday of Advent)

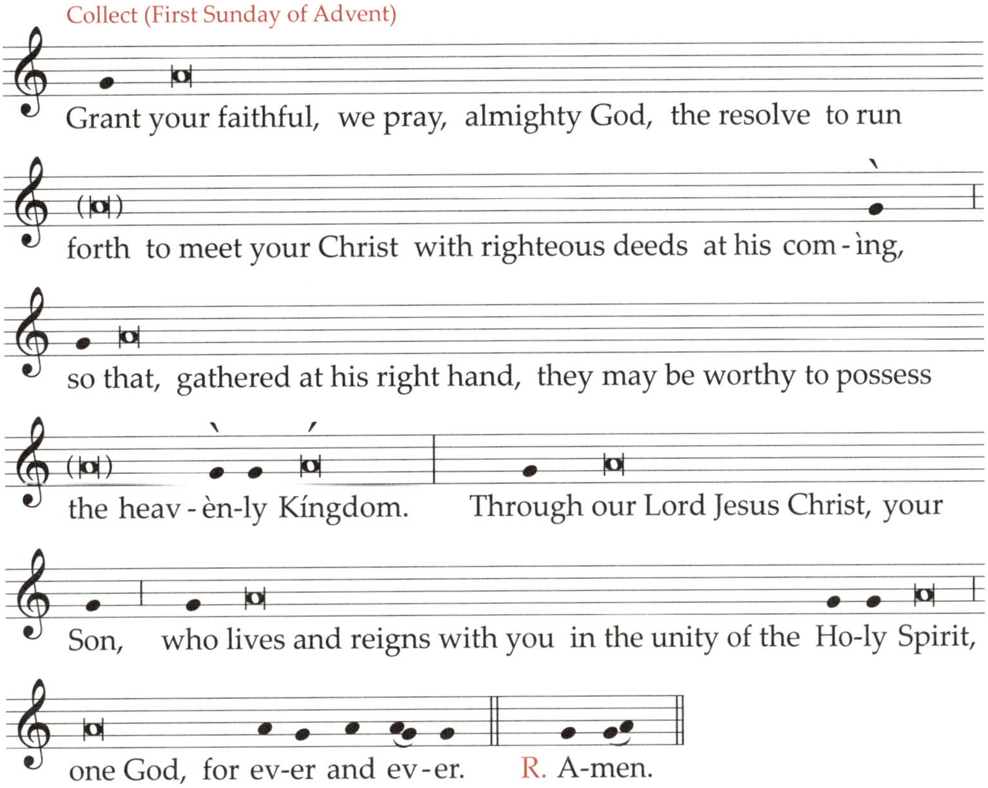

Prayer over the Offerings (The Epiphany of the Lord, The Mass during the Day)

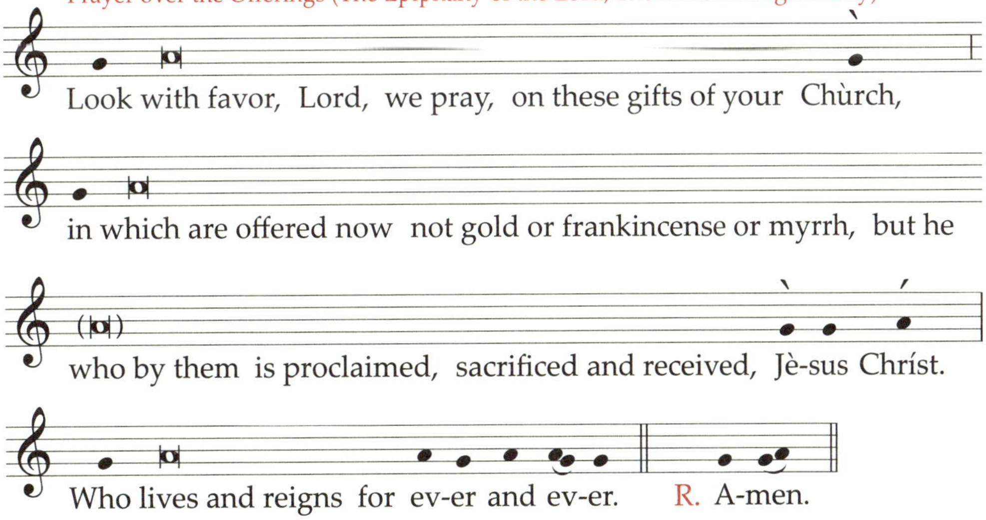

Simple Tone

The presidential prayers (Collects, Prayers over the Offerings, Prayers after Communion) may also be sung according to the simple tone, which follows.

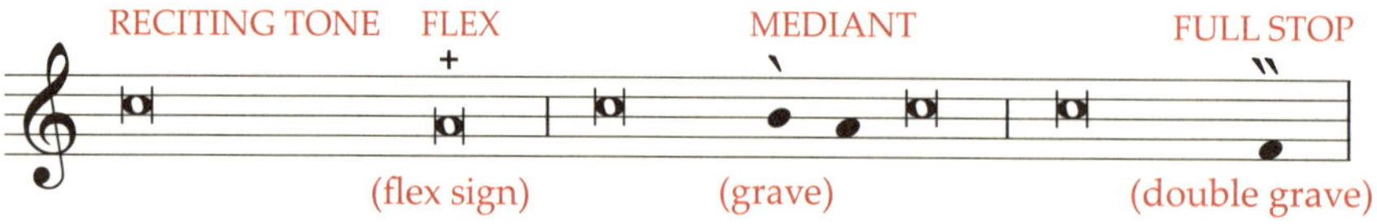

For the Flex and Full Stop, the pointing depends upon where the accent falls. When the final syllable is accented, a flex (+) sign or double grave (\\) is to be given to it. When the final syllable is not accented, this syllable is sung on the Reciting Tone and the flex sign or double grave is to be placed so as to indicate where one descends for the non-accented syllable(s). Examples:

For the Mediant cadence, the grave (\) is placed two syllables before the final accent, without respect to the accentuation of these two syllables.

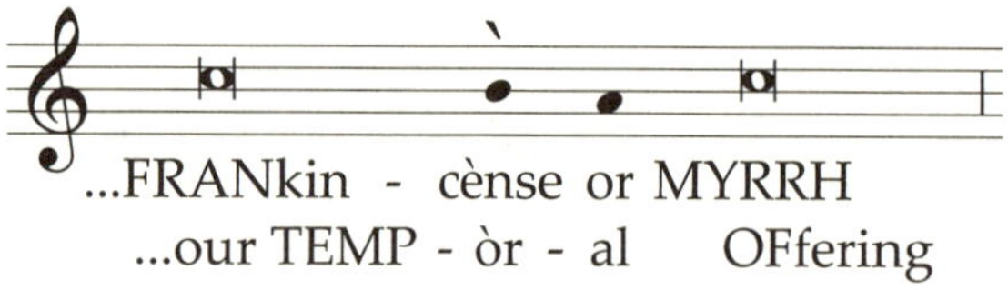

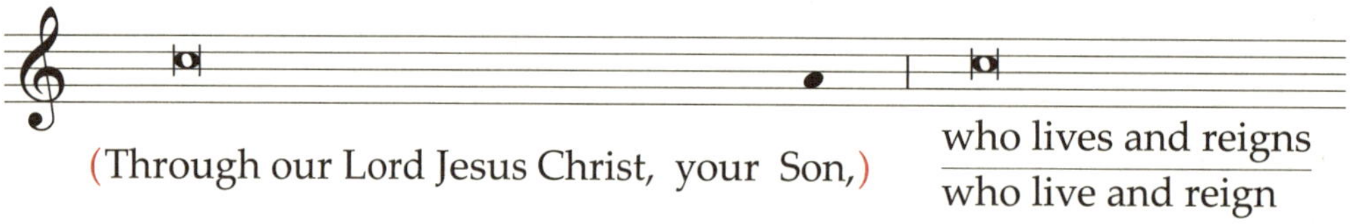

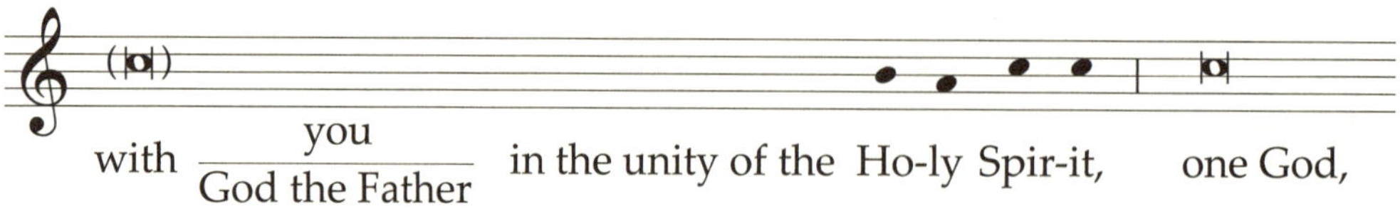

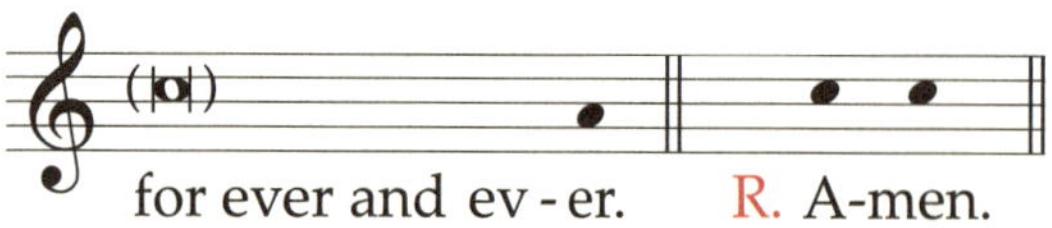

After the other Prayers

Or:

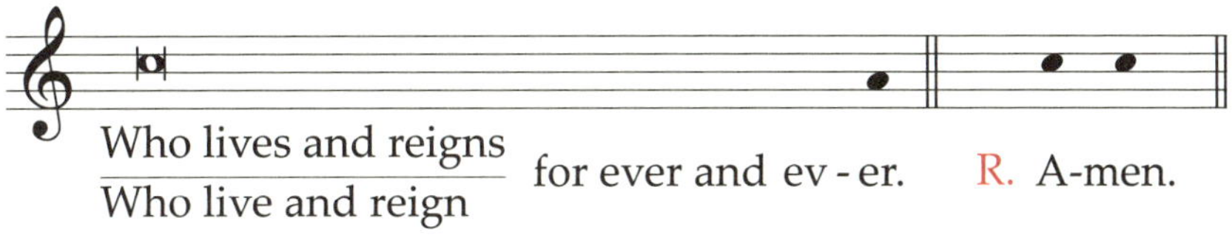

Collect (First Sunday of Advent)

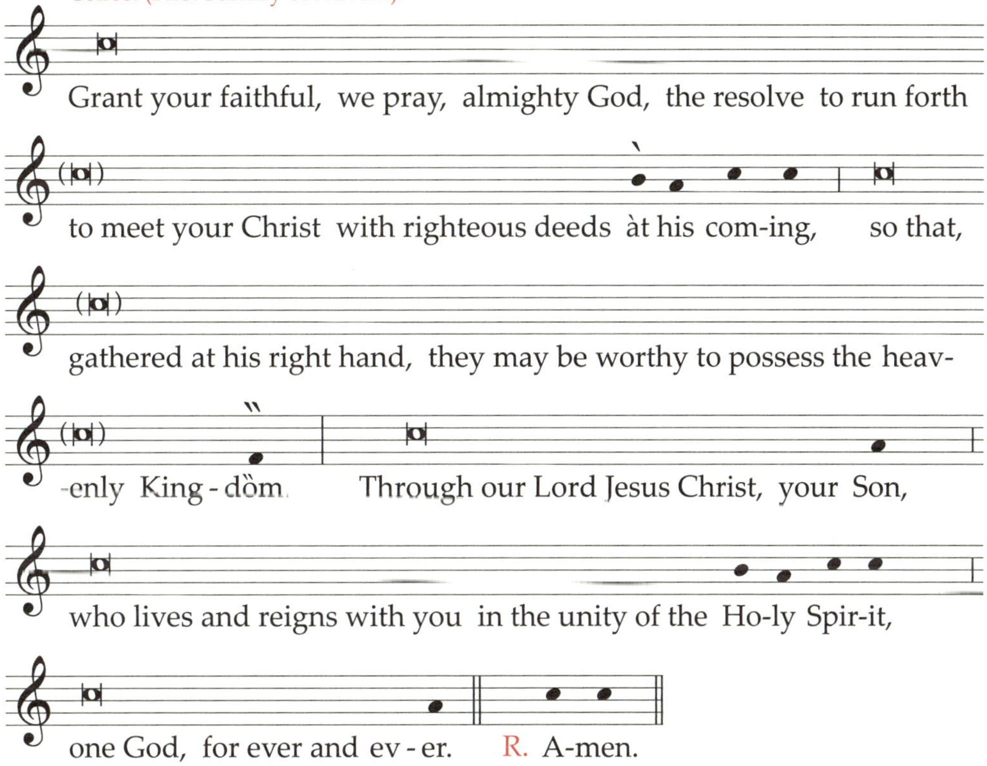

Prayer over the Offerings (The First Sunday of Advent)

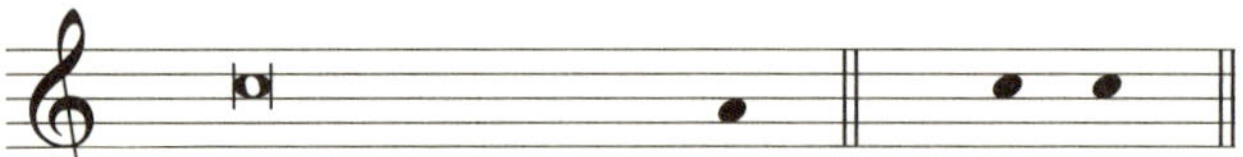

Through Christ our Lord. R. A-men.

Prayer over the Offerings (The Epiphany of the Lord, The Mass during the Day)

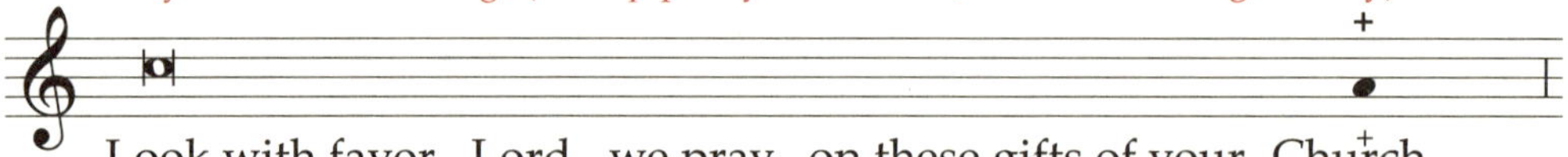

Look with favor, Lord, we pray, on these gifts of your Church,

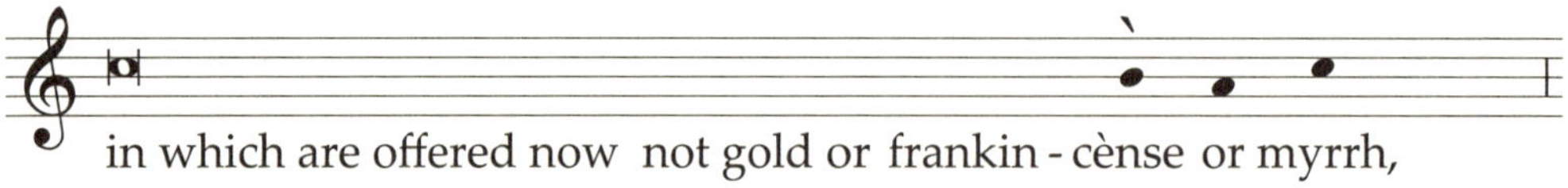

in which are offered now not gold or frankin - cènse or myrrh,

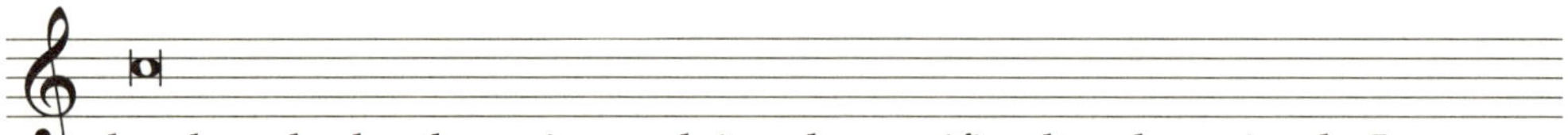

but he who by them is proclaimed, sacrificed and received, Jesus

Christ. Who lives and reigns for ever and ev - er. R. A-men.

Tones for the Readings

I. Old Testament and Acts of the Apostles

INTRODUCTION

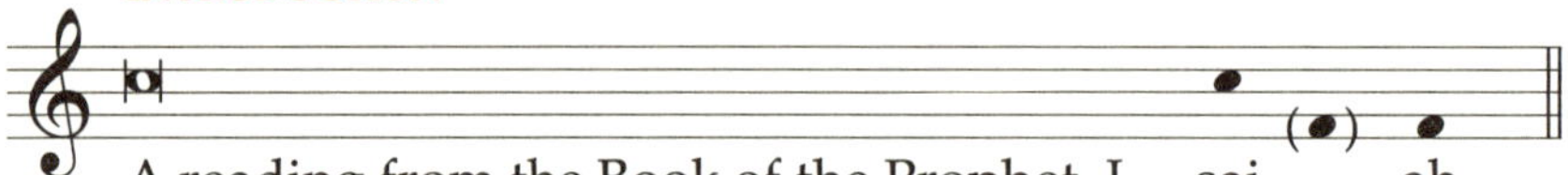

A reading from the Book of the Prophet I - sai - ah.
A reading from the Book of the Prophet E - zek - i - el.
A reading from the first/second Book of Kings.
A reading from the Book of Prov - erbs.
A reading from the Book of Ex - o - dus.
A reading from the Book of Wis - dom.
A reading from the Acts of the A - pos - tles.

RECITING TONE — FLEX — FULL STOP

accent on last syllable — *accent not on last syllable* — *accent on last syllable* — *accent not on last syllable*

QUESTION

CONCLUSION

ACCLAMATION

The flex is used at the end of major clauses within a sentence. In short sentences it may be omitted, and in long sentences it may be used more than once. For the flex, one leaves the reciting tone either on the last syllable or an earlier syllable, as the accentuation demands. The flex should not be used to introduce a question. The full stop is used at the end of every sentence. The question formula is used for all questions, except when the question occurs at the end of a reading. In the question formula, one leaves the reciting tone two syllables before the last accent. In long questions, the ending is used only for the last clause of the question, with the reciting tone for the first clause.

First Reading for the First Sunday of Advent, Year B (NAB)

Isaiah 63:16b-17, 19b; 64:2-7

the heavens and come down, with the mountains quaking be - fóre
you, while you wrought awesome deeds we could not hope for,
such as they had not heard of from of óld. No ear has ever heard,
no eye ever seen, any God but you doing such deeds for those who
wáit for him. Would that you might meet us doing ríght, that we
were mindful of you in our wáys! Behold, you are angry, and
we are sín-ful; all of us have become like unclean people, all our
good deeds are like polluted rágs; we have all withered like leaves,
and our guilt carries us away like the wínd. There is none who
calls upon your name, who rouses himself to clíng to you; for you
have hidden your face from us and have delivered us up to our gúilt.
Yet, O LORD, you are our fá-ther; we are the clay and you the
potter: we are all the work of your hánds.

II. The Epistle and the Book of Revelation

INTRODUCTION

A reading from the [first / second] Letter of the blessed A-pos-tle Paul

to the Co-rin-thi-ans.
to the Ga-la-tians.
to the Phi-lip-pi-ans
to the E-phe-sians.
to the Thes-sa-lo-ni-ans.
to the Ro-mans.
to the He-brews.
to ____ Ti-tus.
to ____ Ti-mo-thy.

Or:

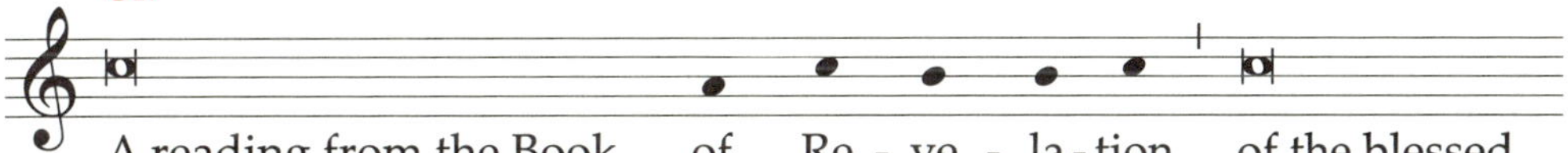

A reading from the Book of Re-ve-la-tion of the blessed
A reading [from the first / from the sec-ond] Let-ter of the blessed

A-pos__ tle John.
A-pos-tle Pe-ter.
A-pos__ tle James.

Each sentence (or group of phrases) in the body of the reading takes the following three elements:

RECITING TONE MEDIANT FULL STOP

The mediant is used at the end of major clauses within a sentence. In short sentences it may be omitted, and in long sentences it may be used more than once. For the mediant, one always leaves the reciting tone three syllables before the last accent, and then completes the line as indicated for last accent on the final syllable or last accent not on the final syllable. The mediant should not be used to introduce a question. The full stop is used at the end of every sentence, with the formula applied as indicated for the various combinations and penultimate accent and last accent. The question formula is used for all questions, except when the question occurs at the end of a reading. In the question formula, one leaves the reciting tone two syllables before the last accent. In long questions, the ending is used only for the last clause of the question, with the reciting tone for the first clause. The conclusion with its two elements is used for the last two lines of the reading. For these two elements, one leaves the reciting tone one syllable before the last accent and then on the last accent.

The Mediant and the Full Stop are pointed according to the following accent patterns.

MEDIANT ACCENT PATTERNS

When the last accent is on the final syllable:

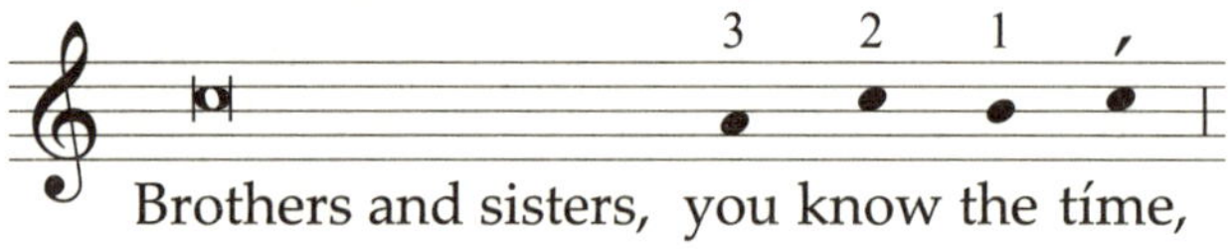

When the last accent does not fall on the final syllable:

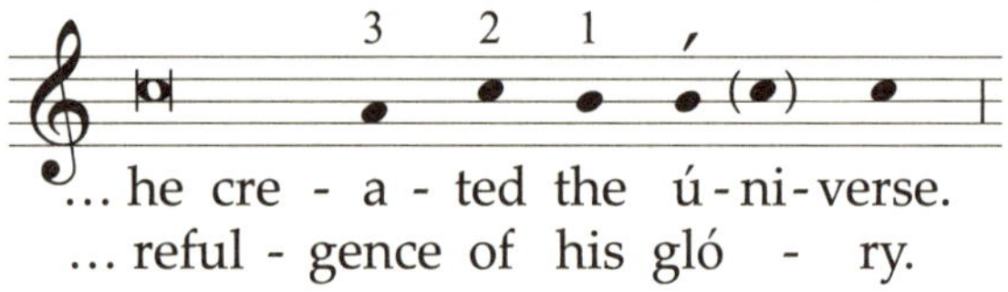

FULL STOP ACCENT PATTERNS

When the last accent is on the final syllable:

Penultimate accent followed by one unaccented syllable: ... ab-sólved__ from sín.
Penultimate accent followed by two unaccented syllables: ... the wón-ders of Gód.
Penultimate accent followed by three unaccented syllables: ... the wón-ders of his lóve.

When the last accent does not fall on the final syllable:

QUESTIONS

Questions are pointed with two syllables before the final accent:

CONCLUSION

The end of the reading is pointed with two elements as follows.

Leave the reciting tone one syllable before the last accent:

Leave the reciting tone on the last accent:

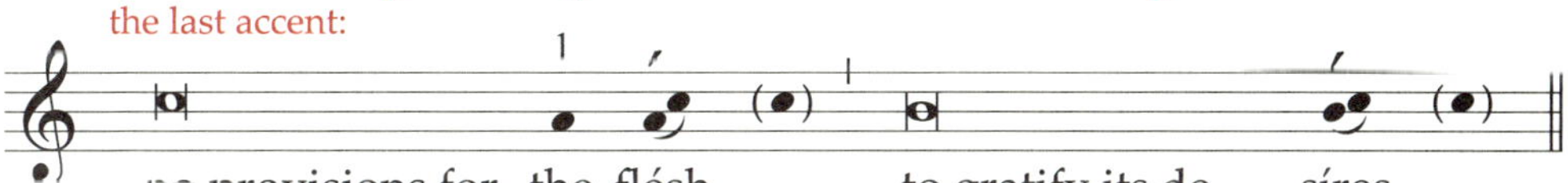

ACCLAMATION

Second Reading for the First Sunday of Advent, Year A (NAB)

Romans 13:11-14

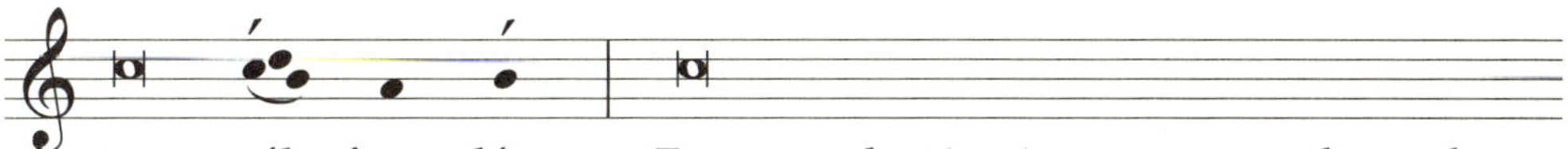

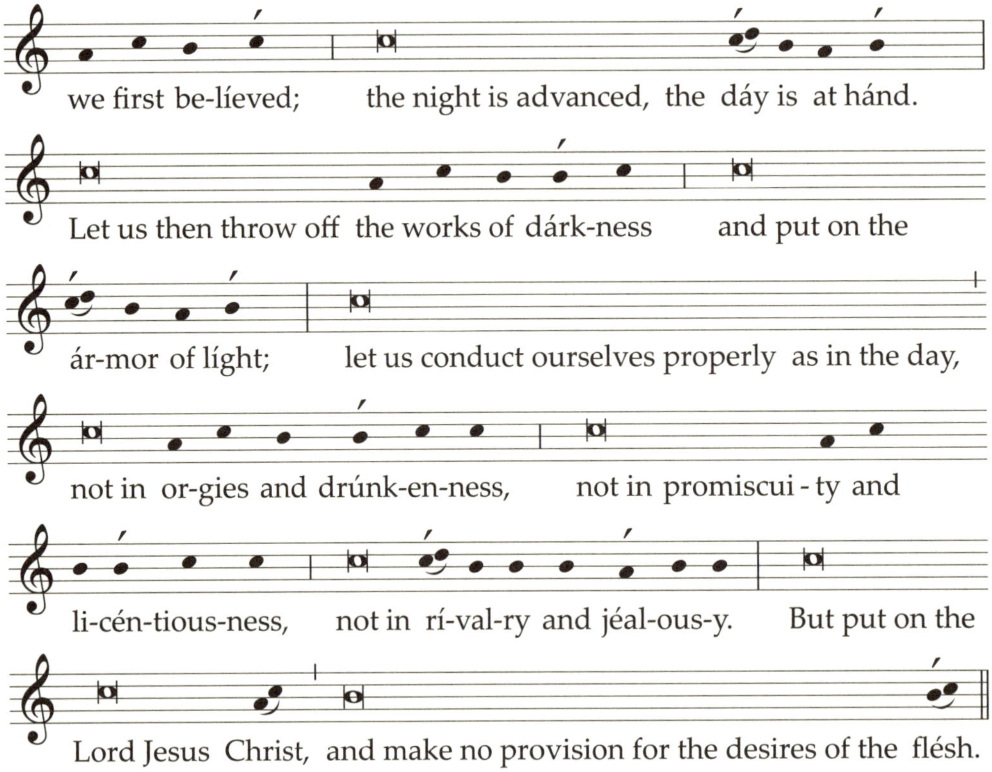

III. The Gospel (Simple Tone)

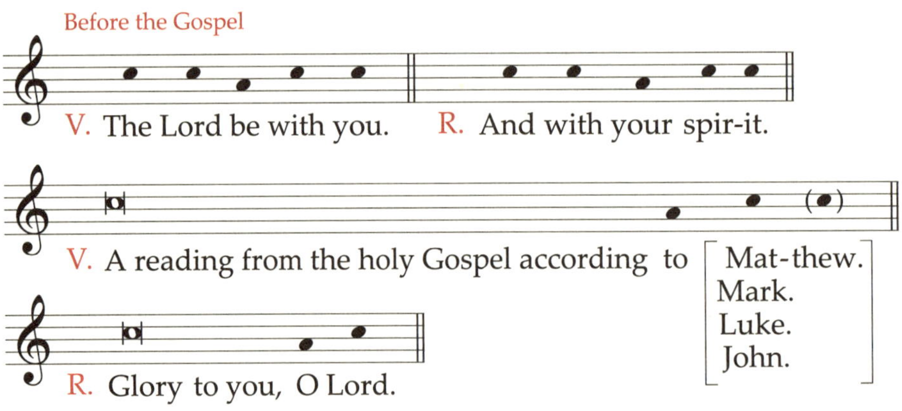

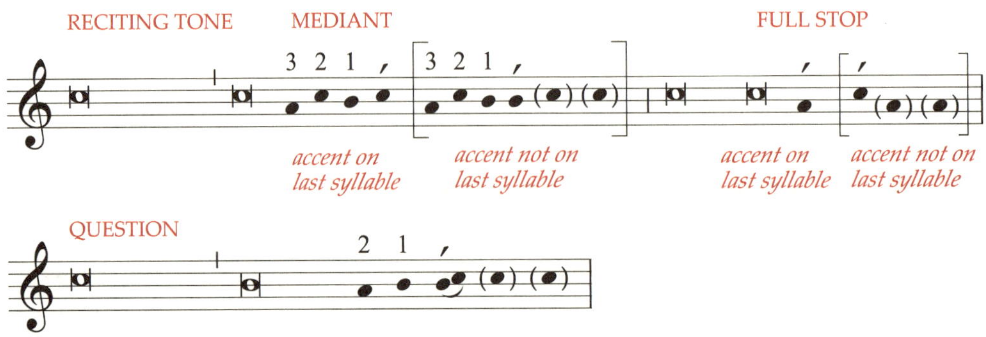

CONCLUSION

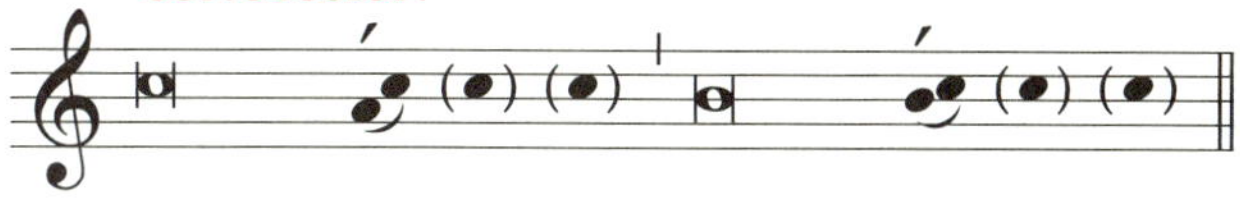

ACCLAMATION

The mediant is used at the end of major clauses within a sentence. In short sentences it may be omitted, and in long sentences it may be used more than once. It should not be used to introduce a question. The full stop is used at the end of every sentence. The question formula is used for all questions, except when the question occurs at the end of a Gospel reading. In the question formula, one leaves the reciting tone two syllables before the last accent. In long questions, the ending is used only for the last clause of the question, with the reciting tone for the first clause. The conclusion with its two elements is used for the last two lines of the reading. For each of these two elements, one leaves the reciting tone on the last accent.

Gospel Reading for Pentecost (NAB)

John 20:19-23

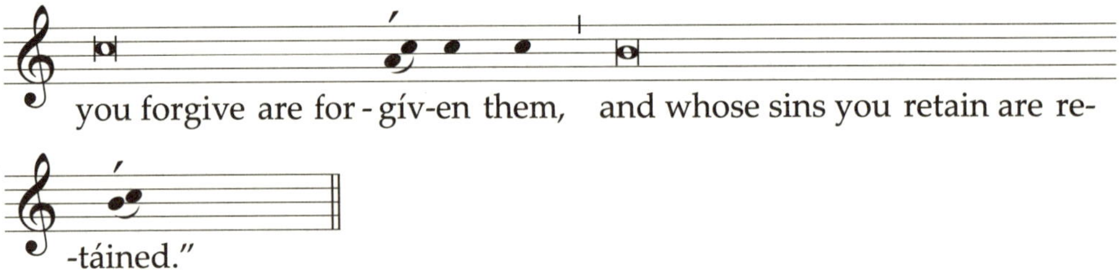

III. The Gospel (Solemn Tone)

Before the Gospel

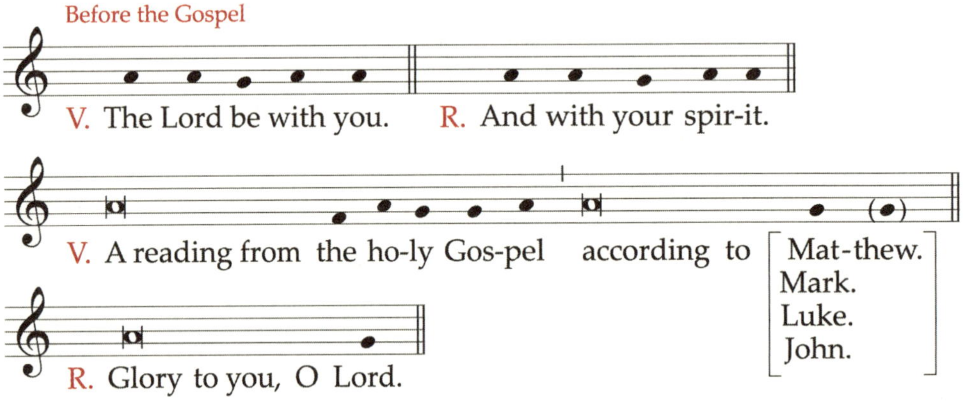

RECITING TONE MEDIANT FULL STOP

QUESTION

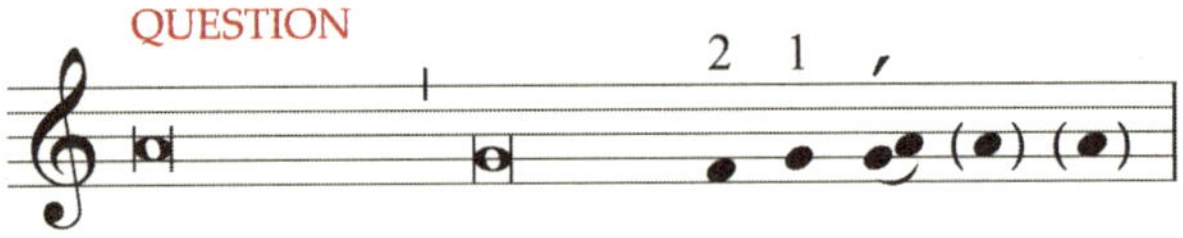

CONCLUSION

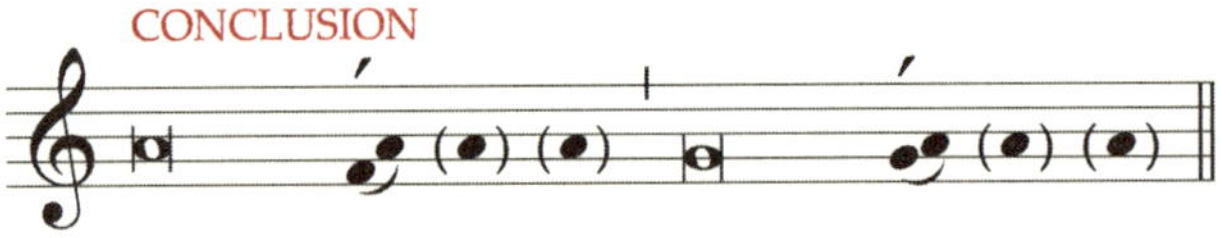

ACCLAMATION

The mediant is used at the end of major clauses within a sentence. In short sentences it may be omitted, and in long sentences it may be used more than once. It should not be used to introduce a question. The full stop is used at the end of every sentence. The question formula is used for all questions, except when the question occurs at the end of a Gospel reading. In the question formula, one leaves the reciting tone two syllables before the last accent. In long questions, the ending is used only for the last clause of the question, with the reciting tone for the first clause. The conclusion with its two elements is used for the last two lines of the reading. For each of these two elements, one leaves the reciting tone on the last accent.

Gospel Reading for Pentecost (NAB)

John 20:19-23

The Creed

Credo III

in ac-cord-ance with the Scrip-tures. He as-cend-ed in-to heav-en
and is seat-ed at the right hand of the Fa-ther. He will come a-gain
in glo-ry to judge the liv-ing and the dead and his king-dom
will have no end.
I be-lieve in the Ho-ly Spir-it, the Lord, the giv-er of life, who pro-
-ceeds from the Fa-ther and the Son, who with the Fa-ther and the
Son is a-dored and glo-ri-fied, who has spo-ken through the
proph-ets. I be-lieve in one, ho-ly, ca-tho-lic and a-pos-tol-ic
Church. I con-fess one Bap-tism for the for-give-ness of sins
and I look for-ward to the res-ur-rec-tion of the dead and the life
of the world to come. A - - men.

Prayer of the Faithful

The text that follows the dagger (†) in the invocations given below can also be used to conclude intentions that are not sung; alternatively, the final words of the individual intentions can take its place.

A

B

C

Or:

D

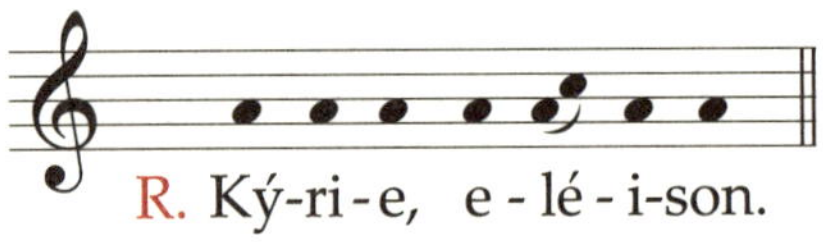

The Lord's Prayer

Tone B (Mozarabic)

After the chalice and paten have been set down, the Priest, with hands joined, sings:

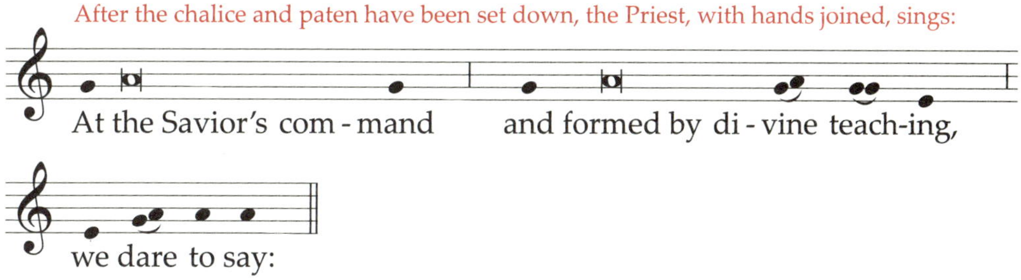

He extends his hands and, together with the people, continues:

Tone C (Solemn Anaphora Tone)

After the chalice and paten have been set down, the Priest, with hands joined, sings:

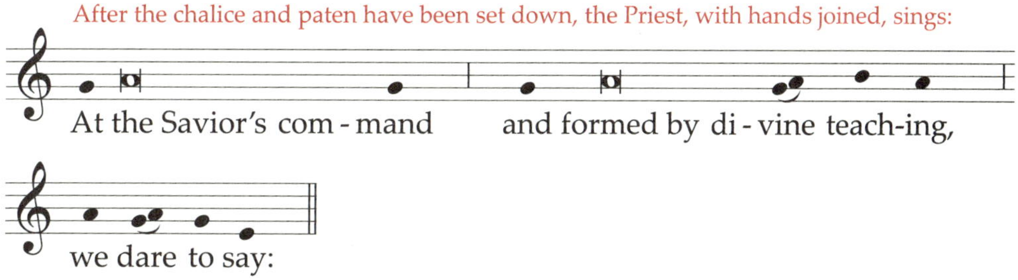

He extends his hands and, together with the people, continues:

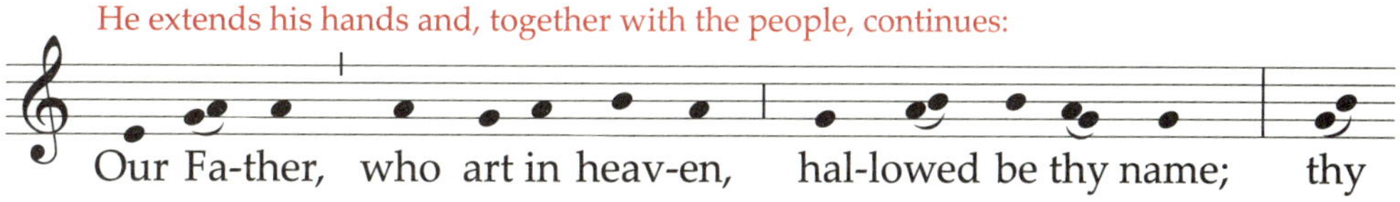

At the Solemn Blessing

Solemn Tone

The Deacon or, in his absence, the Priest himself, sings the invitation:

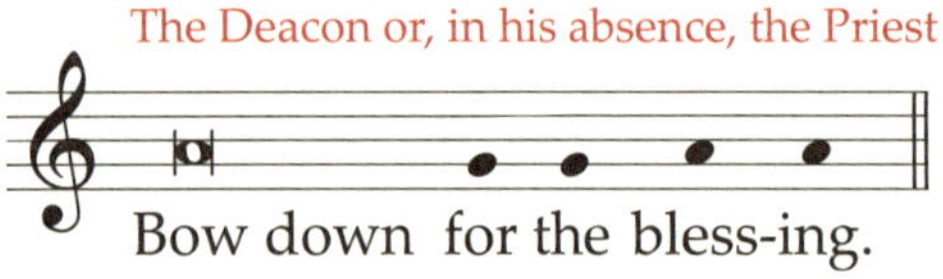

Then the Priest, with hands extended over the people, sings the blessing:

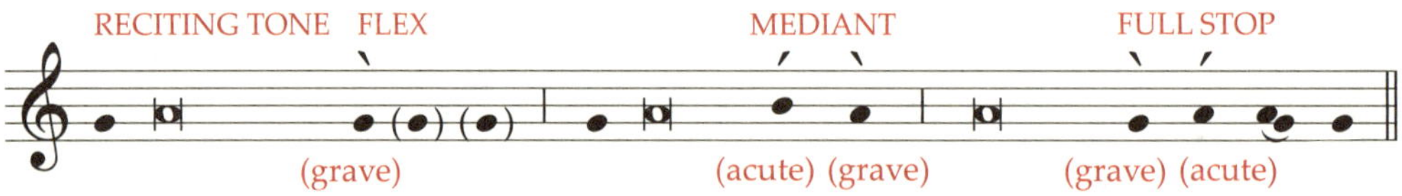

Solemn Blessing for Advent

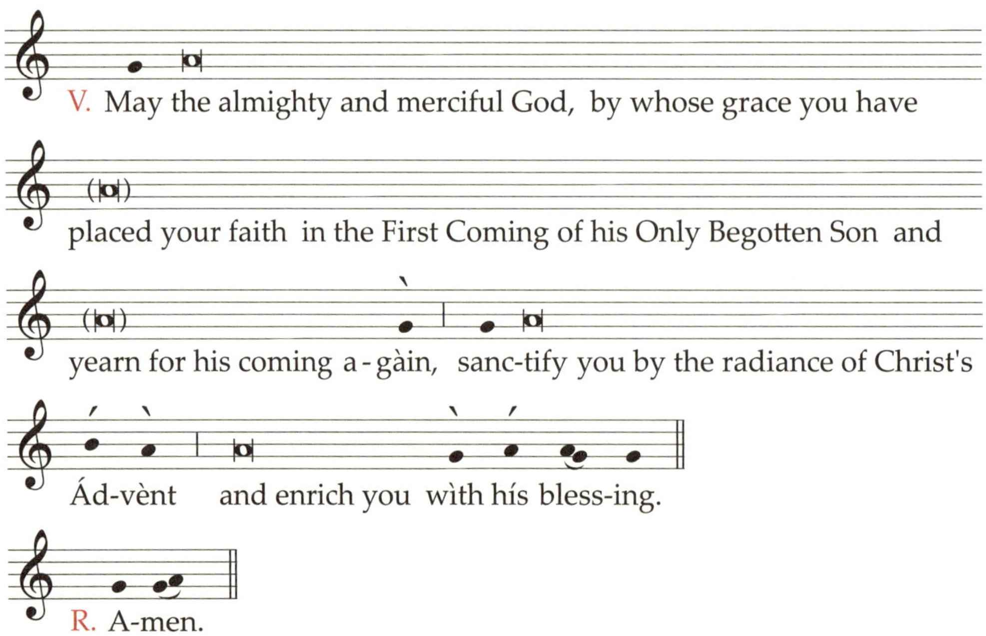

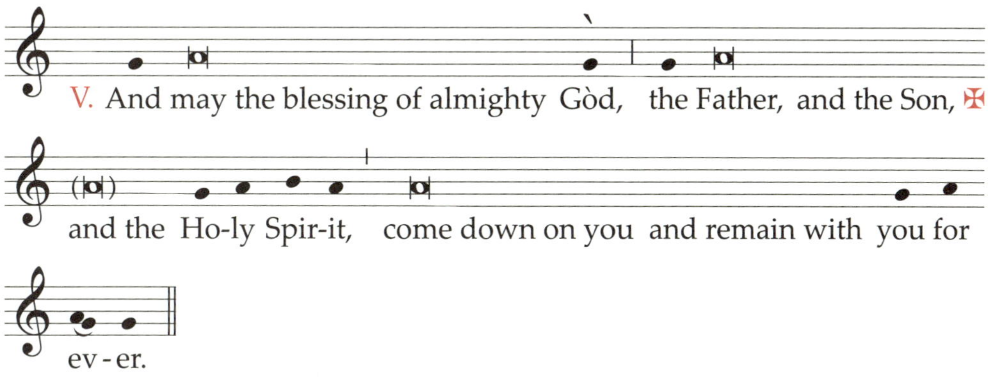

Or, in some Ritual Masses:

Simple Tone

The Deacon or, in his absence, the Priest himself, sings the invitation:

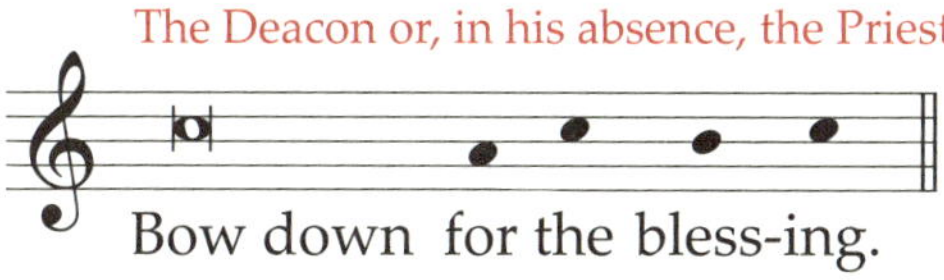

Then the Priest, with hands extended over the people, sings the blessing:

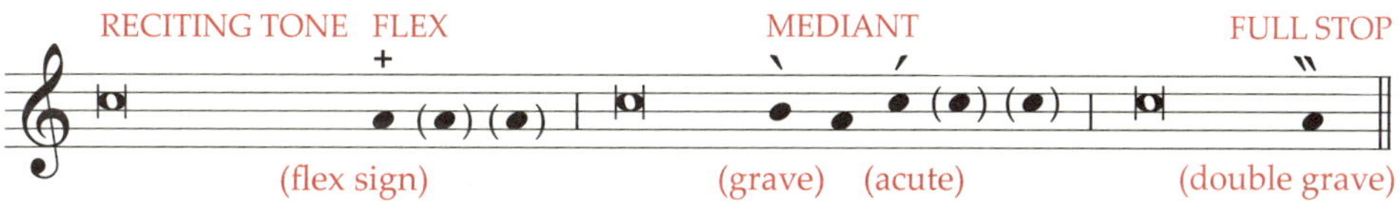

Solemn Blessing for Advent

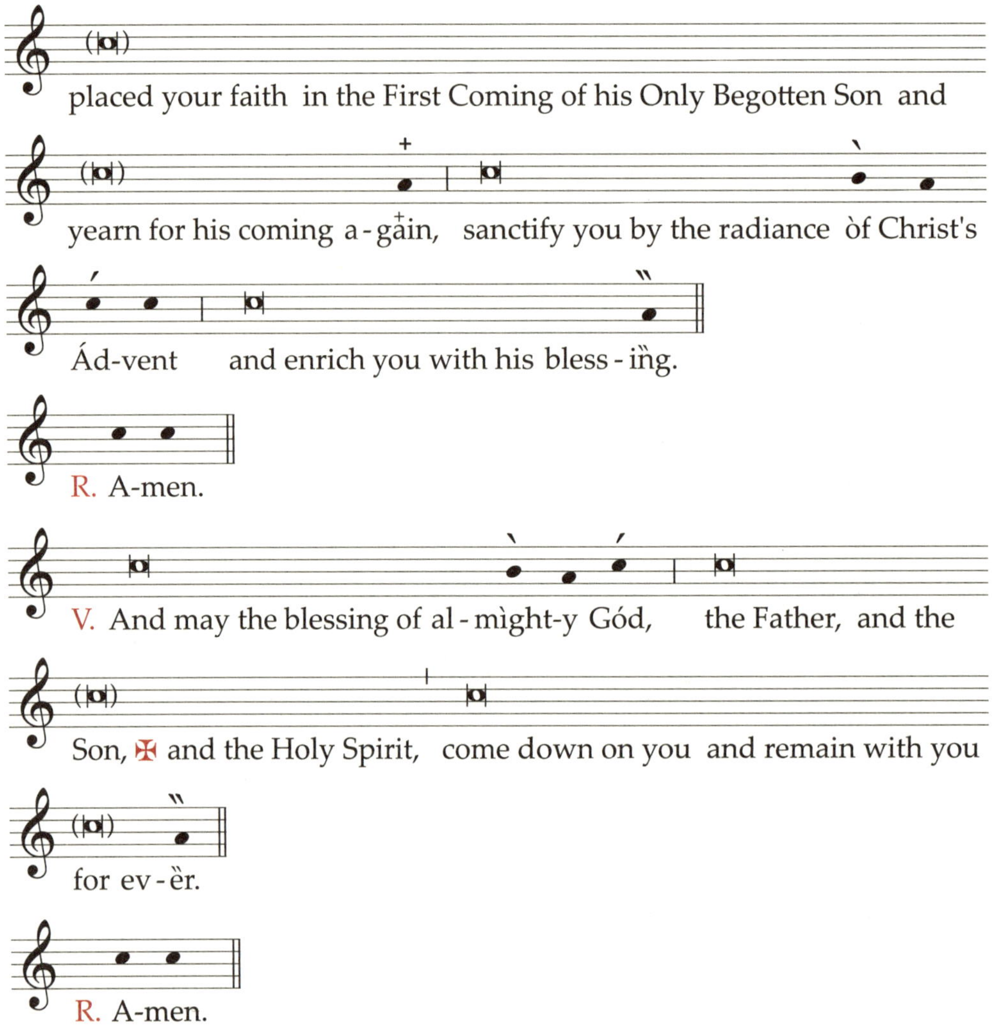

Or, in some Ritual Masses:

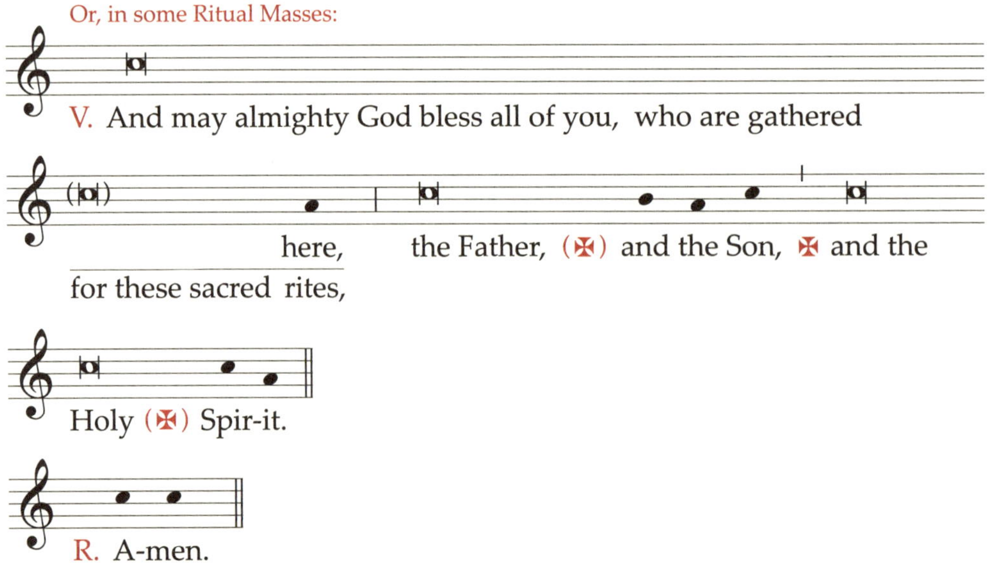

The Announcement of Easter and the Moveable Feasts

On the Epiphany of the Lord, after the singing of the Gospel, a Deacon or cantor, in keeping with an ancient practice of Holy Church, announces from the ambo the moveable feasts of the current year according to this formula:

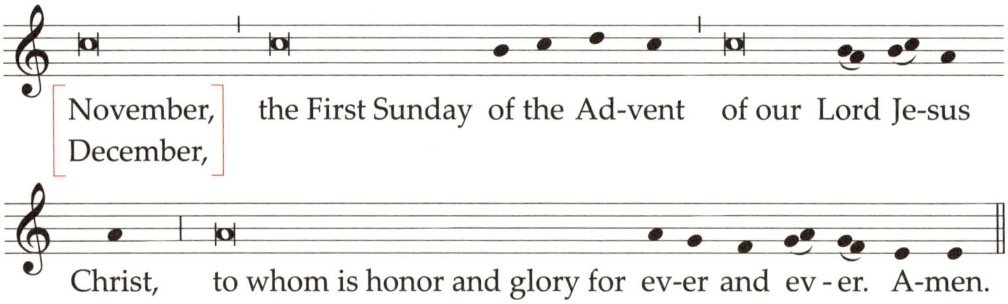

The Nativity of Our Lord Jesus Christ

from the *Roman Martyrology* (USA)

Deacon or other minister:

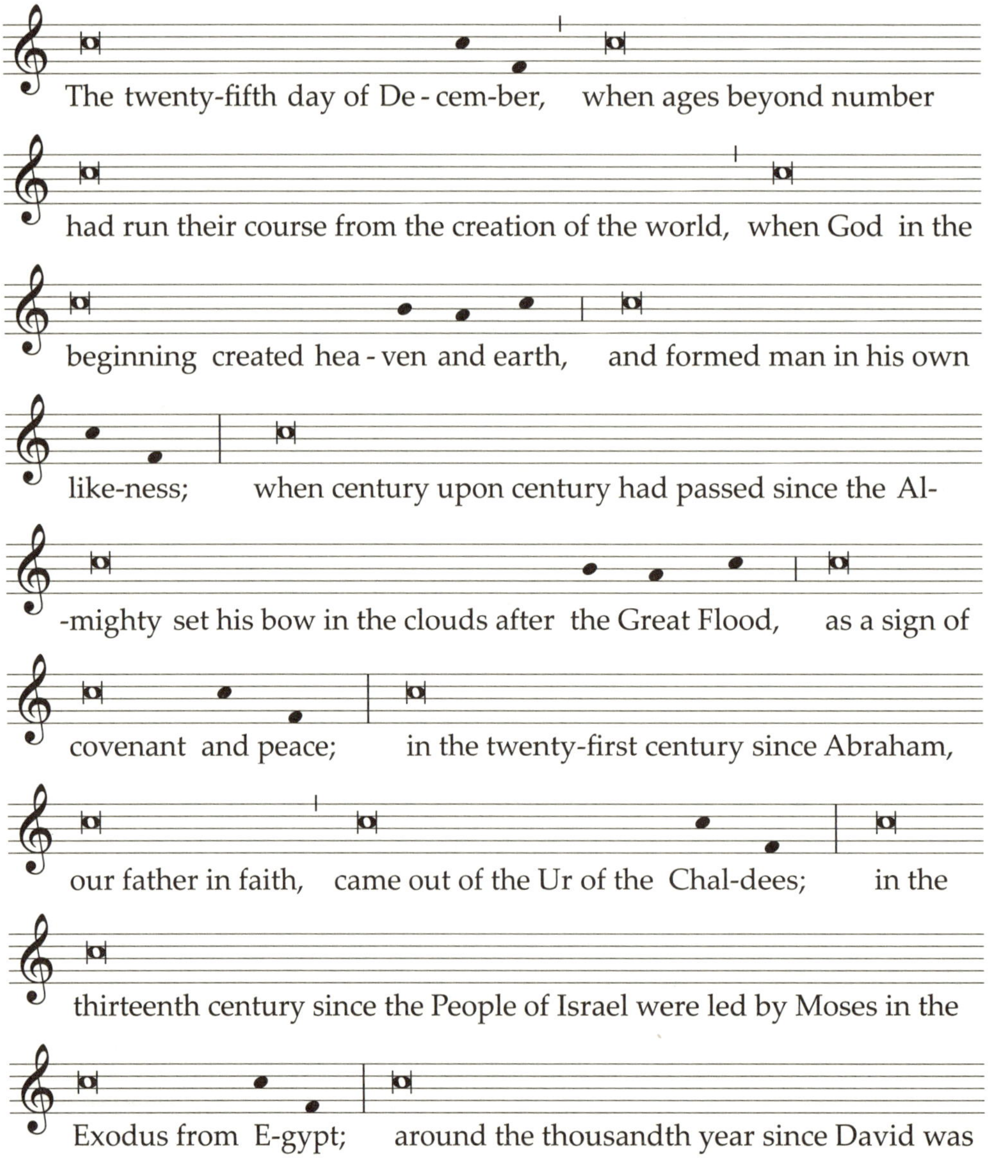

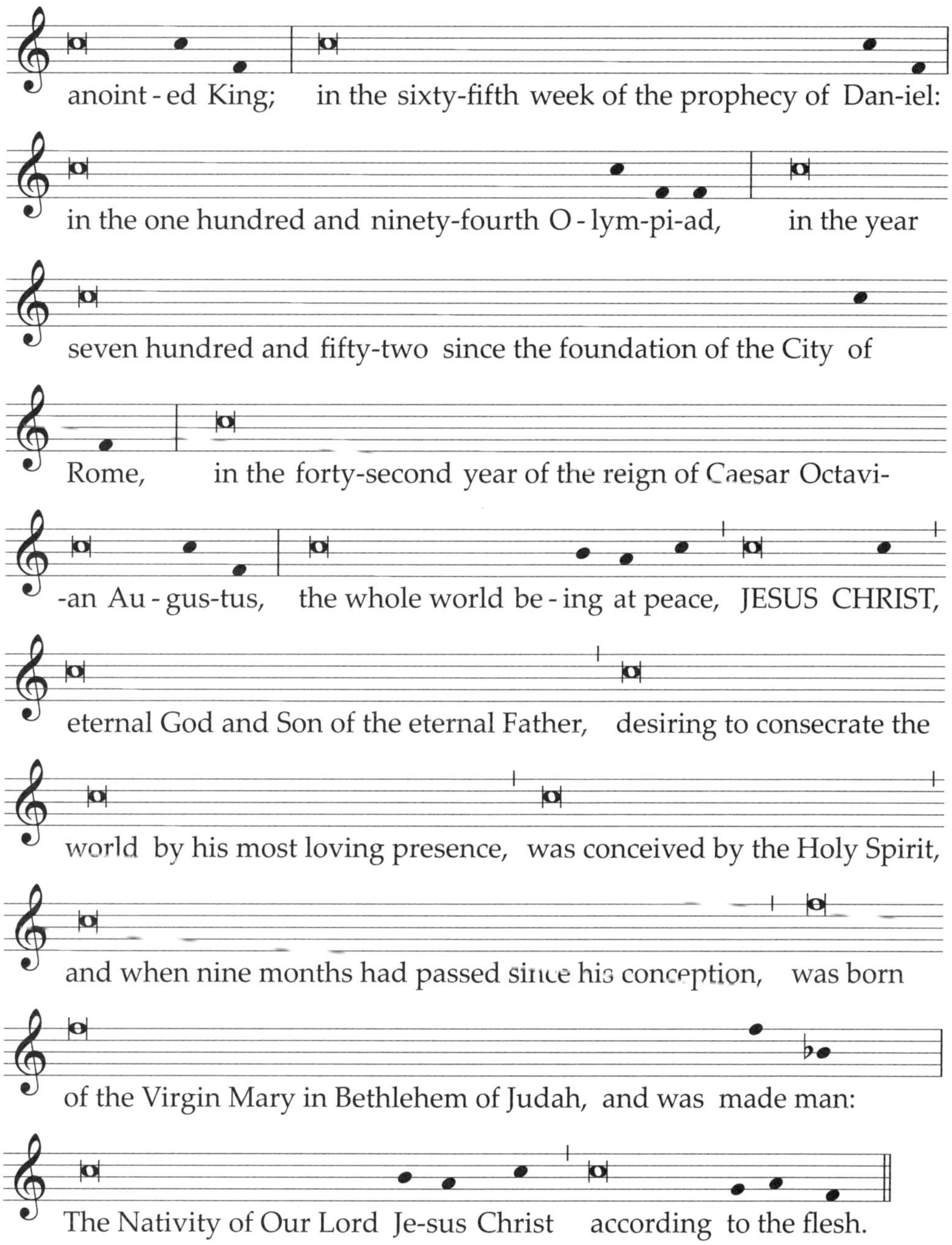
anoint - ed King; in the sixty-fifth week of the prophecy of Dan-iel:
in the one hundred and ninety-fourth O - lym-pi-ad, in the year
seven hundred and fifty-two since the foundation of the City of
Rome, in the forty-second year of the reign of Caesar Octavi-
-an Au - gus-tus, the whole world be - ing at peace, JESUS CHRIST,
eternal God and Son of the eternal Father, desiring to consecrate the
world by his most loving presence, was conceived by the Holy Spirit,
and when nine months had passed since his conception, was born
of the Virgin Mary in Bethlehem of Judah, and was made man:
The Nativity of Our Lord Je-sus Christ according to the flesh.